The Wensleydale Branch

A New History

by
Stanley C. Jenkins MA

THE OAKWOOD PRESS

© Oakwood Press & S.C. Jenkins 1993 & 2002
British Library Cataloguing in Publication Data
A Record for this book is available from the British Library
ISBN 978 0 85361 204 9

First published 1993
Revised Edition 2002
Chapter six updated 2017 by David Haxby

Printed by Blissetts, Roslin Road, Acton W3 8DH.

The Wensley Lime Co. Ltd's Wensley Quarry in 1954. 0-4-0ST No. 1 (Hawthorn, Leslie No. 2412 built in 1899) stands in the quarry with a train of empty wagons, while 0-4-0ST No. 14 (Manning, Wardle No. 1795 built in 1912) approaches with a loaded train. The quarry face is in the background.

R.B. Ledbetter/Alan Rimmer Collection

Title page: Station master Thorpe stands on the platform at Askrigg station during the early 1900s. The gentleman on the extreme right is probably Bill Wilkinson, an Askrigg-based permanent way employee, who died in 1921. *Lens of Sutton*

Front cover: The Stephenson Locomotive Society 'Three Dales Railtour' is seen at Redmire on Saturday 20th May, 1967, with Peppercorn 'K1' class 2-6-0 No. 62005 double-heading the train with type '2' Bo-Bo No. D5160. *Colour-Rail*

Rear cover: Class '37' locomotives Nos. 37668 *Leyburn* and 37667 *Wensleydale* were so named in acknowledgement of their dedicated use on the Wensleydale branch, they are seen here at Redmire in November 1988. The WRA is exploring the possibility of preserving one or both of these locomotives. If you are interested in more information on these engines contact: Barry Wetherall, WRA Class 37 Group, Ashcroft, Oaktree Hill, Darlington Road, North Allerton, N. Yorks, DL6 2PA (tel: 01609 771705). *Arthur Hartley*

Published by The Oakwood Press, 54-58 Mill Square, Catrine, KA5 6RD.
E-Mail: enquiries@stenlake.co.uk   Telephone: 01290 551122
Website: www.stenlake.co.uk

Contents

An ex-NER 'G5' class 0-4-4T, No. 67345, pulls away from Redmire with a Northallerton-bound train on 26th March, 1954.   *R.B. Ledbetter/Alan Rimmer Collection*

Introduction

Running for almost 40 miles across the former North Riding of Yorkshire, the Wensleydale line was one of the longest secondary routes on the North Eastern Railway system. Built in stages, over a 30 year period, this picturesque route eventually formed a link between the east coast main line at Northallerton and the Settle & Carlisle Railway at Garsdale; although mainly a North Eastern route, the westernmost extremity of the line was part of the Midland Railway, and the MR thereby shared in the operation of the line – though the Wensleydale branch was never a 'joint' line in the way that the Midland & Great Northern or Somerset & Dorset systems were joint lines.

In 1980, the Oakwood Press published a short history of the Wensleydale branch, and it was hoped that this publication could be revised and expanded by the original author. However, this was not possible, and the project was therefore taken over by Stanley C. Jenkins – who had recently been working on the history of railways in the Wensleydale area in connection with another publication. As a result, an entirely new book has been produced, and this new history of the line had made much greater use of original sources than its predecessor. The errors that marred the 1980 publication have (hopefully) been eliminated, while much new information has been introduced for the benefit of local historians, railway modellers and other enthusiasts. The story has, moreover, been brought up to date. At about the time the First Edition of this book was published the limestone traffic ceased and the stone facilities were removed. The Wensleydale Railway Company (WRC), which had been formed to try and secure the line's future, submitted a bid to buy part of the line. In the event the Ministry of Defence decided that the line, as far as Redmire, would be of use to them and invested £750,000 in the railway; they also agreed to share the branch with the WRC. Finally in 2000 Railtrack agreed to transfer the 22 miles from Northallerton to Redmire to the Wensleydale Railway and a £2.5m share issue was launched to raise funds for construction and development of the new railway. The transfer was finalised in 2001 and the branch is now held on a 99 year lease from Railtrack, and remains connected to the national network.

The story of the Wensleydale branch is surprisingly complex. The route was built in stages by a bewildering variety of companies, some of which hoped to transform themselves into important main lines, while others were modest branch line schemes. The story is, moreover, a lengthy one in that the first sections of the line were projected in the 1840s, while the final portion between Askrigg and Garsdale was not brought into use until 1878. Most of the route had by that time passed into North Eastern Railway ownership, although the westernmost section of the line from Hawes to Garsdale was always part of the Midland Railway.

This story does, to some extent, lend itself to a chronological treatment, and for this reason *Chapter One* has been devoted to developments at the eastern end of the route, which eventually resulted in the opening of an 18 mile branch between Northallerton and Leyburn. *Chapter Two* deals with the 'second railway mania' of the middle 1860s, with particular emphasis on the Hawes & Melmerby project – an abortive scheme, but one which ultimately resulted in the extension of the line beyond Leyburn to Hawes and Garsdale.

Chapter Three provides details of the line in operation during the 20th century, while the next two chapters describe the stations and route of the Wensleydale line in considerable detail. Finally, the sixth chapter brings the story up to date by describing the closure of the line to regular passenger services, the progressive withdrawal of remaining goods services, the controversial closure proposals made in 1992 and ultimately the transfer of the railway to Wensleydale Railway plc. Writing in the *Sunday Telegraph* in June 2000 a WRC Director said that it was hoped, eventually, to restore the missing 18 miles from Redmire to Garsdale, so the line's history is by no means closed.

Original sources have been used throughout, and in this context one must acknowledge the help provided by the staffs of the University of Leicester Library and the Public Record Office. It would be appropriate to cite every source with extensive footnotes, but a limited number of source notes have been included at the very end of this book – primarily as a guide for further study.

A Note on Proper Nouns, Etc.

The western 'terminus' of the Wensleydale line was originally known as Hawes Junction, but this name was later changed to Hawes Junction & Garsdale. In 1933, the station became Garsdale for Hawes, though it is often referred-to as 'Hawes Junction' or simply 'Garsdale'. To prevent confusion, the latter name has been used throughout this present work and it is hoped that this will clearly distinguish Garsdale from the neighbouring station at Hawes. Similar problems of nomenclature arise in connection with personal names such as Metcalfe, Poulett and Van Straubenzie, which may be spelled in differing ways in newspaper reports, company minutes or trade directories; an attempt has been made to standardise spellings where this is possible.

Other name changes are mentioned in the text, but it may be worth adding here that Jervaulx station was called 'Newton-le-Willows' until 1877, while Leeming Bar was called 'Leeming Lane' until 1902. Less obviously, Appersett viaduct was sometimes referred to as Widdale Beck viaduct, and several other bridges or viaducts may have alternative 'local' names.

Chapter One

Origins and Opening of the Leyburn Line
1845–1860

Situated in the north-western counties of England, the Pennines are a range of desolate hills and moorland, running roughly from north to south and forming a formidable barrier between Lancashire and Yorkshire. These sombre uplands are not a homogeneous geological area, although as a general rule it could be said that the northern part of the Pennine Chain is formed of carboniferous limestone, whereas the southern fells are composed mainly of millstone grit. In historical terms, the Pennines are remembered as the scene of the first industrial revolution, and Pennine towns such as Rochdale and Colne remain to this day as visible reminders of the days when over a million people toiled in the British textile industry.

Early Railway Schemes

The needs of late 18th and early 19th century industry gave rise to the development of improved transport facilities in the form of railways and canals – not only for local transport purposes but also in terms of main line links between England and Scotland. Inevitably, entrepreneurs and industrialists were, at first, concerned primarily with the development of important trunk routes between north and south – and as a result main line railway companies such as the Great North of England Railway and the Lancaster & Carlisle Railway were promoted to forge vital rail links between England and Scotland.

When opened, these new lines became (with their allies to the north and south) integral components of Britain's two great Anglo-Scottish trunk routes – one of which ran northwards through the west Midlands and thence along the west coast, while the other forged northwards along the rival east coast route via York, Northallerton, Newcastle and Berwick-upon-Tweed.

Although much emphasis was placed on the completion of these important main lines, other interests concerned themselves with the creation of useful cross-country links which would, if successfully completed, form east-to-west connecting lines between the east and west coast main lines.

The Newcastle & Carlisle Railway (N&CR) was one of the first of these cross-country routes. Built under Powers obtained on 22nd May, 1829, the line was completed throughout on 21st May, 1839 – by which time the N&CR had become the first line to cross the Pennines from east to west in order to form a coast-to-coast link. Further south, local companies such as the Manchester Bury & Rawtenstall Railway and the Blackburn Clitheroe & North Western Junction Railway were being promoted to serve the Lancashire and West Yorkshire textile-making towns, while in the central Pennines a company known as the North Western Railway was formed in 1846 to build an extension of the Leeds & Bradford Railway between Skipton and Lancaster.

Many of these lines served important industrial areas and, when completed, they would be able to carry large quantities of coal and manufactured goods in addition to local passenger traffic. There were, on the other hand, two possible east-to-west routes across the Pennines which would *not* serve any large industrial centres en route, and although these routes presented few physical barriers for early Victorian railway builders, lack of traffic tended to undermine their potential importance to investors; one of these routes crossed the Pennines via the Stainmore pass, while the other ran from east to west via Northallerton, Leyburn, Bedale and Wensleydale.

In the event, both of these trans-Pennine routes were eventually served by cross-country railways – indeed the Stainmore route did, at least for a time, carry significant mineral traffic between the Durham coalfield and Cumbrian ironworks. As far as the Wensleydale route was concerned the situation was slightly different in that, although there were few obvious sources of industrial traffic, the route did, eventually, form part of an east-to-west trans-Pennine line connecting two main lines. However, this route was not completed until the 1870s, and the resulting Wensleydale branch was never as successful as the Newcastle & Carlisle line or other trans-Pennine routes.

Developments in the 1840s

In order to understand how and why the Wensleydale line was built, it is necessary to sketch-in a few details relating to the connecting lines at Northallerton, with particular reference to the grandly-named Great North of England Railway and the short branch from Northallerton to Leeming Bar.

Northallerton, the county town of the North Riding, was first served by rail in 1841, when the Great North of England Railway was opened between York and Darlington. The Great North of England Railway was leased to the Newcastle & Darlington Junction Railway in 1846, and two years later the Newcastle & Darlington Junction company was itself leased to the York Newcastle & Berwick Railway. Meanwhile, the Leeds Northern Railway had reached Northallerton by means of running powers over the former Great North of England line, and in 1852 the Leeds Northern opened an entirely new line from Melmerby to Northallerton, and thence north-eastwards to Stockton-on-Tees.

These diverse schemes were characteristic products of the 'Railway Mania' of 1845–47 – a period of reckless speculation in which grandiose railway projects were floated with little or no regard for planning or future profitability. One of the more successful schemes emanating from the Mania Years was a line promoted by the Great North of England Railway between Northallerton and Bedale, a distance of 7½ miles.

The Bedale Branch

Authorised by the Newcastle & Darlington Junction Railway (Bedale branch) Act of 26th June, 1846, this modest line was to commence by a junction with the Great North of England Railway at Northallerton 'near the thirty mile post' and terminate at Bedale near the water mill on Bedale Beck.

The authorised route presented no engineering problems, though a small river bridge would be needed over the River Wiske between Northallerton and Ainderby, together with a slightly larger bridge over the River Swale near Ainderby.

The Act provided for the construction of a road link between the termination of the branch and the public highway between Northallerton and Bedale, and the railway was scheduled to cross eight specifically mentioned level crossings. These were defined as:

The Boroughbridge and Piersebridge turnpike road
The highway leading from Northallerton to Romanby
The highway leading from Warlaby to Yafforth
The highway leading from Ainderby Steeple to Thrintoft
The highway leading from Morton-upon-Swale to Thrintoft
The highway leading from Scruton to Bedale
Another highway leading from Scruton to Bedale
The highway leading from Northallerton to Bedale

The Act stipulated that a station or crossing keeper's lodge would be needed at each of these crossings so that road traffic would not present a danger to the trains.

It should, perhaps, be pointed out that the Great North of England Railway and the Newcastle & Darlington Junction Railway were both controlled by the infamous George Hudson (1799–1871), the so-called 'Railway King'. In many ways the embodiment of unbridled capitalism, Hudson – 'Mammon and Belial in one' – was then at the height of his power; he had constructed a network of inter-related companies which, though separate promotions, were controlled entirely by himself. Indeed, the finances of these companies were so complex that Hudson was able to manipulate the railway stock market to an extraordinary degree. In the words of G.M. Young, 'Hudson was one of those not uncommon characters who persuade themselves that an aptitude for business carries with it a genius for fraud. He kept one block of shares in demand by paying the dividends out of capital; with even greater simplicity he helped himself to others which did not appear in the books'.[1] Inevitably, the true nature of Hudson's business activites was eventually revealed, and when this happened the 'Railway King's' fall from power was as dramatic as his rise.

In the middle 1840s, however, Hudson and the Railway Mania seemed unstoppable, and in February 1847 it was announced that the Bedale branch had been commenced and 'would be constructed with the least possible delay'. A year later, on 6th March, 1848, the line was opened between Northallerton and Leeming – though in the event, Hudson's fall (and other developments) ensured that further progress was then halted for several years.

The Yorkshire & Glasgow Union Railway

Meanwhile, other interests were promoting a whole series of lines which, if successfully completed, would have altered the entire railway network in northern England. Many of these schemes envisaged the construction of main line links between York and Carlisle; in 1845, for example, the Yorkshire & Glasgow Union Railway was suggested as a possible line extending from Thirsk to Bedale, and thence west and northwards via Leyburn, Hawes and Penrith – at which point the Lancaster & Carlisle Railway would provide a northwards path towards Scotland.

In its prospectus, the Yorkshire & Glasgow Union claimed that the proposed main line would form part of a 'trunk route from London, Hull, York, Leeds, Lincoln, Boston, Cambridge, Norwich, Yarmouth, and the towns of the eastern portion of England'. These diverse and populous towns and cities would be placed in direct communication with 'Carlisle, Glasgow and Scotland', the result being an 'immense through traffic' which would guarantee healthy dividends for the shareholders once the railway was in operation.

It was, in addition, hoped that the Yorkshire & Glasgow Union line would facilitate the development of local industry, while Wensleydale farmers would be able to cater for the populations of neighbouring industrial conurbations:

> The country through which this railway will pass is one of the most fertile in England, and it supplies the great food consuming districts of Yorkshire with large quantities of corn, cattle and other produce.
>
> In lead, coal, freestone, flags and other minerals, a large traffic is also expected, considerable quantities being at present exported in carts; but from the want of canals, or other proper facilities of communication, the resources of the country have not yet been properly developed. The limestone in the vicinity of the proposed railway is peculiarly adapted for agricultural purposes, and it is estimated that a considerable revenue will be derived from its transport.
>
> The usual steps have been taken to ascertain the amount of traffic, and there is no doubt that it will afford a handsome return on the capital invested; and from a preliminary examination of the country it is found that the engineering works on the line are likely to be of an inexpensive character, and the proposed capital will be amply sufficient for its completion.

The scheme enjoyed considerable local support, and its promoters included a large number of Wensleydale people. As might be expected, the farming and land-owning community was well-represented, but the leading supporters were also drawn from the ranks of the learned professions. There were, for example, at least four Anglican clergymen on the Yorkshire & Glasgow Union Provisional Committee, together with several military gentlemen and a naval officer. Some of these gentlemen appear on the following list of prominent supporters of the scheme.

The Right Hon. Lord Beaumont, Carlton Hall and 18, Curzon Street, London.
The Right Hon. Lord Glasgow, Oak Head, Paisley.
The Hon. J.S. Wortley, MP, Wortley Hall.
Colonel Wood, MP, Littleton Park.
Sir Frederick Hankey, Queen Anne Street, Cavandish Square, London.
Richard Allen, Esq., Hawes, Yorkshire.
Timothy Hutton, Clifton Castle, near Bedale, Yorkshire.
Marmaduke Wyvill, Esq., Burton Hall, near Leyburn, Yorkshire.
Captain Wyvill, RN, Stanton Hall.
The Reverend Edward Wyvill, Finghall, Yorkshire.
Richard Winn, Nappa Hall, near Askrigg, Yorkshire.
The Reverend John Winn, Nappa, near Askrigg, Yorkshire.
S.T. Scroope, Esq., Danby Hall, near Spennithorne, Yorkshire.
Captain Octavious Vernon-Harcourt, Swinton Park and Devonshire Place, London.
William Lodge, Esq., Middleham, near Leyburn, Yorkshire.
Martin Mangles, Esq., Middleham, near Leyburn, Yorkshire.
Thomas Midgley, Esq., Middleham, near Leyburn, Yorkshire.

The Reverend John Morison, Bedale, Yorkshire.
Edward Shepherd, Esq., Bedale, Yorkshire.
Wood Metcalfe, Esq., Askrigg, Yorkshire.
John Fryer, Esq., Newbiggin, near Aysgarth, Yorkshire.
William John Anderson, Esq., Swinithwaite Hall, near Aysgarth, Yorkshire.
James Brand, Esq., New Broad Street, London.
John Chapman, Esq., Thornton Rust, near Aysgarth, Yorkshire.
John F. Clarkson, Esq., Chauntry.
John Harland Cooper, Esq., Carperby, near Aysgarth, Yorkshire.
J.V. Dent, Esq., 7 Clarendon Place, Hyde Park Gardens, London.
Captain Thomas Fothergill, Kingthorpe.
Henry King, Esq., Kingston-upon-Hull, Yorkshire.
Ralph Lodge, Esq., Newhouses.
James Farquhar Morice, Esq., Tulse Hill, London.
Christopher Other, Esq., Elm House, Leyburn, Yorkshire.
James Orton, Esq., Park Hall.
John Pickersgill, Esq., 31 Tavistock Square, London.
William Purchase, Esq., West Burton, near Aysgarth, Yorkshire.
Ralph Robinson, Esq., Castlebank.
George P. Robinson, Esq., West Burton, near Aysgarth, Yorkshire.
Thomas Robson, Esq., Holtby Grange.
Edward Smith, Esq., Huddersfield, Yorkshire.
Edward Spence, Esq., Kingston-upon-Hull, Yorkshire.
John Tomlinson, Esq., Aysgarth, Yorkshire.
Lupton Topham, Esq., Middleham, near Leyburn, Yorkshire.
William Wray, Esq., Eastholme.
The Reverend Richard Wood, Woodhall Park.
Arthur Wellington Wood, Esq., Littleton Park.

It will be noted that many of the Yorkshire & Glasgow Union Railway's supporters lived in the Aysgarth and Middleham areas, and this is entirely consistent with a locally-inspired scheme that had probably originated among a small group of friends and neighbours.

It is unclear who first suggested that a railway could be built through upper Wensleydale, though Marmaduke Wyvill of Burton Hall seems to have been one of the leading supporters. Captain Wyvill of Stanton Hall and the Reverend Edward Wyvill of Finghall appear to have been his relatives, and one can perhaps imagine the enthusiastic Mr Wyvill persuading these gentlemen to put their names down as subscribers to the new scheme!

Other leading supporters appear to have been Timothy Hutton and Christopher Other. Mr Hutton added extra weight to the subscription list in that he was a former High Sheriff, while Mr Other worked tirelessly in support of the project, being 'Honorary Secretary' to the Provisional Committee, as well as an investor in his own right.

The Yorkshire & Glasgow Union Engineer was Hamilton H. Fulton, and the bankers were Messrs Hankey & Co. of London, and the Swaledale & Wensleydale Banking Company of Leyburn, Bedale, Richmond and Hawes. It was hoped that the entire scheme could be accomplished for a little under one and a half million pounds, and the company's capital was provisionally fixed at £1,200,000 in 24,000 shares of £50 each.

The Yorkshire & Glasgow Union scheme attracted much interest throughout the Wensleydale area, and a public meeting held to discuss the projected railway in the Public Rooms at Bedale on Tuesday 24th June, 1845 was very well attended. The speakers included Marmaduke Wyvill, who stated that the railway 'from Thirsk, through Bedale, Leyburn, and Hawes, to near Clifton' would be of great benefit to the landowners and inhabitants of Bedale; he suggested that the completion of a cross-country link between the Great North of England Railway in the east and the Lancaster & Carlisle Railway in the west would 'preserve and promote' the interests of the traders and agriculturalists of Bedale and the surrounding district.

The next speaker was the Reverend John Monson, who proposed that the inhabitants of Bedale and district should give their undivided support to the Yorkshire & Glasgow Union Railway, and that a declaration to that effect should be presented to the Board of Trade.

The meeting was fully reported in the local press, while on Saturday 28th June, 1845, *The Railway Times* printed the following account of the proceedings:

> YORKSHIRE & GLASGOW UNION RAILWAY – A large and influential meeting of the inhabitants of Bedale and its vicinity was held in the Public Rooms in Bedale on Tuesday the 24th instant. Timothy Hutton, Esq., of Clifton Castle, late High Sheriff for the County, presided. Several resolutions were unanimously passed, highly approving of the project, and confirmatory of its essential benefits to Bedale and the district.
>
> The several gentlemen who moved and seconded the resolutions all spoke of the great importance which a railway communication, both to the east and west, would be to the town of Bedale as regards the cattle, corn and butter markets, as also the district generally, and particularly the agriculturalist, who will be enabled to obtain the Blue Mountain lime from the Vale of Wensleydale which is now used as a fertilizer in the district at a moderate cost . . .
>
> The Yorkshire & Glasgow Union Railway passes through one of the most fertile tracts of England, and the district abounds in mineral productions; it was stated that the local traffic would be very extensive, but when the line, as was pointed out by some of the speakers, was a through trunk line between London and Glasgow, the advantages must be very great, not only to the neighbourhood of Bedale but to the public generally, as it will have the advantage of being the best and newest route by near 30 miles between these two important places.

In engineering terms, the Yorkshire & Glasgow Union Railway was an entirely feasible proposition, and with its strong local support, there seemed no reason why the scheme should not have enjoyed early success. However, the Yorkshire & Glasgow promoters were not alone in their desire to bring railway communication to the area, and in 1845 a rival scheme for a line from Northallerton to Penrith was brought before the public.

The York & Carlisle Railway

The York & Carlisle and Durham, Westmorland & Lancashire Junction Railway (to give it its full name) was to run from a point on the Great North of England Railway near Northallerton, using part of the projected branch to Richmond (then under construction) and then diverging from it to follow the south side of the Tees valley via Stainmore, Brough and Kirkby Stephen. From here the route would continue along the Eden Valley to Appleby and thence to Penrith, where the line would converge with the Lancaster & Carlisle Railway – the intention being that York & Carlisle trains would reach their destination by means of running powers over L&CR metals. It was also suggested that there might be a branch from Stainmore, through Ravenstonedale, to join the Lancaster & Carlisle Railway between Orton and Borrow Bridge.

The total distance from Northallerton to Penrith would be about 61 miles, of which 55 would be new construction; the branch to Orton would involve the building of a further 17 miles, and the whole scheme would therefore involve the construction of 72 miles of railway.

To pay for their scheme the York & Carlisle promoters intended to raise a capital of £1,500,000 in 30,000 shares of £50 each. It was anticipated that the Lancaster & Carlisle Railway would provide one third of the capital, and in this context it is interesting to note that Cornelius Nicholson (1804–1889), a leading supporter of the Lancaster & Carlisle Railway, was also a promoter of the York & Carlisle scheme.

Other supporters of the York & Carlisle scheme included Henry Howard of Greystoke Castle, John Wakefield of Sedgwick House, Major Maclean of Carlisle, Joseph Salkeld of Penrith, Dr. Thomas Proudfoot of Kendal, Robert Addison of Appleby, John Gandy of Kendal, Joseph Paxton of Chatsworth, James Hibbert Wanklyn of Manchester, Thomas Meynell of York, Henry Pease of Darlington, Henry Tootal of Wakefield, Sir George Musgrave, Bart., of Edenhall, and Colonel Henry Lowther, the Member of Parliament for Westmorland.

Significantly, many of these gentlemen were Directors of neighbouring railways – Henry Howard, John Wakefield and H.D. Maclean being Directors of the Lancaster & Carlisle Railway, while John Salkeld was the L&CR Auditor. Henry Tootal and James Hibbert Wanklyn were Directors of the Trent Valley line, and Henry Pease was a Director of the Stockton & Darlington Railway.

Joseph Paxton (the designer of the Crystal Palace) was a notable supporter of the York & Carlisle scheme, but otherwise the subscription list of the proposed railway included the usual collection of bankers, vicars and country gentlemen. Most of the subscribers seem to have resided in the Westmorland area, and it is likely that the majority of these investors were also connected with the Lancaster & Carlisle scheme.

In retrospect, there is ample evidence to suggest that the York & Carlisle project was – in its early stages at least – a subsidiary of the Lancaster & Carlisle Railway. It is possible that Cornelius Nicholson and his fellow-Lancaster & Carlisle supporters viewed the York & Carlisle scheme as a defensive measure which would prevent the Yorkshire & Glasgow Union Railway from reaching L&CR territory, but at the same time the York & Carlisle scheme would have acted as a useful feeder to the L&C main line, and in this respect the York & Carlisle prospectus contained an optimistic assessment of the volume of freight traffic that would flow onto the parent system:

In addition to the proceeds from passengers and goods, a very large income will accrue from the extensive mineral resources of the country. A better access will be made to the lead mines of Middleton-in-Teesdale, and to those in Westmorland.

The line will run near a large district of iron-stone, and become the channel for the coal of Durham to pass into East Cumberland, Westmorland, the north-west of Yorkshire, and Lancashire north of the Wyre.

It will form a junction between the Baltic ports of the Wear and Tees and the western ports of Lancaster, Fleetwood and Liverpool. To increase the traffic to these large importing harbours, new docks are now making at Hartlepool, and the Tees river has been declared a 'free port' to all vessels.

There are no canals in the district, and no direct competing railways. The local traffic is now conveyed in carts, while the through traffic is conveyed from Manchester to Newcastle by York on the one hand, or by Carlisle on the other. Stainmore is the route for the agricultural produce of Cumberland passing into the colliery and mining districts of Durham.

The general traffic has been estimated to yield an adequate return for the proposed capital.

The prospectus added that a branch would also be built to West Auckland, in the hope that this would 'give that town a road to the south-west and to the north'. The proposed branch would (hopefully) carry lucrative coal traffic from the Durham coal field.

The cost of the entire scheme would have been about £20,000 per mile, and there would have been six tunnels, including one of about 3,482 yds beneath Stainmore summit.

The Northern Counties Union Railway

Although the Yorkshire & Glasgow Union Railway and the York & Carlisle scheme would have followed different routes, they would both tap the same sparsely-populated region, and despite the extravagant claims set out by the rival promoters, it was obvious that the district between Northallerton and Penrith could not support two new railways. Accordingly, in 1846, the two schemes were combined in a slightly amended form as the 'Northern Counties Union Railway'.

The revised scheme was presented to Parliament in 1846, the result being an Act of incorporation for the Northern Counties Union Railway, which received the Royal Assent on 27th July, 1846. This Act (9 & 10 Vic.cap.260) provided for the construction of railways from Thirsk or Northallerton to Penrith, with branches from Kirkby Stephen to Tebay and from Kirkby Stephen to Bishop Auckland.

Capital of no less than £3,000,000 was authorised, and it was hoped that the Lancaster & Carlisle Railway would help to finance the projected branch between Tebay and Kirkby Stephen.

The authorised route of the Northern Counties Union Railway passed through Bedale and near Leyburn, and in 1847 the York & Newcastle Railway applied to Parliament for Powers to construct a short connecting line between the Northern Counties Union line and the Bedale branch. (This connection was authorised on 9th July, 1847.) In February 1847 the Northern Counties Union announced that construction would commence

NORTHERN COUNTIES UNION RAILWAY COMPANY.

At an ORDINARY and SPECIAL MEETING of the SHAREHOLDERS of this Company, held at the London Tavern, Bishopsgate-street, in the City of London, on Wednesday, the 24th day of February 1847, the Directors' Report was laid before the Meeting.

ORDINARY MEETING.

WILLIAM BERESFORD, Esq., M.P., was unanimously called to the Chair.

It was resolved unanimously,—That the Report now read be received, adopted and circulated amongst the subscribers.

It was resolved unanimously,—That William Beresford, M.P., Henry Pease, William Rickford Collett, M.P., John Whitwell, Joseph Middleton and Christopher Other, Esqrs., the directors retiring by rotation, be now re-elected.

It was resolved unanimously,—That Richard Dutton, Esq., who retires from the Auditorship, be now re-elected.

It was resolved unanimously,—That the Meeting approves the terms of the amalgamation agreed to by the deputation of this Company, appointed at the last Special Meeting, with the Liverpool, Manchester and Newcastle-upon-Tyne Junction Railway Company, and authorizes the Board to conclude the agreement.

SPECIAL MEETING.

It was resolved unanimously,—That the bill now submitted to this meeting to enable the Northern Counties Union Railway Company to make certain alterations in the parishes of Aysgarth and Wensley, in the North Riding of the county of York, is hereby approved, and the directors be requested to proceed with the same, embodying the clause authorizing the Directors after a vote of any general meeting to proceed upon the construction of any portion or portions of the railway antecedently to other parts thereof.

It was resolved unanimously,—That the thanks of this meeting be given to the deputation of this company appointed to negotiate terms of amalgamation with the Liverpool, Manchester and Newcastle-upon-Tyne Junction Railway Company.

WM. BERESFORD, Chairman.

The Chairman having vacated the chair, it was resolved unanimously,—

That the cordial thanks of this meeting be given to William Beresford, Esq., M.P., for his able and impartial conduct in the chair.

CHAS. LOCOCK WEBB, Secretary.

Company's Offices, Poet's Corner, Westminster,
24th of February, 1847.

THE NORTHERN COUNTIES UNION RAILWAY COMPANY.

NOTICE IS HEREBY GIVEN, that the ORDINARY HALF-YEARLY MEETING of the Shareholders of this Company will be held at the London Tavern, Bishopsgate-street, in the City of London, on Wednesday, the 24th day of February next, at the hour of 12 for half-past 12 o'clock, upon General Business; when the Report of the Directors will be submitted for their approval.

And NOTICE IS HEREBY FURTHER GIVEN, that at the said Meeting, pursuant to notice already published, and in compliance with the Standing Orders of the House of Lords, the Bill, for which a petition is already deposited, to enable the Northern Counties Union Railway Company to make certain Alterations in their Railway in the parishes of Aysgarth and Wensley, in the North Riding of the county of York, will be submitted to the approval of the Shareholders.

WM. BERESFORD, Chairman.
CHAS. LOCOCK WEBB, Secretary.

The Register of Transfers will be closed, and remain so, from the 12th day of February until the 24th day of February 1847, both days inclusive. CHAS. LOCOCK WEBB, Secretary.

Dated Company's Offices, 1, Poet's-corner, Westminster,
Feb, 3, 1847.

Two extracts from *The Railway Chronicle*, the one at the bottom being an announcement of a shareholders' meeting to be held on 3rd February, 1847, while the main extract provides brief details of the business conducted at that meeting.

between Wath (near Melmerby) and Leyburn 'without delay', so that advantage could be taken 'to secure the traffic from the district of Wensleydale to the south'. The Directors also intended to begin work at the Tebay end of the line, although they warned that these works would entail a call of 30 shillings per share.

The Lancashire & North Yorkshire Railway

Another scheme projected at this time was the Lancashire & North Yorkshire Railway, which would have run from Skipton to Richmond. This line, which was surveyed by John Hawkshaw (1811–1891), would presumably have connected with the Blackburn Burnley Accrington & Colne Extension Railway (and other constituents of the Lancashire & Yorkshire Railway) – thereby changing the whole complexion of railway politics in the central Pennine region.

The Lancashire & North Yorkshire scheme was a combination of two competing Railway Mania projects, both of which originated in 1845. The original Lancashire & North Yorkshire Railway emanated from 'a large body of influential landowners and other parties' who desired a better mode of transport in the Skipton, Masham and Bedale districts. These aims were largely shared by another group of landowners and entrepreneurs who had formed a provisional committee with the aim of constructing a 'Lancashire & North Riding Junction Railway' serving roughly the same area. In July 1845, these two schemes were very sensibly combined, and a joint prospectus was issued within a matter of days. This document explained that the promoters hoped to secure a means of direct communication between Manchester, the manufacturing districts of Lancashire, and the important industrial centres around Newcastle-upon-Tyne.

The proposed line would have left the Leeds & Bradford Extension Railway near Skipton, and run northwards via Grassington, Kettlewell, Middleham and Spennithorne to a junction with the Richmond branch of the Great North of England Railway. As usual, the promoters claimed that their chosen route would serve an area abounding with lead ore, limestone, slate and 'flags of a superior quality', the implication being that a lucrative freight business could be developed.

To build their line, the promoters hoped to raise the sum of £900,000 in 45,000 £20 shares, and those interested in the scheme were invited to send a deposit of £1 2s. per share.

The list of initial subscribers revealed that support for the Lancashire & North Yorkshire Railway was particularly strong in the Leeds and Manchester areas, and many of the promoters were connected with the Manchester & Leeds Railway; Henry Houldsworth, for instance, was the Manchester & Leeds Chairman, while Samuel Brooks, Robert Gill, James Hatton and Henry Wickham Wickham were Manchester & Leeds Directors.[2] There was, however, a modicum of support for the Lancashire & North Yorkshire scheme in the Wensleydale area, and Major Clark of Bedale, Christopher William Carter Chaytor of Spennithorne Hall, Marmaduke Wyvill of Burton Hall, John Maughan of Jervaulx Abbey and William Lodge of Middleham were also included among the list of subscribers.

The Liverpool Manchester & Newcastle-upon-Tyne Railway

Meanwhile, other railway schemes were coming thick and fast – among them the Liverpool Manchester & Newcastle-upon-Tyne Railway, which was authorised on 26th June, 1846 to construct a line from Skipton to Aysgarth and thence eastwards through Wensleydale to Finghall, and finally north-eastwards to join the Richmond branch at Scorton, to the east of Catterick; at Aysgarth, a short branch would have run westwards to Hawes.

Like the Lancashire & North Yorkshire Railway, the Liverpool Manchester & Newcastle-upon-Tyne Railway was intended to provide 'the shortest possible communication' between the manufacturing districts of Lancashire and the mining areas of Durham and Northumberland.

In the event, none of these ambitious schemes were ever implemented. An unexpected failure of the potato crop at the end of 1845 sparked off a major economic crisis, and when, in the following year, both the corn and the potato harvests failed the Victorian financial system was thrown into utter confusion. Poor harvests in 1848 and 1849 led to riots and revolutions throughout Europe, and in these grave and unhappy circumstances the railway stock market collapsed. Many of the wild schemes hatched during the mania years were abandoned in their entirety, while established companies were obliged to reduce their expenditure on new lines; one of the casualties was the projected branch from Northallerton to Bedale which, as we have seen, had got no further west than Leeming by 1848.

The Bedale & Leyburn Railway

Leeming remained the western terminus of the line from Northallerton for seven years, but improved trading conditions in the early 1850s enabled the York Newcastle & Berwick Railway to give its support to a proposed eleven mile extension from Leeming to Leyburn, which received Parliamentary sanction on 4th August, 1853.

Although the Bedale & Leyburn Railway was no more than a local branch line scheme it was, in many ways, a lineal descendant of the earlier Yorkshire & Glasgow Union Railway. As we have seen, the latter scheme had enjoyed significant local support, and in this respect it had been unlike many of the other Railway Mania schemes (which had been promoted mainly by non-local interests). The failure of the Yorkshire & Glasgow project had left a pool of support for a more modest branch line scheme, and this ensured that there was adequate financial backing for the proposed branch from Leeming to Leyburn.

Many of the former Yorkshire & Glasgow supporters were active in the promotion and management of the Bedale & Leyburn Railway – one of the most enthusiastic promoters being Marmaduke Wyvill, who seems to have been unswerving in his desire to bring railway communication to Wensleydale.

The newly-formed company was favourably received, not only by local people, but also by The Railway Times. This influential shareholders' journal (which was read by a large proportion of the Victorian investing public) pointed out that the Bedale & Leyburn Railway showed a 'strong local interest' and gave 'satisfactory evidence of vigour' in its councils. The Board of Directors, added the paper, contrasted favourably with those of other companies, 'not so much in amount of individual subscriptions', but in terms of political and economic influence in the district through which the railway would be built.

In support of these claims, The Railway Times printed a list of the Bedale & Leyburn Railway's principal supporters, and this list of subscribers clearly showed how local gentlemen such as Marmaduke Wyvil and Christopher William Carter Cheytor were able to rally their friends and neighbours in support of a new railway scheme. The full list of supporters was as follows:

> The Right Hon. Lord Bolton, Bolton Hall, Yorkshire.
> Marmaduke Wyvill, Esq., Burton Hall, near Leyburn, Yorkshire.
> John Chapman, Esq., Thornton Rust, near Aysgarth, Yorkshire.
> John Hammond, Esq., West Burton near Aysgarth, Yorkshire.
> James Pullein, Esq., Crakehall, Yorkshire.
> Henry Van Straubenzie, Esq., West Burton, near Aysgarth, Yorkshire.
> Samuel Weston, Esq., Leeds, Yorkshire.
> Thomas Kirkby, Esq., Leeds, Yorkshire.
> George Place, Robinson, Esq., West Burton, near Aysgarth, Yorkshire.
> Frederick Liddell, Esq., The Grove, Leyburn, Yorkshire.
> Peter Buck, Esq., Leyburn, Yorkshire.
> Christopher Other, Esq., Elm House, Leyburn, Yorkshire.
> Timothy Hutton, Esq., Clifton Castle, near Bedale, Yorkshire.
> Ralph Stapleton-Dobson, Esq., Leyburn, Yorkshire.
> Charles Heneage, Esq., Elsley, Yorkshire.
> Christopher William Carter Cheytor, Esq., Leyburn, Yorkshire.

The subscribers lost no time in organising a committee of provisional Directors, and these included John Hammod, Christopher Other, James Pullein, Frederick Liddell, Henry Van Straubenzie and Ralph Stapleton-Dobson, together with the Honourable Amias Orde Poulett (who did not appear on the list of subscribers published by The Railway Times). The Chairman of the new company was Marmaduke Wyvill, and its authorised capital was £50,000.

As authorised by the Bedale & Leyburn Act of 4th August, 1853 (16 & 17 Vic. cap. 137) the Bedale & Leyburn Railway would commence at Leeming 'by a junction with the Bedale Branch of the York Newcastle & Berwick Railway at the Leeming Station in the Township of Aiskew (otherwise Aiskew with Little Leeming) in the Parish of Bedale in the North Riding of the County of York' and 'terminate in a field adjoining the Highway leading from Leyburn to Middleham in the Township of Leyburn and Parish of Wensley, all in the said North Riding of the County of York.'

The line began by the engine shed west of Leeming Lane station, and ran from the 100 ft datum point by generally rising gradients of around 1 in 104. The Engineer had wanted to take the line clear of Bedale village to the north-east, but was persuaded to put in a rather obvious loop of about three miles, bringing the line to the edge of the settlement. Similarly the original terminus of the line was to be west of the Leyburn to Middleham road south of the final location, the deviation taking the route through Harmby village.

The Act also mentioned a tramroad or 'branch railway' commencing 'from out of the said first mentioned Intended Railway at, or near, or contiguous to the village of Harmby in the Parish of Spennithorne aforesaid, and terminating in a Pasture field known as Leyburn High Town Pasture belonging to the Right Hon. Lord Bolton.'

The authorised route presented few engineering problems, and no tunnels or major bridge works would be necessary. It was expected that one or two intermediate stations would be provided between Bedale and Leyburn, although the exact location of these wayside stopping places was by no means clear. For this reason some local residents (fearing that their hoped-for stations would not be provided) sent a 'memorial' to the Bedale & Leyburn Directors asking for stations to be opened at Crakehall and Stoop House.

The first public meeting of the newly-incorporated Bedale & Leyburn Railway Company was held in the Bolton Arms at Leyburn on Wednesday 11th January, 1854, and in an atmosphere of renewed optimism, the supporters of the scheme listened attentively as Marmaduke Wyvill outlined the progress that had been made since the passing of the Act in the previous summer. Remembering the chaos and profligacy of the Railway Mania, Mr Wyvill presented a picture of prudent financial management; the Directors had, he claimed, enforced 'the strictest economy in the engineering and surveying departments', and having selected the cheapest possible route between Leeming and Leyburn his fellow Board members were keen to begin construction of the 11 mile branch.

On a note of caution, the Chairman warned that the works would not be commenced until sufficient money was available to complete the project, but he hoped that a contract for construction of the line would be let as soon as 'one thousand additional shares had been taken up by the landowners and inhabitants of the district'.

Some discussion followed, and at the end of the meeting it was announced that no less than 600 additional shares had been taken up. This was an encouraging development, but there were still not enough subscribers, and the meeting was adjourned for one month in order that the Directors could 'ascertain the feelings of the district upon the question of increasing the subscription list'.

Happily, the inhabitants of the area were now determined to see their hoped-for railway in operation without further delay, and at a further meeting held on Saturday 11th February, 1854 Mr Wyvill was able to report that 'upwards of a thousand shares' had been issued – 'principally to the inhabitants of the immediate neighbourhood'. It was, in consequence, now possible to begin work on the new branch line, and the Bedale & Leyburn Chairman told his delighted listeners that the works would be commenced 'without delay'. At the close of the meeting, Mr Wyvill congratulated the assembled shareholders on the progress that had been made, and he looked forward to the 'line being made with as little delay as possible'.

Completion to Bedale & Leyburn

Construction evidently began within the next few weeks, and by the end of the year the new railway was taking tangible shape in the pleasant Yorkshire countryside. The York Newcastle & Berwick Railway subscribed £5,000 towards the new branch line – this modest sum being intended to pay for the short section of line between Bedale and the existing railhead at Leeming Bar. Good progress was made on this initial section, and the 1¾ mile link between Bedale and Leeming was ready for opening by the end of 1854.

First, however, it was necessary for the newly-constructed line to be examined by a government Inspector from the Railway Department of the Board of Trade, and after an exchange of official correspondence it was agreed that this compulsory BoT inspection would be carried out on 26th January, 1855. The Inspecting Officer would be Lt Colonel George Wynne, RE.

There had, by this time, been an important development in that the York Newcastle & Berwick Railway had joined forces with the Leeds Northern and the York & North Midland railways to form the North Eastern Railway. A provisional agreement for the joint working of the three lines came into force on 1st April, 1853, with Thomas E. Harrison (1808–1888) of the York Newcastle & Berwick Railway as General Manager and A.C. Sherriff of the York & North Midland as traffic superintendent. A year later, on 31st July, 1854, these arrangements were formalised by an Act of Parliament (17 & 18 Vic. cap 211), and over 700 miles of railway were officially vested in the North Eastern Railway Company.

As a result of this amalgamation the Bedale branch passed into NER ownership, and when, on 26th January, 1855, Colonel George Wynne inspected the Leeming to Bedale extension line, he treated this 1 mile 57 chain section of the Bedale & Leyburn Railway as an integral part of the North Eastern system.

The new section of line ran south-westwards from Leeming, and there were no intermediate stations or major engineering works. As far as the engineering was concerned, Colonel Wynne was well-pleased with the line; his BoT report, dated 29th January, 1855, started as follows:

29th January, 1855

Sir,
    I have the honour to acquaint you, for the information of the Lords of the Committee of Privy Council for Trade, that on the 26th instant I inspected an extension of 1 mile 57½ chains of the Bedale Branch of the North Eastern Railway into the town of Bedale.
    Besides the earthworks and station buildings there are no other constructions on the line.
    I found the permanent way very well laid, and as far as the constructed part of the line is concerned, I can report favourably of the extension, but the line is a single one, and the regulations under which the Directors propose to work it I consider very objectionable.[3]

At this point the Inspector explained that the single line extension would be worked by a 'pilotman', who would accompany each train on the line to ensure that two trains would never be on the extension at the same time. Colonel Wynne saw no objection to the employment of a pilotman as a means of ensuring safety on a single line, but he objected most strongly to certain paragraphs in the North Eastern Railway's operating instructions for pilotmen working on the extension, which he considered to be ambiguous and potentially-dangerous.

The Leeming to Bedale line was a single line section and, as such, it could only be worked by one engine in steam (or two coupled together). However, the NER proposed to introduce a rule whereby *two* trains could follow each other onto the line. If one of the trains was a goods working it was intended that the engine of the goods train would become a 'pilot engine', which would be coupled to the passenger train while the goods train was left behind in the sidings at Leeming. Both engines would then proceed onto the single line with the pilotman on the goods engine, and when the double-headed passenger train reached Bedale the pilot engine would return to the other end of the section to collect its own train.

Paragraph six of the proposed operating instructions for pilotmen was supposed to ensure safe working in the case of a passenger working overtaking a slower goods train. In this case, the instructions were as follows:

> In case the first train you despatch from one end shall be a goods train you will of course wait and accompany the succeeding passenger train; and in case the passenger train should overtake the goods train your duty will be to remain with the goods train and accompany it to the junction.[4]

The Board of Trade Inspector pointed out that this mode of operation was dangerous because it presupposed that there would be two trains on the single line at the same time. Moreover, if the pilotman travelled to the end of the section on a 'pilot engine', there was an implicit assumption that the pilot engine would immediately return to the other end of the single line section when the first train had reached Bedale. This would, in turn, mean that one of the trains on the single line would be travelling in a contrary direction, and although the general meaning of the NER instructions was clear enough, the Colonel considered that the *principle* of single line working would be negated. As he explained in his inspection report:

> The principle of working the train by a pilot is violated, and the goods engine will travel over the line in a contrary direction to the passenger train, and without a pilot, and the goods engine driver may be left without being under proper control.
>
> I . . . consider the sixth paragraph objectionable for it being proposed to work more than one train on the line at the same time, but in the same direction; it will nullify the principle of safety if the pilot is permitted to proceed on any but the last train.

In Colonel Wynne's view, there could only be one train on the single line at any one time, and although he was perfectly happy with the construction of the line he refused to pass it for passenger traffic. He therefore concluded his report as follows:

> For the reasons above stated I must report that, owing to this objectionable working
> arrangement for the extension of the Bedale Branch, I am of the opinion that the
> line cannot be opened without danger to the public using it.
>
> I am, etc.,
> George Wynne,
> Lt. Colonel, RE

The Bedale & Leyburn Directors were saddened to learn that their line had failed its Board of Trade inspection, but they were unable to rectify this sorry situation because operational matters had been left entirely in the hands of the NER. The North Eastern General Manager was, for his part, annoyed that Colonel Wynne should have questioned operating procedures which the NER considered to be perfectly consistent with public safety. It was, nevertheless, necessary for the NER to agree with Board of Trade recommendations – otherwise, permission to open the line would simply be withheld. Accordingly, on 30th January, 1855, the North Eastern Railway General Manager wrote the following, slightly petulant, letter to the Board of Trade.

> 30th January, 1855
>
> Sir,
> Understanding that the opening of the extension of the Bedale Branch will not
> receive the sanction of the Railway Department of the Board of Trade except on the
> condition that the branch be so worked that two engines in steam are not to be on
> the extension at one time. I understand, on the part of the Company, that the traffic
> shall be worked in the condition prescribed.
> The Company being of the opinion that the requirement is not necessary for the
> public safety under all circumstances, but that the same need may be attained by
> different . . . rules, will however bring this request again under the notice of the
> Board of Trade should further extension of the Bedale Branch, or any other
> arrangement, render it, in their judgement, expedient to do so with a view to it
> being done.
>
> I am, etc.,
> T.E. Harrison

Having received this grudging reply from the North Eastern General Manager, Colonel Wynne immediately agreed that the extension line could be opened to traffic 'without danger to the public',[5] and on 1st February, 1855, the 1¾ mile section between Leeming and Bedale was brought into use.

Work was now proceeding apace on the remaining section between Bedale and Leyburn, and with no physical obstacles to hinder the railway builders, this major section of the Bedale & Leyburn Railway was substantially complete by the summer of 1855.

Finance was, as always, a major problem, and some shares had not been taken up. Nevertheless, by maintaining the strictest economy in every form of expenditure, the Directors were confident that the Bedale & Leyburn Railway would be a success. The normal half-yearly meeting of the company was held at Leyburn on 27th August, 1855, and this gathering was reported as follows in *The Railway Times* on Saturday 8th September:

> BEDALE & LEYBURN RAILWAY – The half yearly meeting was held on 27th ultimo at Leyburn, Mr M. Wyvill in the chair. The report stated that the works would soon be ready for inspection by the government inspector, and the Directors hoped to be able to open the line for the public conveyance of passengers and goods in the early part of September.
>
> The Directors recommended that the salary of the Secretary, from the opening of the railway, should be eighty pounds per annum. The capital account to 30th June last showed that £26,003 had been received, and £44,128 expended, leaving a balance of £18,125 due to the company's bankers.
>
> The Chairman said that the balance due to the company's bankers was covered to the extent of £16,000 in bonds which the company had the power to issue. Every economy which the Directors could devise had been adopted with regard to the expenditure on the line. Mr Plews seconded the motion, which was adopted, as was also the recommendation with respect to the Secretary's salary.
>
> The Directors were authorised to dispose of the unissued shares upon such terms as they might deem proper, to indemnify them from any loss on account of any liability they might incurr in completing the railway; with the understanding that the shares would, in the first instance, be offered to the existing shareholders.

In the event, Mr Wyvill's prediction that the railway could be opened in September 1855 was somewhat over-optimistic, though the line was sufficiently complete for the carriage of goods traffic to commence on 24th November, 1855. A few months later, on 19th May, 1856, the Bedale & Leyburn Railway was opened throughout for passenger and goods traffic, and the first 18 miles of the Wensleydale branch was thereby brought into use.

Opening Day was celebrated in appropriate style by the inhabitants of Leyburn and the surrounding district – though, after the many trials and tribulations of the Railway Mania years, the Bedale & Leyburn supporters no doubt felt that a certain amount of self-congratulation was in order!

The completed line was, nevertheless, no more than an 18 mile branch from the east coast main line at Northallerton, which carried local traffic and served the transport needs of small communities such as Leeming, Bedale and Constable Burton. At Northallerton, the branch joined the main line by means of an awkward, north-facing connection that was sited about a mile to the north of the station; trains from Leyburn had to reverse into and out of the platforms – and there was, as yet, no branch bay.

The Bedale & Leyburn line was, from its inception, worked by the North Eastern Railway which, as successor to the York Newcastle & Berwick Railway, had inherited an operating agreement that had earlier been made between the YN & BR and the Bedale & Leyburn company. The line was worked as simply as possible as an 11 mile extension of the original branch to Leeming, and there were around four or five trains daily between Northallerton and Leyburn.

Although the Bedale & Leyburn Railway had originated as an independent company with its own corporate identity, the owners of the railway took little interest in the day-to-day operation of the line. Most of the proprietors were content to let the North Eastern Railway operate the branch in return

for a share in the receipts, while others were quite open in their wish to sell
out completely to the NER.

Perhaps surprisingly, Marmaduke Wyvill was vocal in his support for a
policy of amalgamation with the NER, and at the half-year Bedale & Leyburn
meeting held at Leyburn on 4th February, 1857 the Chairman recommended
that the entire undertaking should be transferred to the NER. Discussions
between the Bedale & Leyburn and the North Eastern Railway had evidently
taken place, and the Bedale & Leyburn Directors explained the terms under
which a transfer might be carried out; it was suggested that the Bedale &
Leyburn shareholders could be paid guaranteed dividends of 3 per cent for
the first two years, 3½ per cent for the next two years, and then 4 per cent in
perpetuity.[6]

The proposed terms were, in many ways, appealing, and Marmaduke
Wyvill urged the assembled shareholders to accept the North Eastern's offer.
In the words of *The Railway Times*, a 'warm discussion' ensued, and after
much heart-searching the proposed transfer was put to the vote – the result
being a rejection of the terms by 603 to 439 votes.

In the event, the independent life of the Bedale & Leyburn Railway was
now coming to an end, and having considered the matter further many of the
shareholders realised that the proposed amalgamation was, in fact, the best
option. Accordingly, at a further meeting held on 19th August, 1857 the rank
and file proprietors agreed that the transfer of their undertaking should go
ahead.

In order to carry out the amalgamation, the Bedale & Leyburn Railway had
to obtain Parliamentary consent. Before this, however, the company took
steps to increase its share capital from £50,000 to £60,000, and this was
accomplished under the terms of an Act obtained in 1857 (20 & 21 Vic. cap.
10). A few months later on 8th August, 1859 an Act 'for amalgamating the
Bedale & Leyburn Railway with the North Eastern Railway Company' (22 &
23 Vic. cap 91) received the Royal Assent, and the NER thereby assumed full
control of the 18 mile branch from Northallerton to Leyburn.

The terms of the amalgamation were similar to those proposed by Mr
Wyvill in February 1857, and in retrospect one suspects that, despite their
earlier misgivings, the Bedale & Leyburn proprietors were more than happy
to sell their undertaking to the North Eastern Railway in return for guaranteed NER dividends.

As far as Marmaduke Wyvill and his fellow proprietors were concerned,
the Bedale & Leyburn Railway had been formed to bring rail communication
to the locality, and once that aim had been successfully accomplished the
local Directors saw no need to continue their direct involvement in the
scheme. Amalgamation with the NER had always been a distinct possibility,
and the final arrangements whereby the North Eastern Railway absorbed the
local company were clearly satisfactory to all concerned.

Leyburn Branch.

DOWN. (July 1867)

	1	2	3	4	5	6	7	8	9
	Fridays only Mkt train	Diarton Coal and Gds train	PASS.	Pick-up Goods.		PASS.	PASS.	PASS.	
	a.m.	a.m.	a.m.			p.m.	p.m.	p.m.	
N'thallerton ... Dep.	7 55	9 45	10 25	...	...	1 55	3 20	8 45	...
Ainderby	8 0		10 35	...	...	2 2	3 30	8 56	...
Scruton	8 9		10 39	...	...		3 34	8 59	...
Leeming Lane ...	8 13	10 10	10 44	...	...	2 14	3 39	9 4	...
Bedale .... Arr.	8 25	10 20	10 50	...	...	2 20	3 45	9 10	...
Bedale .... Dep.	8 30	10 30	10 52	1 10	...		3 47	9 12	...
Crakehall	8 37	10 38	11		...		3 51	9 18	...
Newton-le-Willows	8 45		11 7	1 35	...		3 58	9 29	...
Pinghall Lane ...	8 55		11 13	1 40	...		4 9	9 34	...
Constable Burton	9 0		11 18	1 50	...		4 14	9 39	...
Spennithorne ...	9 10	11 15	11 23		...		4 16	9 43	...
Leyburn .... Arr.	9 15	11 20	11 30	2 10	...		4 20	9 45	...

UP. (July 1867)

	1	2	3	4	5	6	7	8	9	10
				Goods Pick-up		Fridays only Mkt train	PASS.	Diarton Coal and Gds train	PASS.	
	a.m.	a.m.		noon		p.m.	p.m.	p.m.	p.m.	
Leyburn ...... Dep.	8 21		...	12 0	...	3 10		3 15	5 43	...
Spennithorne ...	8 30		...	12 5	...				5 50	...
Constable Burton	8 34		...	12 9	...				5 53	...
Pinghall Lane ...	8 38		...	12 13	...				5 55	...
Newton-le-Willows	8 48		...	12 19	...	3 30		3 55	6 0	...
Crakehall			...	12 23	...				6 8	...
Bedale .... Arr.	8 54		...	12 29	...	3 40		4 45	6 14	...
Bedale .... Dep.	8 56		...	12 51	...	3 50	4 0	4 0	4 30	6 16
Leeming Lane ...	9 5		...	12 57	...	4 4	4 15		4 20	6 22
Scruton	9 10		...	12 43	...	4 8	4 25		6 32	
Ainderby	9 15		...	12 47	...	4 12	4 45		6 43	
W'thallerton Arr.	9 27		...	1 0	...	4 20	3 45		4 46	

NOTE.—On Fridays a Coal Train for the Leyburn branch will leave Darlington at 6-10 a.m. the engine will leave the train at the Bedale branch Junction, (Y. N. B.) then run to Northallerton and take the 7-55 a.m. Market Train to Leyburn; it will return to the Bedale Junction, (Y. N. B.) and take the Train of Coal to Leyburn; it will then bring the 3-10 p.m. Market Train to Northallerton, and leave there for Darlington at 4-35 p.m. with Goods and Coal Wagons.

No. 4 runs from Bedale to Leyburn when necessary, it also runs as extra trip to Northallerton when required.

Staff Stations—Northallerton Junction, Leeming Lane, Bedale, Newton-le-Willows, and Leyburn.

Every Tuesday a Leeds Cattle Train arrives at Bedale at 10-30 a.m. and returns at 12-0 noon.

The Working Timetable for the Leyburn branch, dated July 1867.

Courtesy J.F. Addyman

The Working Timetable for the Leyburn branch, dated April 1870.

Courtesy J.F. Addyman

Leyburn Branch.

DOWN. (April 1870)

	1	2	3	4	5	6
	PASS.	Diarton Coal and (Gds. train)	PASS.	PASS.	PASS.	PASS.
	a.m.	a.m.	a.m.	p.m.	p.m.	p.m.
N'thallerton Dep.	7 32	9 40	10 25	1 53	3 25	8 45
Ainderby	(A)		10 41	2 1	3 33	8 56
Scruton	7 50	10 0	10 46		3 41	9
Leeming Lane ...	7 55	10 6	10 52	2 14	3 54	9 12
Bedale } Dep.	7 58	10 20	11 0	2 20	4 0	9 20
Crakehall	(A)		11 6			9 26
Newton-le-Willows	8 6	9 12	11 16		4 12	9 37
Finghall Lane ...	8 15	9 50	11 10		4 17	9 42
Constable Burton	(A)	1 10	11 17		4 22	9 43
Spennithorne ...	8 30	1 25	11 22			
Leyburn ...... Arr.			11 30		1 30	9 30

A—Stop when required.
B—Stops at Scruton Lane for 1st Class passengers to Northallert'n and stations beyond.
C—On Fridays a carriage is attached to convey Market passengers to Ainderby and Intermediate stations.

Staff Stations—
Northallerton Junction.
Leeming Lane Bedale.
Newton-le-Willows, and Leyburn.

Every Tuesday a Leeds cattle train arrives at Bedale at 10-30 a.m., & returns at 12-0 noon.

NORTHALLERTON and HAWES BRANCH.

UP	1 Pass.	2 Pass.	3 Leeds Cattle.	4 Leeds Cattle	5 Pass.	6 Coal, &c.	7 Pass.	8 Goods	9 Pass.	10 Midland (de. from Carlisle)	11 Pass.	12	13	Staff Stations.—Northallerton Junction, Leeming Lane, Bedale, Jervaulx Leyburn, Aysgarth, Askrigg, and Hawes.
	a.m	a.m	a m	p m	a m	p m	p m	p m	.a m	p.m	p m	p m		
Hawes Junction..... Dep.	...	7 25	...	...	1046	...	1 5	...	...	5 55	6 20	...	...	
Hawes................... „	...	7 37	...	...	1058	...	1 17	3 0	4 45	6 15	6 32	...	...	
Askrigg ....{ Arr.	...	7 47			11 8	...	1 27	3 30	4 55	...	6 42	...	...	
Aysgarth .... „	...	7 57			1118	...	1 37	A	5 15	...	6 52	...	...	
Redmire .... „	...	8 5			1126	...	1 45	A	5 23	...	7 0	...	...	
Wensley .... „	...	8 10			1131	...	1 50	A	5 28	...	7 5	...	...	
Leyburn ....{ Arr.	...	8 16			1137	...	1 56	4 30	5 33	...	7 10	...	...	
	6 10	8 26			1139	1230	1 58	4 55	5 35	...		...	...	
Spennithorne ....„	6 15	8 31			1144	...	2 3	...	5 39	...		...	...	
Constable Burton ...„	6 19	8 34			1148	A	2 7	A	5 42	...		...	...	
Finghall Lane ....„	6 23	8 37			1152	A	2 11	A	5 45	...		...	...	
Jervaulx ....„	6 28	8 42			1157	1 20	2 16	5 25	5 49	...		...	...	
Crakehall ....„	6 33	8 47			12 2	...	2 21	...	5 54	...		...	...	
Bedale............{ Arr.	6 38	8 52			12 7	1 36	2 26	5 35	5 59	...		...	...	
	6 40	8 54	9 55	1215	12 7	1 36	2 26	5 35	5 59	...		...	...	
Leeming Lane.........„	6 44	8 59	10 5	A	1214	2 10	3 33	6 20	6	...		...	...	
Scruton ....„	6 49	9 5	...	...	1218	...	2 37	...	6 10	...		...	...	
Ainderby ....„	6 55	9 7	...	...	1222	A	2 41	A	6 14	...		...	...	
Nallerton ....Arr.	7 1	9 14	1030	1240	1230	2 40	2 49	6 50	6 20	...		...	...	

DOWN	1 Coal, &c.	2 Pass.	3 Goods.	4 Leeds Cattle.	5 Leeds Cattle.	6 Pass.	7 Pass.	8 Midland Goods to Skipton	9 Pass.	10 Pass.	11 Pass.	12	13	B—No. 4, when required this train will leave Bedale after the arrival of the 9.1 a.m. up passenger train and run to Jervaulx, returning from there at 9.35 a.m.
	a m	a m	a m	a m	a m	a.m.	p m	p m	p.m.	p m	p.m.			
Northallerton.........Dep.	7 15	7 40	7 45	8 0	9 45	10 46	1 50	...	4 0	...	9 20	...	...	
Ainderby ....„	A	7 47	A	...	...	10 53	1 58	...	4 8	...	9 28	...	...	
Scruton ....„	...	7 50	...	...	...	10 57	2 2	...	4 12	...	9 32	...	...	
Leeming Lane.........„	9 15	7 54	8 50	8 25	10 20	11 6	2 6	...	4 16	...	9 36	...	...	
Bedale ....{ Arr.	3 10	7 58	9 0	8 35	10 30	11 6	2 11	...	4 21	...	9 41	...	...	
	3 10	8 0	1015			11 8	2 28	...	4 23	...	9 43	...	...	
Crakehall ....„	...	8 5	...			11 13	2 33	...	4 28	...	9 48	...	...	
Jervaulx ....„	9 30	8 9	1030			11 18	2 38	...	4 33	...	9 53	...	...	
Finghall Lane ....„	A	8 13	A			11 22	2 42	...	4 37	...	9 57	...	...	
Constable Burton ...„	A	8 17	A			11 26	2 46	...	4 41	...	10 1	...	...	
Spennithorne ....„	A	8 21	...			11 30	2 50	...	4 45	...	10 5	...	...	
Leyburn ....{ Arr.	1010	8 26	1110			11 35	2 55	...	4 50	...	10 10	...	...	
	...	8 30	11 50			11 39	2 59	...	4 54	7 30	...	...	...	
Wensley ....„	...	8 36	A			11 45	3 5	...	5 0	7 36	...	...	...	
Redmire ....„	...	8 41	A			11 5	3 10	...	5 5	7 41	...	...	...	
Aysgarth ....„	...	8 49	1 40			11 58	3 18	...	5 13	7 49	...	...	...	
Askrigg ....{ Arr.	...	8 59	A			...	...	...	7 59	...	...	...	
	...	8 59	A			12 8	3 28	...	5 23	...	...	...	...	
Hawes ....{ Arr.	...	9 9	2 15			12 18	3 38	...	5 33	8 9	...	...	...	
	...	10 10	...			12 19	...	6 45	5 34	8 10	...	...	...	
Hawes Junction.......Arr.	...	10 25	...			12 34	...	7 5	5 49	8 25	...	...	...	

The Working Timetable for the whole branch, dated 1887.

Chapter Two
Extension to Hawes & Garsdale 1860–1908

As explained in the preceding chapter, the branch line that was eventually built between Northallerton and Leyburn represented the culmination of a variety of conflicting schemes, most of which had envisaged the construction of some form of through route between Northallerton, Thirsk and the west coast main line at Penrith. The supporters of these ambitious schemes had hoped that, by building such a main line, they would attract lucrative passenger and freight traffic from beyond the confines of their own system, yet, at the same time, local landowners and traders continued to press for the implementation of more modest schemes which would provide much-needed local transport facilities.

Although the route was not particularly profitable in its own right, the line from Northallerton to Leyburn fulfilled a useful role as an 18 mile feeder branch. In the 1860s, however, a series of unexpected developments on the western side of the Pennines ensured that the Leyburn branch would eventually be completed as an east-to-west cross country route linking two important main lines. In retrospect, it is clear that there had been no preconceived plan for such a line through remote and beautiful Wensleydale, and by analysing events as they took place, we can see that the line came about largely by default.

The Hawes & Melmerby Railway Scheme

The Bedale & Leyburn Railway – a modest, but ultimately successful concern – satisfied the transport needs of people living in and around lower Wensleydale, but there was still demand for improved transport in upper Wensleydale, and the inhabitants of towns and villages such as Askrigg, Hawes, Aysgarth and Redmire continued to hope that their hitherto railway-less district could be linked to the existing railhead at Leyburn.

There was, in fact, still considerable interest in the concept of a Leyburn to Hawes extension line, and in the middle 1860s the supporters of a company called the 'Hawes & Melmerby Railway' came very near to success in their attempt to build a new line between Hawes, Leyburn and the North Eastern Railway at Melmerby.

As its name implies, the Hawes & Melmerby Railway was intended to provide a cross-country connecting line between the places mentioned in its title. The scheme was submitted to Parliament in 1865, and on 5th July, 1865 an Act for 'making and maintaining the Hawes & Melmerby Railway' received the Royal Assent (28 & 29 Vic. cap. 244). Capital of £350,000 was authorised, this sum being sub-divided into 35,000 ten pound shares; an additional £116,000 could be borrowed when all of the shares had been taken up. The Act allowed a period of three years for the purchase of land and five years for completion of the works.

As usual in Victorian Railway schemes, the route of the proposed railway was carefully defined, and for ease of reference the authorised line was treated as three distinct railways. The most important part of the scheme was, perhaps, the connecting line between Hawes and the former Bedale &

Leyburn terminus at Leyburn. This was described as follows in the 1865 Act:

> A railway commencing in the township of Hawes, in the Parish of Aysgarth, in the North Riding of the County of York, in a field belonging to Thomas Metcalfe and others, and numbered 103 on the deposited plans, and terminating in the Parish of Wensley in the said North Riding by a junction with the Bedale and Leyburn branch of the North Eastern Railway.

The second line would diverge south-eastwards from Leyburn to reach the North Eastern Railway near Melmerby, and as defined in the Act the actual junction between railways one and two would be on the east side of Leyburn station; this second line was described as:

> A railway commencing in the Parish of Fingall by a junction with the said Bedale and Leyburn branch, and terminating in the Parish of Wath in a field belonging to the Marquis of Ailesbury, numbered 16 on the deposited plans.

Finally, a third and much shorter line would provide a link between the above-mentioned railway and the nearby North Eastern Railway line at Melmerby. This last section of the Hawes & Melmerby scheme was described as:

> A railway, wholly in the said Parish of Wath, commencing by a junction with the railway secondly authorised, in a field belonging to the Marquis of Ailesbury and occupied by Francis Wells, and terminating by a junction with the North Eastern Railway near the Melmerby station.

Another part of the 1865 Act dealt with running powers over the Bedale & Leyburn section, and in this context the Hawes & Melmerby Railway was given full use of the line through Leyburn station to the point at which the Melmerby line would diverge from the Northallerton route. The relevant section of the Act allowed the Hawes & Melmerby Company to:

> Run over, work and use, with their engines, carriages and servants, or those of any other company or person, and for the purposes of traffic of all kinds, so much of the Bedale & Leyburn branch of the North Eastern Railway Company as lies between the points of junction with each of the railways firstly and secondly by this Act authorised, and . . . also use all stations between those points and the Leyburn, Spennithorne and Melmerby stations; and the booking offices, sidings, works and conveniences and accommodation of, or connected with, those stations.

Henry Van Straubenzie, Lightly Simpson, George Lightfoot, Harry Stephen Thompson, George Leeman, Henry Pease, Isaac Wilson and William Rutherford Hunter were mentioned by name as the first Directors, and these individuals were to remain in office until the first ordinary meeting of the Hawes & Melmerby Company. The shareholders would then be given a chance to elect a new body of Directors, or so many new Directors as were required 'to supply the places of those not continued in office'.

The North Eastern Railway was permitted to subscribe half of the capital needed to build the line from Hawes to Melmerby, while four of the Hawes & Melmerby Directors were NER representatives. The entire scheme was, in effect, a North Eastern venture – and it thus comes as something of a surprise to discover that the western section of the Wensleydale line owed its existence not to the North Eastern Railway but to the ambitions of the expanding

Midland Railway Company which, in the 1860s, found itself in conflict with the rival London & North Western Railway.

The North Western and the Midland railway companies had originated during the hectic days of the Railway Mania, both companies being amalgams of a number of smaller lines which, in the 1840s, had joined together to create larger, and more efficient undertakings. As a result of these amalgamations the London & North Western Railway found itself in possession of the west coast main line between London Euston, Preston, Lancaster and Carlisle, while the Midland (which also aspired to trunk route status) could get no further north than Ingleton.

Midland Railway Plans

In theory, it was possible for Midland Railway expresses to reach Scotland via Leeds, Ingleton and thence via LNWR metals to Carlisle. Unfortunately, the London & North Western Railway showed little inclination to smooth the path of Midland ambitions, and the arrangements at Ingleton were therefore made as awkward as possible. Through travellers were forced to change trains at both Ingleton and Tebay, and in these circumstances it is hardly surprising that most Anglo-Scottish passenger traffic flowed northwards along the LNWR route. The entire exercise was obviously designed to frustrate the Midland, and in this situation it was inevitable that, sooner or later, the Midland Railway would hit back by building its own, independent main line to Carlisle. Thus, in 1866, in the midst of a second 'Railway Mania', the Midland Railway lodged a Parliamentary Bill seeking consent for the construction of a main line railway from Settle to Carlisle.

Interestingly, the Settle & Carlisle scheme had originated in 1865 when, as part of a flurry of renewed speculation, the engineers John Hawkshaw and James Brunlees (1816–1892) had planned an 88 mile line running from Settle, through Ribblesdale to Hawes, and then heading due eastwards to Leyburn via Askrigg and Aysgarth. An extension would have continued beyond Leyburn to Richmond, beyond which the projected line would have struck across country to a junction with the West Hartlepool Harbour & Railway at Carlton, near Stockton. This ambitious scheme was known, appropriately enough, as 'The North of England Union Railway'.

The Midland Railway was not interested in serving the north-east of England, but the company was aware of the potential importance of the western part of the North of England Union route. By following the Ribble Valley as far as Garsdale the scheme formed a useful extension to the existing Leeds & Bradford Extension line; further north, the Eden Valley provided a corresponding route towards the south, and the Midland engineers realised that if an intervening tract of high moorland could be crossed the MR would have a ready-made main line to Carlisle. The Midland Railway therefore took over the North of England Union project and replanned the scheme to achieve a 1 in 100 ruling gradient between Settle and Garsdale. A route northwards to Carlisle was surveyed, while the unwanted extension to Carlton was quietly dropped. Thus, the original North of England Union scheme was transformed into the Midland Railway Settle &

Carlisle Bill,[7] and in this amended form the Bill passed through the complex Parliamentary process in the early months of 1866.

Despite strenuous opposition from the London & North Western Railway the Settle & Carlisle Bill passed successfully through Parliament, and on 16th July, 1866, the Settle & Carlisle scheme received the Royal Assent.

The newly-passed Act (29 & 30 Vic. cap. 223) provided for the construction of an 80-mile scheme which, for convenience, was treated as three distinct lines. Significantly, the first part of the line included a branch to Hawes, this southernmost section of the Settle & Carlisle route being defined as follows:

> A railway twenty-eight miles and one furlong or thereabouts in length, to commence in the Parish of Giggleswick and township of Settle in the West Riding of the County of York, by a junction with the North Western Railway, and terminating in the Parish of Aysgarth and township of Hawes in the North Riding of the County of York.

This line would form a junction with the recently-authorised Hawes & Melmerby Railway, and as explained by the Midland Railway Chairman at the February 1866 MR half-yearly meeting, Midland Railway trains would then be able to run through to Leyburn 'where they would join the North Eastern system and form the shortest route between the manufacturing towns and iron districts of East Yorkshire and the port of Liverpool'.[8] It was expected that the combined Midland-North Eastern route between Settle, Hawes and Leyburn would carry a 'considerable local traffic', although the Midland Railway Directors admitted that there would be little through traffic between Leyburn, Hawes and Scotland.

The next portion of the Settle & Carlisle line would form a junction with Railway No. 1 at Garsdale, and this part of the authorised route was described as:

> A railway twenty-five miles five furlongs four chains and fifty links or thereabouts in length, to commence in the Parish of Sedbergh . . . by a junction with the railway hereinbefore described, and terminating in the Parish of St Martin Appleby . . .

Finally, the northernmost part of the Settle & Carlisle route would commence in the Parish of St Martin Appleby by a junction with Railway No. Two and terminate in the Parish of St Cuthberts, Carlisle, by a junction with 'the Newcastle & Carlisle Railway of the North Eastern Railway Company on the east side of the River Petteril'.

The Midland was given running Powers over the North Eastern Railway and into Carlisle Citadel station, and additional share and loan capital of £2,000,000 was authorised to pay for this ambitious new main line through the high Pennines.

The proposed branch to Hawes was, in many ways, a minor part of the Settle & Carlisle scheme, yet this modest line served as a reminder that the North Eastern Railway was keen to see the proposed Settle & Carlisle scheme brought to fruition. At the same time, by projecting its own line into Wensleydale, the Midland effectively blocked any future North Eastern Railway incursions into Garsdale – if the NER was going to expand westwards, it would do so in alliance with the Midland Railway rather than in opposition to it!

A Change of Plan

In fact, the North Eastern company *was* still very interested in the proposed line through Wensleydale, as we have seen, the Hawes & Melmerby scheme which had received Parliamentary sanction in the previous year was intimately connected with the NER. However, the Midland's sudden and unexpected decision to build an independent route to Carlisle transformed the entire course of railway development in the Wensleydale area. If the proposed main line from Settle to Carlisle was built, the Wensleydale branch would be able to function as a cross-country link between the North Eastern main line at Northallerton and the new Midland route at Garsdale. This meant, in turn, that the authorised Hawes & Melmerby route between Hawes and Leyburn would become of particular importance, whereas the remaining sections of the Melmerby line would be relegated to branch line status.

There were, moreover, problems in terms of finance for the Hawes & Melmerby project, and indeed, virtually no funds were available for the proposed line between Leyburn and Melmerby. Few individual investors had actually bought Hawes & Melmerby shares, and in these circumstances the North Eastern Directors decided to amend the original Hawes & Melmerby scheme; the southern sections of the route would be abandoned, and the Hawes to Leyburn portion would be built as a link to the Midland's authorised line from Settle to Hawes.

The 1865 Hawes & Melmerby Act had allowed five years for completion of the works, but as the revised scheme involved the abandonment of part of the authorised route the North Eastern Railway prepared a new Bill, seeking consent for the amended Leyburn and Hawes branch and the abandonment of the authorised lines from Leyburn to Melmerby.

The revised scheme passed through Parliament in 1870. There was, at first, some opposition from landowners in the areas between Leyburn and Melmerby, and the NER had to promise to construct a branch from Melmerby to Masham, in return for which the objectors withdrew their opposition to the new Bill.

The North Eastern Railway (Leyburn & Hawes) Bill received the Royal Assent on 4th July, 1870, and as a result the NER was empowered 'to make and maintain' with 'all proper stations, approaches, works and conveniences' a 16¼ mile-long railway between Leyburn and the authorised Midland Railway branch at Hawes. The authorised line was described as:

A railway, sixteen miles, two furlongs and five chains or thereabouts in length, commencing in the Township of Leyburn and Parish of Wensley in the North Riding of the County of York, by a junction with the Bedale and Leyburn branch of the North Eastern Railway, and terminating in the Township of Hawes and Parish of Aysgarth, in the said North Riding, by a junction with the authorised line of the railway first described and sanctioned by the Midland Railway (Settle to Carlisle) Act 1866.

A period of five years was again allowed for completion of the works, and the Act also contained elaborate provisions relating to the Midland Railway. The latter company was given running powers over the new NER line between Hawes and Leyburn, the appropriate section of the Act being as follows:

> The Midland Railway Company may pass over and use the railway by this Act authorised, and all stations, watering places, water, booking offices, warehouses, wharves, sidings, works and conveniences connected therewith, including the station of the Company at Leyburn.

The authorised Hawes and Leyburn line traversed some relatively difficult terrain, but the chosen route through upper Wensleydale presented very few problems. There would be one river crossing near Hawes, together with some relatively deep cuttings at Leyburn and elsewhere. The line would pass by or near Wensley, Redmire, Aysgarth and Askrigg, and it was expected that small stations would be built at each of these places.

Second Thoughts?

There had, by this time, been much vacillation in relation to the Settle & Carlisle scheme. The main line from Settle to Carlisle had been staked out for much of its length by September 1866, but the Midland Railway had made no attempt to begin construction. This was, at least in part, a reflection of the Midland's financial problems in the wake of the sudden failure of bankers Overend & Gurney in the previous May; it had become increasingly difficult for railway companies to raise money for new schemes, and the Midland Directors may have decided to postpone construction until the overall business climate became more congenial. On the other hand, it is possible that the whole Settle & Carlisle scheme was a gigantic bluff designed to bring the hitherto-unhelpful London & North Western Railway to the negotiating table vis-à-vis Ingleton and the Anglo-Scottish traffic. If this was indeed the case the ploy was highly successful, and the LNWR Directors sued for peace in their war with the Midland.

Having obtained a better deal from the London & North Western Railway the Midland Directors decided to abandon the Settle & Carlisle scheme, but when the necessary Abandonment Bill was sent up to Parliament in 1869 it faced bitter and sustained opposition from other railways – notably the North British Railway and the Lancashire & Yorkshire Railway (both of which had welcomed the Settle & Carlisle as a means of breaking the LNWR monopoly south of Carlisle).

If the Settle & Carlisle project had been abandoned in the summer of 1869 the Hawes line would also have been dropped, but in the event Parliament decided that the Abandonment Bill should be thrown out, and the Midland Railway was thereby obliged to begin construction of the Settle & Carlisle line – an expensive 'white elephant' which, by 1869, the company no longer wanted!

Work on the 72 mile-long main line was rapidly put into effect, and with construction proceeding apace at several different places the new main line soon began to take shape in the bleak uplands around Dent and Kirkby

Stephen. The line was inspected by Colonel Rich of the Board of Trade in February 1876, but he refused to pass the route for passenger traffic until additional catch points and improved drainage works had been completed.

In the meantime, it seems that the line was opened for at least some forms of freight traffic, and a report printed in *The Railway Times* mentioned that goods traffic had commenced on 1st August, 1875. The Board of Trade Inspector returned in April, and finally, on 25th of that month he belatedly passed the Settle & Carlisle Railway for passenger traffic.

A week later, on 1st May, 1876 the line was ceremonially opened, the official 'first train' being a long-distance special from London St Pancras to Glasgow St Enoch. A few hours earlier, Kirtley 2–4–0 No. 806 had hauled the first public service over the line; this historic working had been driven by John Mayblin of Carlisle, and its triumphant passage through the raw new earthworks marked the culmination of seven years of toil and effort amid the bleak moors and waste fells.

Completion of the Scheme

The branch to Hawes was not yet finished, but with the Settle & Carlisle in full operation the Midland and the North Eastern companies were understandably keen to see the lines from Leyburn to Hawes and from Hawes to Garsdale brought into use. The North Eastern pressed ahead with work on its extension of the branch from Northallerton to Leyburn, Messrs Gibb & Sons being the main contractors. The new line followed a generally easy course beside the River Ure, and although much of this NER line was carried on embankments or through cuttings there were no tunnels or major viaducts on the 16½ mile route.

The Midland Railway, in contrast, was faced with somewhat greater problems on the section of line between Hawes and Hawes Junction. This western extremity of the Wensleydale line crossed numerous roads, rivers and streams, and the nature of the surrounding terrain dictated that there would be several, quite substantial, earthworks. The largest engineering features included the 375 ft-long Appersett viaduct and a 245 yard tunnel at Mossdale Head, together with a second, slightly smaller viaduct near the east portal of the tunnel.

Good progress was made on the NER part of the line, the Leyburn to Askrigg portion of the route being ready for its Board of Trade inspection by the Autumn of 1876. The Board of Trade was officially notified that the railway was ready for the carriage of passengers, and the BoT wrote back to the NER, informing the company that the new line would be inspected by Lt Colonel Hutchinson in October.

The Board of Trade inspection accordingly took place at the end of the month, and having traversed the 12¼ mile section from end to end the BoT Inspector produced an extensive report. Writing quickly in a difficult to read hand, the Inspector provided a valuable eye witness account of the new line from Leyburn to Askrigg, and parts of his report is worth quoting extensively.

The report, dated 31st October, 1876, started in the usual way, with an elegant introduction followed by an outline summary of the works:

                                                          31st October 1876

Sir,

I have the honour to report, for the information of the Board of Trade, that in compliance with the instructions contained in your minute of the 24th instant, I have inspected that portion of the Leyburn to Hawes Railway of the North Eastern Railway which commences at Leyburn and terminates at Askrigg, a length of 12 miles 20 chains.

The line is single throughout, with sidings or passing places at Wensley, Redmire, Aysgarth and Askrigg, the new stations on the line.

It joins end-on with the existing Northallerton and Leyburn Railway at Leyburn, and will, when completed, form a junction with the Midland Company's Carlisle line at Hawes.

The permanent way consists of double headed iron rails in 24 ft lengths, weighing 82 lbs per yard, fished at the joints; secured by outside keys in cast iron chairs weighing 40 lbs each to the sleepers by two cast iron twisted spikes in each. The sleepers are of Scotch fir, creosoted, 9 ft by 10 in. by 5 in., laid transversely 2 ft 8 in. apart.

The ballast is of broken limestone, sand and slag, and has a stated depth of 12 in. below the . . . sleepers.

Land has been purchased and the overbridges constructed with a view to the future doubling of the line. The fencing is post and rail, post and wire and stone walls.[9]

The report then described the various bridges en route to Askrigg, with brief details of the methods of construction employed. There were, in all, no less than 46 bridges on the 12¼ mile line, 10 of these being overbridges while the remainder were underbridges; the longest spans were 45 ft in the case of overbridges and 41 ft in the case of underbridges. In general, the Inspector was satisfied that the bridges had 'sufficient theoretical and practical strength', though he expressed reservations with regard to two underbridges with 'cast iron main girders'.

Turning his attention to signalling matters, Lt Colonel Hutchinson reported that 'the signalling arrangements' had been 'carefully carried out with . . . new cabins, two at Leyburn and one at each of the new stations'.

Unfortunately, the Inspector had not been entirely pleased with what he had seen on the new line, and he listed a number of faults which would have to be rectified before the railway could be opened for public traffic. At Wensley, for example, some 'safety points' had been provided in the coal depot sidings, but these were too far from the facing points and would have to be moved. At Leyburn, the up platform had no shelter for waiting passengers, while clocks were required 'in the signal cabins and booking offices'.

More seriously, the underbridges with cast iron girder spans were considered to be potentially dangerous – the bridges concerned being at 8 miles 47 chains and 11 miles 76 chains. The Inspector could, perhaps, have ignored the missing clocks but he was unable to ignore the suspect bridges, and he therefore refused to 'pass' the line for public opening. His report concluded as follows:

I must now report that, by reason of the incompleteness of the works, the new line between Leyburn and Askrigg cannot be opened for passenger traffic without danger to the passengers using the same.

                     I have the honour, etc.,
                        C.S. Hutchinson,
                        Lt Colonel, RE[10]

It was agreed that public opening would be postponed while the various deficiencies identified by Lt Colonel Hutchinson were rectified, and in the next few weeks workmen struggled to rebuild the bridges and complete the other modifications required by the Board of Trade.

Lt Colonel Hutchinson carried out a re-inspection in December, and his second report, dated 11th December, 1876, noted that the underbridges at 8 miles 47 chains and 11 miles 76 chains had been strengthened. The clocks had been ordered, although they were not yet in place. Otherwise, the Inspector was satisfied that his earlier requirements had been complied with, and he therefore 'Passed' the line between Leyburn and Askrigg for the carriage of passengers.

Having finally passed its Board of Trade inspection, the Wensleydale line was opened between Leyburn and Askrigg on 1st February, 1877. Opening Day was treated as a public holiday, and the official 'first train' along the 12¼ mile railway was greeted by cheering crowds as it steamed in triumph through the dale. The stations were decorated with flags and bunting, and church bells were rung in many of the local churches. On arrival at Askrigg the first train was welcomed by a band playing martial music and traditional airs, and the celebrations then continued with a village tea party, speeches, and a grand firework display in the evening.

Although the railway was now opened from Northallerton to Askrigg (30 miles) the route through to Garsdale was not yet complete. Engineering difficulties had delayed the works on the Midland Railway section between Hawes and Garsdale, and the contractors (Messrs Benton & Woodiwiss) were struggling with a series of problems including landslips and unexpectedly hard rock. The tunnel at Mossdale Head was not yet finished, and as a result of these and other problems the cost of the 5¾ mile Midland branch had risen to over £40,000 per mile.

There were, moreover, disputes over the operation and status of the western portion of the line. It is possible that, as originally planned, the Hawes to Garsdale line would have been worked as part of the Midland Railway, with passengers changing between the Midland and NER systems at Hawes. As an alternative, most trains could be operated by the North Eastern Railway – though in the latter case the NER and Midland companies would need to reach an amicable agreement over the division of receipts, the manning of Hawes station, rents from coal wharves, and a variety of other issues.

It was, after much argument, finally agreed that the passenger services between Northallerton and Garsdale (originally called Hawes Junction) would be worked by NER locomotives and rolling stock. The station at Hawes would be staffed by North Eastern employees, and there would be certain payments between the two companies in respect of rents, working expenses and other considerations.

As the summer of 1877 turned inexorably to Autumn, the Hawes to Garsdale line at last began to take tangible shape in the bleak landscape around Mossdale Head. The viaducts and other engineering features were complete by the following summer, and on 1st June, 1878 goods trains started running between Askrigg and Hawes.

The 5¾ mile section between Hawes & Garsdale was 'passed' for goods traffic on 1st August, and on 6th August, 1878 the line was declared ready for the carriage of passengers. It now appeared that the line would be opened throughout from Northallerton to Garsdale, but, sadly, the Midland and North Eastern companies had not yet resolved their differences *vis-à-vis* operational matters, and for this reason the public opening of the Hawes to Garsdale line was delayed until 1st October. The North Eastern section between Hawes and Askrigg was opened simultaneously on that same day, and thus, some 32 years after the passing of the first Act for a railway from Northallerton to Bedale, the Wensleydale line was brought into full use throughout its 39¾ mile length.

As mentioned earlier, this tenuous, single track link between the North Eastern Railway at Northallerton and the Midland Railway at Hawes Junction had not been planned as a single entity. It was, in many ways, merely a series of historically-distinct lines placed end-to-end, but the completed route via Leyburn and Wensleydale was, nevertheless, a viable route through the Pennine barrier. The line had been opened in six stages, and the following table will, hopefully, clarify the situation regarding opening dates, distances, and companies of origin.

Table 1
OPENING DATES, DISTANCES AND COMPANIES OF ORIGIN

Section of Line	Distance	Opening Date	Company
Northallerton–Leeming	5¾ miles	6th March, 1848	York Newcastle & Berwick Rly*
Leeming–Bedale	1¼ miles	1st February, 1855	Bedale & Leyburn Rly†
Bedale–Leyburn	10 miles	19th May, 1856	Bedale & Leyburn Rly
Leyburn–Askrigg	12¼ miles	1st February, 1877	North Eastern Railway
Askrigg–Hawes	4¼ miles	1st October, 1878	North Eastern Railway
Hawes–Hawes Junction (Garsdale)	5¾ miles	1st October, 1878	Midland Railway

Notes:
*York Newcastle & Berwick Railway vested in NER 31st July, 1854.
†Bedale & Leyburn Railway absorbed by NER by Act of Parliament dated 8th August. 1859.

It will be seen that the route was owned by two companies, though the line was never jointly worked in the way the (for example) Cockermouth Keswick & Penrith Railway was jointly worked. There were, however, arrangements whereby the Midland Railway was permitted to run trains over the NER between Hawes and Leyburn, while in return the North Eastern had Running Powers over the Midland Railway between Hawes and Settle. (These arrangements, initially provided for in the Acts of 1865, 1866 and 1870, were later clarified and expanded in NER-Midland operating agreements for the Hawes to Garsdale and Hawes to Leyburn sections of the line.)

Early Locomotives and Train Services

The early locomotive history of the Wensleydale line is obscure, but by analogy with neighbouring North Eastern Railway branches it may initially have been worked by various ex-main line engines inherited from the Great North of England Railway or other constituents of the NER. If this supposition is correct one might reasonably assume that former Great North of England 2–2–2s and 0–6–0s appeared on the line during the 1850s and 1860s.

A photograph taken at neighbouring Richmond around 1860 shows ex-Great North of England 2–2–2 No. 69 at the head of a train of four-wheel coaches,[11] and it is likely that similar engines worked on the Leyburn branch at that time. No. 69 was a typical Hawthorn 2–2–2, with an open cab, tall chimney, and a characteristic Hawthorn 'mushroom' dome. Somewhat similar 2–2–2 engines were built for the Great North of England Railway by Tayleurs, and it is known that engines from both manufacturers worked in the Northallerton area.

As a great coal and mineral-carrying railway, the North Eastern owned large numbers of 0–6–0 tender engines, many of which were 'long boiler' locomotives with their coupled wheels placed ahead of their fireboxes (thereby producing a slightly unbalanced appearance). These engines are likely to have been used on goods workings on the Wensleydale route – albeit in comparatively small numbers.

Tank engines may also have been used, and in this context it is worth recording that NER 2–4–0T No. 84 worked on the nearby Masham branch during the 1870s; this engine had started life as an 0–6–0 goods engine, but it was rebuilt as a 2–4–0 saddle tank in 1876, and in this rebuilt form it worked local branch services in the Northallerton area.[12]

The coaches used on the line in these early days were exclusively four-wheelers with four or three compartments. They were lit by oil lamps, and the guards' compartments were equipped with raised look-outs. These vehicles were painted dark red, and in the 1850s and 1860s they sported cream or white upper panels.

In a sense, recorded locomotive history in the Wensleydale area really begins with the opening of the line throughout to Hawes and Garsdale in 1878. Photographic evidence suggests that the line was then being worked by newly-built 'Bogie Tank Passenger' 0–4–4 well tanks, one of the first engines of this type to appear on the branch being No. 588, which is said to have headed the first train to Hawes.

The original train service of around four or five trains each way remained the same for many years (apart from minor changes in times of arrival and departure). There were, prior to 1878, usually four trains in each direction between Northallerton and Leyburn, with one or two short distance workings to and from Bedale. The opening of the extension between Leyburn and Garsdale did not materially alter the train service, although most workings were of course extended throughout to Garsdale. Shorter distance services continued to run to or from either Bedale or Leyburn.

Improving the Line

The Wensleydale branch was worked by train staff during the 19th century, the staff stations being Northallerton Junction, Leeming, Bedale, Jervaulx, Leyburn, Aysgarth, Askrigg and Hawes.

Signal boxes, as such, were unknown in the earliest days, though they had certainly appeared by the 1870s – by which time most of the intermediate stations between Northallerton and Hawes had been equipped with typical North Eastern Railway 'Southern Division' style cabins. These structures were unusual in that they were constructed entirely of stone or brickwork – wooden components being used only for floors, roof members and window frames.

The stations between Leyburn and Hawes had single storey cabins, but Bedale boasted a very fine two-storey 'Southern Division' brick cabin. Later, at the turn of the century, a number of stations or level crossings were given conventional timber-framed or brick-and-timber cabins. (Hawes and Garsdale stations were of course built by the Midland Railway, and there signal boxes reflected MR practice.)

As a general rule, the signal boxes erected during the Victorian period were brick or stone-built 'Southern Division' style cabins, whereas those boxes built in the early years of the 20th century were timber-framed structures supported on brick bases. The largest of these brick and timber boxes was that at Leeming Bar, where a new, 36-lever box was installed in 1907–8 (*see Chapter Four*).

The branch was signalled with NER-type slotted post semaphores, some of which were graced by stylish, 4 ft high McKenzie & Holland type finials – though a number of others had simple wooden pointed tops to their posts. All of these signals had lower quadrant arms, the distant arms being distinguished by their 'fish tail' ends (in NER days all signals, both home and distants, were painted red).

The Wensleydale line was improved in a variety of ways during the late 19th and early 20th centuries, one of the most significant innovations made at this time being the installation of a short section of double track between Leeming and Bedale. Additionally, some hitherto single platform stations were given second platforms and new or improved crossing loops, so that they could be used for passing passenger trains. The stations concerned included Wensley and Leeming, both of which were given new up platforms during the early 20th century.

Apart from these changes the most important development in terms of infrastructure took place at the Northallerton end of the line, where the unsatisfactory junction arrangements whereby branch trains joined the NER main line via a north-facing connection had always caused problems. As the station at Northallerton was situated to the *south* of the junction it was necessary for branch trains to reverse in and out of the platforms, and to eradicate this problem the NER decided to build a new, 'inner' curve between Northallerton station and the branch. This new curve would leave the station at Northallerton High Junction and, diverging north-westwards, it would meet the branch at a new junction to be known as Northallerton Inner Junction; the old alignment between Northallerton Inner Junction and Castle Hills Junction would be retained as the west-to-north arm of a triangle.

Work on the new curve was carried out on 1881–82, and the new connecting line was inspected by Major-General (formerly Lt Colonel) C.S. Hutchinson of the Board of Trade on 18th March, 1882. Having examined the curve, together with its junction at each end, the Inspector reported as follows:

18th March, 1882

Sir,

I have the honour to report, for the information of the Board of Trade, that in compliance with the instructions contained in your minute of the 27th ultimo, I have inspected the junction of the Northallerton Curve with the Bedale Branch of the North Eastern Railway.

The arrangements in connection with this junction have been satisfactorily carried out, with the exception that the locking of the facing point is not so close as is desired. The Engineer has promised to have this deficiency remedied, and I can accordingly recommend the Board of Trade not to object to this new junction being brought into use.

I have the honour, etc.,

C.S. Hutchinson, Major-General, RE[13]

Maps prepared in conjunction with the BoT inspection reveal that the new line was a single track curve that converged with the original branch by a facing connection. Northallerton Inner Junction box (later Northallerton West) was a small, 10-lever cabin on the down side of the line, and its frame contained one spare lever.

There was, as yet, no branch bay at Northallerton, but in 1911 the latter station was substantially remodelled, and as a result of these changes Wensleydale branch trains were given their own bay at the north end of Northallerton's down platform.

Some Abortive Schemes

The Wensleydale route featured in a surprising variety of abortive schemes, many of which have already been mentioned in connection with the Yorkshire & Glasgow Union, Bedale & Leyburn, Hawes & Melmerby and Settle & Carlisle schemes. There were, in general, two great periods of railway speculation during the Victorian era, the Railway Mania of the 1840s being followed, some 20 years later, by a further period of expansion during the middle 1860s.

The Hawes & Melmerby and the North of England Union railways were the two dominant schemes of the 1860s, and although neither of these projects was immediately successful, they both resulted in the creation of new lines – the Hawes & Melmerby Railway being the precursor of the Leyburn to Hawes line, while the North of England Union scheme was quickly transformed into the Midland Railway's Settle & Carlisle scheme. One might add, however, that several other projects were mooted during the 1860s boom – notably the Sedburgh & Hawes Railway and the Skipton Wharfedale & Leyburn Railway. The Sedburgh & Hawes promoters had intended to build an extension of the Hawes & Melmerby Railway beyond Hawes to a junction with the London & North Western Railway's Ingleton branch, while the Skipton & Wharfedale supporters hoped to build a line connecting Gargrave, Kettlewell, Middleham and Leyburn. Both of these projects were abandoned.

Another scheme suggested during the 1860s was the East & West Yorkshire Union Railway, which would have run from Melmerby to Sedburgh via Leyburn, Wensleydale and Garsdale; this scheme was bitterly opposed by the North Eastern Railway, though it later emerged, in an amended form, as the Hawes & Melmerby Railway.

In retrospect, it can now be seen that the core of Britain's railway network was laid down during the 1840s or 1850s (the majority of BR's InterCity routes were built during this period). The schemes of the 1860s tended to produce branch lines and cross country lines – many of which are now closed – while many later schemes were largely superfluous in that they duplicated existing routes. In truth, the railway system was more or less complete by the 1880s (if not the 1860s), and it follows that most of the lines promoted at the end of the 19th century were doomed to failure; there was still a great need for urban and suburban lines, but otherwise most travellers and manufacturers were satisfied with the size and scope of the late Victorian railway system. This fact did not, however, deter over-optimistic promoters from planning a further series of lines in the Wensleydale area, and in the 1880s and 1890s persistent attempts were made to complete a rail link between Wharfedale and the NER at Leyburn or Richmond.

Many of these final schemes envisaged the construction of a line from the Midland Railway at Skipton, which would have run via Grassington and Kettlewell to some convenient point on the Wensleydale route. Thus, in 1880, the Skipton & Kettlewell Railway sought Parliamentary consent for a railway running through Bishopsdale to Aysgarth. The North Yorkshire & Lancashire Railway of 1881 was a somewhat similar scheme which would, however, have taken a more easterly route via Coverdale to a junction with the Wensleydale branch near Spennithorne. The Skipton & Kettlewell proposal was followed by the substantially-similar Skipton & North East Junction Railway scheme of 1883, while at around the same time the Richmond & Hawes Railway was seeking financial backing for a line through the lead-mining area of Swaledale.

None of the 1880s schemes were successful. This was, in great measure, because money for such projects was becoming hard to find; there was, moreover, growing opposition from people who would today be called 'conservationists' – all of whom objected most strongly to what they saw as the despoilation of the River Ure by unnecessary railway construction.

Further proposals were made public during the 1890s, though the only scheme to enjoy any kind of success was the Yorkshire Dales Railway. Originally seen as part of a grandiose scheme linking Skipton, Grassington, Kettlewell, Middleham and Darlington, the project was later cut down to become no more than a modest branch line scheme, and on 6th August, 1897 the promoters obtained Parliamentary consent for a short branch from Skipton to Grassington. In this form the line was eventually opened on 29th July, 1902, and although there were various other proposals for railways or tramways in upper Wharfedale, Grassington was destined to remain the end of the line until its closure to passengers in 1930, and to freight traffic in 1969.

It would, finally, be worth adding that the passing of the Light Railways Act of 1896 led to a series of proposals for a light railway link between Hellifield and the Richmond branch at Scorton. These schemes were, in effect a revival of the earlier Yorkshire Dales Railway. The revised scheme – known as the North Yorkshire Dales Railway – emerged in 1903 and again in 1912; indeed, the promoters managed to obtain a Light Railway Order for a short line from Richmond to Reeth, but World War I intervened, and the project was abandoned for once and all in 1922.

Directors and Promoters – A Further Note

We have seen in Chapters One and Two, how the constituent parts of the Wensleydale branch were promoted by small groups of land-owning gentlemen, and it may be worth adding a few more notes on these public-spirited individuals before examining the subsequent history of the line.

It is often assumed that railways, mines and other large scale industrial ventures were promoted largely by the Victorian middle classes, but in practice most railways seem to have been built through the efforts of local landowners. In this respect the Yorkshire & Glasgow Union Railway and the Bedale & Leyburn scheme were entirely typical, and there is no doubt that land owning interests were predominant during the promotion of these companies. This was, at least in part, because land was the most expensive component of any railway scheme, and in this respect landowners were well-placed to play a leading role as the Chairmen and Directors of large numbers of local railways. Marmaduke Wyvill of Burton Hall was, perhaps, a typical railway promoter, in that he was a minor landowner with a direct interest in the creation of improved transport links for himself and for his neighbours.

Speculative investors seem to have been largely absent during the promotion of the Bedale & Leyburn and other local lines, though one notes a large number of professional people such as doctors and clergymen on the subscription lists of many companies. In reality, some of these subscribers were friends or relatives of the local landowners, and they may well have been persuaded to participate in the various schemes by their fathers or elder brothers.

Finally, a third group of promoters were the nominees or representatives of larger companies. Henry Pease, for example, sat on the Hawes & Melmerby Board as one of three NER representatives, while his name had earlier appeared as a subscriber to the abortive York & Carlisle scheme. Cornelius Nicholson was another notable railway promoter whose name was associated with other lines, while Lightly Simpson (a Director of the Hawes & Melmerby Railway) was closely connected with the Great Eastern Railway and its constituents. Some of this third group of promoters may have combined duty to the community with an element of speculative self-interest, but the fact nevertheless remains that the Wensleydale line was built and originally owned by land owners, and the manufacturing classes seem to have shown little or no interest in the railway.

NORTHALLERTON and HAWES—Weekdays.

DOWN.

M.C.	Station	1 PASSENGER	3 B Goods	4 D Goods	5	6	7	8 B Mineral Empties	9 PASSENGER	10	11	12 B Mineral	13
		arr. dep.	arr. dep.	arr. dep.	arr. dep.			arr. dep.	arr. dep.				
		a.m. a.m.	a.m. a.m.	a.m. a.m. (E)	a.m. a.m.			a.m. a.m.	a.m. a.m.			p.m.	
....	**Northallerton** +	— 7 0		— 7½20					— 10 50				
0 53	Castle Hills Inner J. ⊕	7 4	—	7 3½	— 8 35			9½6	10 53			—	
2 76	Ainderby ⊕		7 8		A				10 58			—	
4 33	Scruton		7 12		A				11 2			—	
5 70	Leeming Bar ⊕		7 16	7 44	9 20 10 20			9 39	11 6			—	
7 42	**Bedale** ⊕	7 20 7 22		8 *	10 27 12 10			9 44	11 10 11 11			—	
9 67	Crakehall		7 28									—	
11 41	Jervaulx ⊕		7 3?		12 25 12 50				11 18			—	
13 20	Finghall Lane		7 36		A				11 22			—	
14 26	Constable Burton ⊕	7*40	7 42		1 7 1 32				11 26			—	
15 67	Spennithorne		7 46									—	
....	*Harmby Quarry*											1 5	1 10
17 44	**Leyburn** ⊕	7 50 7 59		8 42 9 42	1 45 —			10 20 10½45	11 32 11 38			—	
....	*Ord & Maddison's Q'ry*												
19 72	Wensley ⊕		8 5	9 49 10 7	—			10 55	11 44			—	
21 78	Redmire ⊕		8 10	10 14 10 35	—			—	11 49			—	
24 75	Aysgarth ⊕ †	8 17	8 18	10 42 11*30	—			—	11 56 11 57			—	
29 51	Askrigg +	8 28	8 29	11 43 12*40	—			—	12 7			—	
33 73	Hawes +	8 38	8 C42	12 52	—			—	12 16 12c18			—	
39 68	**Hawes Junction and Garsdale**	8 57	—	—	—			—	12 33 —			—	

DOWN.

Station	14	15 B Mineral	16	17 PASSENGER	18 L.M.&S. PASSENGER	19 L.M. & S. Goods D	20 PASSENGER	21 PASSENGER	22 PASSENGER S O	23	1	2 Empty Train	3	4
				arr. dep.			arr. dep. arr. dep. (B)					arr. dep.		
		p.m.		p.m. p.m.	p.m. p.m.		p.m. p.m p.m. p.m.		p.m.			p.m. a.m.		
Northallerton +		—		1 39	—	—	4 11 7 14		9 15			— 11 55		
Castle Hills Inner J. ⊕		—		1 42	—	—	4 14 7 17		9 18					
Ainderby ⊕		—		1 46	—	—	4 19 7 21		9 22					
Scruton		—		1 50	—	—	4 23 7 25		9 26					
Leeming Bar ⊕		—		1 54	—	—	4 27 7 29		9 31					
Bedale ⊕		—		1 58 1 5?	—	—	4 31 4 33 7 34 7 36		9 36			12 10		
Crakehall		—		2 4	—	—	4 39		—					
Jervaulx ⊕		—		2 8	—	—	4 43 4 44 7 45 7 48		—					
Finghall Lane		—		2 13	—	—	4 48 7 53		—					
Constable Burton ⊕		—		2*17 2 20	—	—	4 52 7 57		—					
Spennithorne		—		2 24	—	—	4 56		—					
Harmby Quarry									—					
Leyburn ⊕		1 55		2 29 2 36	—	—	5 11 5 7 8 3 8 10		—			12k25 12 32		
Ord & Maddison's Q'ry		2 0							—					
Wensley ⊕		—		2 42	—	—	5 13 8 16		—			12t40		
Redmire ⊕		—		2 47	—	—	5 18 5 19 8 22		—			12t4?		
Aysgarth ⊕ †		—		2 55	—	—	5 26 5 28 8 3½		—			12t55		
Askrigg +		—		3 5	—	—	5 38 5 39 8 43		—			1t 7		
Hawes +		—		—	4 22 4 45	—	5 48 5C51 8c52 8 56		—			1 15 —		
Hawes Junction and Garsdale		—		—	4 36 5 5	—	6 8 9 11		—					

B—Horse boxes and carriage trucks are not conveyed by this train, except racehorses for Leyburn, when there are not sufficient boxes to justify a special being run.   E—Runs as D Goods from Leyburn.   t—Sets down empty milkcans.   †—Low Yard.

The Working Timetable of the branch for September 1926.

HAWES and NORTHALLERTON—Weekdays.

		UP.	1	2	3	4	5	6	7	8	9	10	12	13	14
Distance from Hawes Junction				PASSENGER.						PASSENGER.	Mineral	B Light Engine.		PASSENGER.	
M.C.				arr. dep.						arr. dep.				arr. dep.	
	Hawes Jun.			a.m. a.m.						a.m. a.m. p.n. p.m.				p.m. p.m.	
	and Garsdale			N 6C23						10c31		—		1C5	
5 75	Hawes .. ⊹			6 31 6 37						10 42 10 46	—	—		1 16 1 20	
10 17	Askrigg .. ⊹			6 45 6 48						10 53 10 57	—	—		1 28	
14 73	Aysgarth .. ⊕⊹			6 56 6 59						11 5 11 9	—	—		1 37	
17 70	Redmire .... ⊕			7 5 7 8						11 15 11 19	—	—		1 44	
19 76	Wensley .. ⊕			7 13 7 15						11 24 11 25 12 30	—			1 49	
	Ord & Maddison's Q'ry														
22 24	**Leyburn** .. ⊕			7 20 7 27						11 30 11 38 12 40 12 55	—			1 54 2 5	
	Harmby Quarry ..										12 58					
24 1	Spennithorne			7 31 7 33						11 42	—	—		2 10	
25 42	Constable Burton....⊕			7 37 7 46						11 46	—	—		2*15 2 19	
26 48	Finghall Lane			7 49 7 50						11 49 11 50	—	—		2 22	
28 27	Jervaulx .... ⊕			7 53 7 54						11 53 11 56	—	—		2 26	
30 11	Crakehall			7 58						12 0	—	—		2 30	
32 26	**Bedale** .... ⊕			8 3 8 5						12 6 12 8	—	—		2 36 2 38	
33 78	Leeming Bar .. ⊕			8 10 8 13						12 13 12 14	—	—		2 43 2 45	
35 55	Scruton			8 18						12 19	—	—		2 49	
36 72	Ainderby .. .. ⊕			8 22						12 23	—	—		2 53	
39 15	*Castle Hills Inner J.* ⊕			8 27						12 28	—	—		2 58	
39 68	**Northallerton** ⊹			8 30						12 31	—	—		3 1 —	

	UP.	15	16	17	18	19	20	21	22	24	25	2	3
		B Mineral.	D Goods.	D Goods. TX	D Goods. TO	D L.M.& S. Goods.	PASSENGER.	L.M.& S. PASSENGER.		PASSENGER.	S O PASSENGER.	MILK TRAIN.	
		arr. dep.	arr. dep.	arr. dep.	arr. dep.		arr. dep.			arr. dep.		arr. dep.	
	Hawes Jun.	p.m. p.m.	p.m. p.m.	p.m. p.m.	p.m. p.m. J	p.m.	p.m. p.m.	p.m.		p.m. p.m.	p.m.		p.m. p.m.
	and Garsdale	— —	— —	— —	— — J	—	— —	4 1		6C30	—		— —
	Hawes .. ⊹	— —	— —	2 0 1 50	2 0	3 0	— —	4 12		6 41 6 45	—	Sundays.	— 1 30
	Askrigg .. ⊹	— —	— —	2 30	2 10 2 4	3 20	— 3 20	—		6 53 6 58	—		1 37 1 42
	Aysgarth .. ⊕⊹	— —	— —	2 41 3*10	2 34 3*17	—	.. 3 29	—		7 4 7 7	—		1 50 1 59
	Redmire	— —	— —	3 17 3*42	3 22 3*45	—	.. 3 36	—		7 13 7 14	—		2 4 2 7
	Wensley .. ⊕	— —	— —	3 47 4	3 59 4 25	—	.. 3 41	—		.. 7 21	—		2 11 2 16
	Ord & Maddison's Q'ry	— —	2 20			—		—			—		
	Leyburn .. ⊕	2 25 2 40	3 20	4 11 5 10	4 40 5 40	—	3 46 3 53	—		7 26 7 32	—		2 21 2 25
	Harmby Quarry	3 23 3 33				—		—			—		
	Spennithorne ..	.. ..				—	.. 3 57	—		—			.. ..
	Constable Burton ..⊕	.. ..	3 42 4*12			—	4 2	—		.. 7 39	—		B ..
	Finghall Lane ..	.. ..	A			—	4 6	—		7 43	-		.. ..
	Jervaulx .... ⊕	.. ..	4 29 5 0			—	4 9 4 10	—		7 46 7 47	—		.. ..
	Crakehall	.. ..				—	.. 4 14	—		—			.. ..
	Bedale .... ⊕	3 13 3x18	5 12 6 20	5 38	6 8	—	4 19 4 21	—		7 55 7 57	9 51		2 46 2 48
	Leeming Bar .. ⊕	3 27	6 27 7 31	5 43	6 13	—	4 26 4 29	—		8 2 8 3	9 56		2 53 2 54
	Scruton	.. ..	A			—	4 33	—		.. 8 7	10 0		.. ..
	Ainderby .. .. ⊕	.. ..	.. ..			—	4 37	—		8 11	10 4		3 2
	Castle Hills Inner J.⊕	3 48	8 8 3 45	6 0 6 20	6 20 6 50	—	4 42	—		3 16	10 9		3 7
	Northallerton ⊹	4 10	8 55	6 35	7 0	—	4 45	—		8 19	10 12		3 10

B—Stops to take up milk traffic.
J—Detaches North wagons at Castle Hills. Class B from Leyburn.
N—Will not convey horse boxes except from Leyburn, Bedale, and Leeming Bar.
x—Brakes
⊹—Low Yard.

Class 'S3' 4-6-0 No. 843, seen here at Leyburn on 29th June, 1927 having just hauled one of the eclipse specials and, *below*, a further London special arriving on the same day with No. 711 and No. 1372 at its head. *H.C. Casserley*

Chapter Three
The Line in Operation 1908–1948

The Wensleydale line served a sparsely-settled rural area, and passenger traffic was never of massive proportions. Train services were, as a general rule, worked by the North Eastern Railway – Garsdale being the usual western 'terminus' for passenger services. In the Edwardian period the Midland Railway ran one train each way on weekdays between Hellifield and Hawes, and for some reason this train (and its successors) were known to local railwaymen as the 'Bonnyface'.

Train Services

There were usually about four or five trains in each direction between Northallerton and Garsdale, together with a limited number of local workings to Leyburn or Bedale. This pattern of operation remained fairly constant throughout the years, though there were attempts to increase the level of service to the public during the Edwardian period. In this context, the summer 1908 public timetable is particularly interesting in that there were no less than seven trains in each direction at that time. Indeed, the July 1908 timetable was one of the fullest ever provided on the bucolic Wensleydale route.

Services began with the departure of an early morning up train from Leyburn to Northallerton at 6.00 am. This service called by request at many of the smaller intermediate stopping places, though the more important stations at Bedale, Leeming and Ainderby were scheduled stops. The train reached its destination at 6.50 am, and it is assumed that the same locomotive and rolling stock then formed the 7.18 am service to Garsdale (arr. 10.25 am). Meanwhile, another engine had left Garsdale with the 6.42 am working to Northallerton, and this eastbound working passed the westbound 7.18 am from Northallerton in the crossing loop at Jervaulx.

The 6.42 am from Garsdale reached its destination at 8.28 am. A little over half an hour later, at 9.07 am, an unbalanced up service left Hawes, and this working reached Northallerton at 10.22 am. A second down train had, by this time, departed from Northallerton (9.48 am) en route for Hawes, while at 10.54 am another up train departed from Garsdale; the latter service reached Leyburn at 11.44 am, and having passed a corresponding down working from Northallerton (dep. 10.50 am) the 10.54 am reached its destination at 12.33 pm.

The afternoon service continued with further down workings from Northallerton at 1.38, 3.55, 6.33 and 9.40 pm while, in the opposite direction, up trains departed from Garsdale at 1.05, 3.40 and 6.25 pm. There was, in addition, an afternoon service from Hawes at 3.35 pm, and this last-mentioned working reached Northallerton at 5.02 pm. On Sundays, a train left Hawes at 5.30 pm, this solitary unbalanced service being provided primarily to serve the needs of local dairy farmers, who needed a means of transporting their milk churns out of the dale.

From a peak in 1908, branch train services declined slightly – though the basic service still offered around half a dozen trains each way. In 1914, for example, there were five trains running through from Northallerton to

45

Garsdale and six returning from Garsdale or Hawes, together with one up
service from Leyburn to Northallerton and an evening down train from
Northallerton to Leyburn; there was also an unbalanced short distance
service to Bedale.

On Sundays, the line was served by just one up train which left Hawes at
5.20 pm and called at all stations to Northallerton (the latter train had
arrived earlier in the day as an empty stock working). Journey times
averaged a little under two hours, though study of the following times will
reveal that some trains waited for over an hour at Hawes, and these lengthy
pauses increased the journey time to about three hours!

In 1914, down (westbound) passenger trains left Northallerton for
Garsdale at 7.16, 10.52 am, 1.30, 3.55 and 6.33 pm, while in the up direction
balancing eastbound workings departed from Garsdale at 6.41, 10.54 am,
1.05, 3.15 and 6.25 pm. The full 1914 branch time table is shown overleaf:

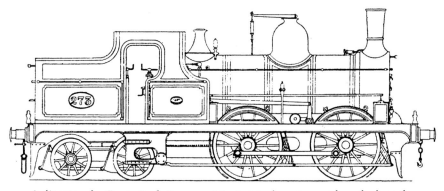

A diagram of a 'Bogie Tank Passenger' 0–4–4 tank engine used on the branch.

Fletcher 'Bogie Tank Passenger' class 0–4–4T No. 321 at Askrigg in August, 1900.
K. Taylor Collection

DOWN		am	am	am	pm	pm	pm	pm
Northallerton	dep:	7.16	9.48	10.52	1.30	3.55	6.33	10.00
Ainderby	dep:	7.23	9.55	10.59	1.37	4.02	6.40	10.07
Scruton	dep:	7.27	9.59	11.03	1.41	4.06	6.44	11.11
Leeming Bar	dep:	7.31	10.03	11.07	1.45	4.10	6.48	11.15
Bedale	arr:	7.35	10.07	11.11	1.49	4.14	6.52	11.18
	dep:	7.37		11.13	1.51	4.16	6.54	11.21
Crakehall	dep:	7.43		11.19	1.57	4.22	7.00	11.27
Jervaulx	dep:	7.55		11.23	2.13	4.30	7.05	11.32
Finghall Lane	dep:	8.00		11.28	2.18	4.35	7.10	
Constable Burton	dep:	8.04		11.32	2.22	4.39	7.14	11.41
Spennithorne	dep:	8.08		11.36	2.26	4.43	7.18	
Leyburn	arr:	8.12		11.40	2.31	4.47	7.22	11.47
	dep:	8.18		11.46	2.37	4.54	7.30	
Wensley	dep:	8.24		11.51	2.43	5.00	7.36	
Redmire	dep:	8.29		11.56	2.48	5.05	7.41	
Aysgarth	dep:	8.36		12.03	2.55	5.12	7.49	
Askrigg	dep:	8.46		12.13	3.05	5.22	7.59	
Hawes	arr:	8.55		12.22	3.14	5.31	8.08	
	dep:	10.10		12.24	4.15	5.33	8.10	
Garsdale	arr:	10.25		12.38	4.27	5.47	8.25	

UP		am	am	am	am	pm	pm	pm
Garsdale	dep:		6.41		10.54	1.05	3.15**	6.25
Hawes	arr:		6.51		11.05	1.16	3.27	6.36
	dep:		6.53	9.05	11.06	1.17	3.35	6.38
Askrigg	dep:		7.02	9.13	11.14	1.25	3.44	6.49
Aysgarth	dep:		7.12	9.22	11.23	1.34	3.53	7.00
Redmire	dep:		7.19	9.28	11.29	1.41	4.00	7.07
Wensley	dep:		7.24	9.33	11.34	1.46	4.05	7.13
Leyburn	arr:		7.29	9.38	11.39	1.51	4.10	7.18
	dep:	6.10	7.36	9.42	11.44	1.56	4.14	7.25
Spennithorne	dep:		7.40		11.49		4.18	7.29
Constable Burton	dep:		7.44	9.48	11.54	2.05	4.22	7.33
Finghall Lane	dep:		7.47		11.56	2.08	4.25	7.36
Jervaulx	dep:		7.51	9.54	12.00	2.12	4.29	7.40
Crakehall	dep:		7.55		12.05	2.17	4.34	7.45
Bedale	arr:	6.29	8.00	10.01	12.10	2.22	4.39	7.50
	dep:	6.32	8.02	10.02	12.12	2.24	4.41	7.52
Leeming Bar	dep:	6.37	8.08	10.07	12.17	2.29	4.46	7.58
Scruton	dep:		8.13	10.11	12.21	2.33	4.50	8.02
Ainderby	dep:	6.44	8.18	10.15	12.25	2.37	4.54	8.06
Northallerton	arr:	6.52	8.26	10.22	12.33	2.45	5.02	8.13

** = Midland Railway connecting service.

Goods services were provided by both the Midland and the NER companies, the Midland running at least one train a day on the western section of the line between Hawes and Garsdale, while the North Eastern provided a more complex pattern of services between Northallerton, Leyburn and Hawes.

The Midland working generally left Hawes in the late afternoon at around 3.25 pm, while the NER pick up goods working usually left Northallerton at about 7.20 am. At the very end of the NER era, the latter train ran non-stop to Leyburn and then called *en route* at the smaller stations between Leyburn and Hawes. A second NER mixed freight working usually departed from Northallerton at around 8.30 am, and this service shunted at the intermediate stations between Northallerton and Leyburn.

There were, in addition, a variable number of NER mineral trains which ran empty from Northallerton to Leyburn, Wensley or Hawes and returned fully laden in the early afternoon; in 1923, for example, a loaded mineral train left Leyburn at 3.10 pm. These mineral workings were augmented (as required) by one or two short distance trips between Leyburn and the neighbouring stone quarries.

In 1916 (by which time the effects of World War I had resulted in an altered pattern of freight train operation) a daily North Eastern Railway goods working was booked to leave Thirsk at 7.15 am, and this service called at most of the intermediate stations as shown below:

DOWN		am	UP		pm
Thirsk Down Yard	dep.	7.15	Leyburn	arr.	12.55
Northallerton	arr.	7.35		dep.	1.35
	dep.	7.39	Constable Burton	arr.	1.46
Inner Junction	pass	7.42		dep.	2.28
Ainderby	arr.	7.49	Finghall Lane	arr.	2.33
	dep.	8.03		dep.	2.38
Scruton	arr.	8.09	Jervaulx	arr.	2.45
	dep.	8.19		dep.	3.00
Leeming Bar	arr.	8.25	Bedale	arr.	3.12
	dep.	9.25		dep.	3.55
Bedale	arr.	9.32	Leeming Bar	arr.	4.02
	dep.	10.25		dep.	5.00
Jervaulx	arr.	10.40	Scruton	arr.	5.06
	dep.	11.10		dep.	5.15
Finghall Lane	arr.	11.17	Ainderby	arr.	5.24
	dep.	11.22		dep.	5.45
Constable Burton	arr.	11.28	Castle Hills	arr.	5.54
	dep.	11.50		dep.	6.15
		pm	Northallerton Low Yard	arr.	6.25
Leyburn	arr.	12.03	Light engine to Thirsk	arr.	6.45
	dep.	12.30			
West Quarry	arr.	12.35			
	dep.	12.50			

On Saturdays the train ran back fast to the Low Yard, arriving there at 3.55 pm. The line was, by this time, worked mainly by electric train tablet, though the older train staff and ticket system was employed at the eastern end of the branch between Northallerton and Northallerton West Junction, and on the western section between Aysgarth and Garsdale. There was a 1¾ mile double track section between Bedale and Leeming Bar, but otherwise the line was single track with crossing loops at Leeming, Jervaulx, Constable Burton, Leyburn, Wensley, Redmire, Aysgarth, Askrigg and Hawes.

Passenger trains could not cross at Redmire or Askrigg because these stations had only one platform. It was possible, however, for two freight workings or one passenger and one goods train to pass each other at these stations; a similar situation pertained at Bedale – although in this case passenger trains were allowed to pass each other on the double track section to the east of the single platform (see Chapter Three and Appendix Three).

Those who knew the Wensleydale line during the early 1900s regarded the route as an archetypal rural branch, and in this context it would be fitting to conclude this survey of operations in the pre-Grouping period with an eye-witness account of a journey made on the line around 1915. The journey – on Hawes market day – was made by an anonymous traveller known only as 'F.H.G.':

> The train proceeds slowly up the dale, disgorging sundry parcels and newspapers at each stopping place, but picking up passengers, for it is market day at Hawes, and on arrival there we are probably carrying a paying load. Farmers and dealers, for the most part, they present varying types of the British agriculturalist. Others have arrived mounted on stout Galloways; a good many have driven and some have come on foot, and the main street of the little grey town, nestled among the fells, presents an unusually animated appearance.[14]

Motive Power in the NER Era

Train services between Northallerton and Hawes Junction were worked, for many years, by Fletcher 0-4-4T Bogie Tank Passenger ('BTP') engines. These engines had been introduced in 1874, and they were employed throughout the NER system. No less than 124 were built, and several of these served on the Wensleydale line, typical numbers, at various times, being Nos. 15, 28, 69, 71, 188, 189, 322, 324, 357, 465, 588 and 1432. No. 465 was involved in an accident at Bedale in 1901 (see Chapter Three).

In 1920, Northallerton's allocation included five BTP 0-4-4Ts including Nos. 188, 189, 207, 264 and 357; Nos. 188, 207 and 357 were withdrawn in 1922. Sister engine No. 324 had a narrow escape in 1913 when it was almost hit by a main line train; the locomotive had been signalled into the up platform at Northallerton station when someone suddenly noticed that the next up express train was approaching against its signals. With commendable promptitude the driver set the little engine in motion and jumped clear before No. 324 disappeared in the Thirsk direction, giving the following driver time to realise the situation and bring the heavy train to a stand. (The runaway 'BTP' 0-4-4T was, fortunately, halted on the approaches to Thirsk.)

The BTP 0-4-4Ts were progressively withdrawn during the 1920s, and in their place the branch was worked by T.W. Worsdell's 'A' class 2-4-2Ts. Introduced in 1886, the NER class 'A' engines were remarkably similar to the 'M15' 2-4-2 tanks designed by Worsdell for the Great Eastern Railway. With their 5 ft 7¼ in. diameter coupled wheels, the Worsdell 2-4-2Ts were, perhaps, better-suited to fast suburban work than toiling up and down hilly branch lines, but the class 'A's were nevertheless employed on a number of North Eastern rural lines during the 1920s and early 1930s.

Top: Fletcher 'Bogie Tank Passenger' 0−4−4T No. 71 standing at Askrigg station in August 1900.

Middle: 'BTP' class 0−4−4T No. 588 on a local service at Hawes station in the 1900s.

Bottom: 'BTP' class 0−4−4T No. 465 on a branch service at Garsdale station in 1900.

All courtesy K. Taylor Collection

There were 60 class 'A' 2–4–2Ts in all, and they were numbered at random between 21 and 1606. Several members of the class appeared on the Wensleydale line, including Nos. 40, 279, 418, 420, 423, 469 and 1603, all of which were seen on the branch at various times from 1923 onwards. They worked from Northallerton shed, where up to half a dozen could be housed, along with a handful of 0–6–0 tender engines for local goods work. No. 423 was a later arrival, and it spent some time out-stationed at Hawes Junction (as did No. 469). The last locally-based 2–4–2T was No. 40, which moved to Tyne Dock in 1935.

Other locomotives used on the branch during the pre-Grouping period included NER class 'P1' 0–6–0s, and possibly class 'B1' 0–6–2Ts. Midland train services, meanwhile, were worked by venerable Kirtley double-framed 2–4–0s, Kirtley or Johnson 0–6–0 tender engines, and various other standard MR types. For Edwardian locomotive enthusiasts, these Midland Railway engines, with their distinctive crimson-lake livery, brought colour and variety to an otherwise exclusively-North Eastern scene. The greatest variety was of course to be found at the western end of the line between Hawes and Garsdale, where NER and Midland locomotives and rolling stock effectively shared the working of the branch.

In Edwardian days, Hawes and Garsdale were colourful places; NER and Midland trains were always well turned-out, the red Midland engines contrasting favourably with the light green North Eastern locomotives. Both companies favoured an overall dark-red livery for passenger vehicles, while the two railways painted their freight rolling stock light grey.

A Note on Locomotive Sheds

Locomotives used on the Wensleydale line were shedded at Northallerton, or in the single road sheds at Leyburn and Garsdale, with some engines working through from Hellifield or elsewhere.

Northallerton shed originated in 1857, but a new shed was erected in 1881 at a cost of £647 10s. Four years later, in 1886, an extension was provided at a cost of £290.[15] There were, typically, around ten engines based at Northallerton at any one time, and in the NER period roughly half of these were tank engines.

The small shed at Garsdale belonged to the Midland Railway, but it was rented by the NER from 1881 for £2 per month, plus an additional 9s. per week for the use of three railway cottages. Here, a North Eastern engine was outstationed (no doubt as an object of wonder or mirth to the MR men) to work trains to Northallerton. The shed had two sets of men who worked out and back trips to Northallerton with fill-in turns of shunting. There was also a cleaner whose duties included 'night firing' so that the engine would always be ready for its first turn of duty at around 6.30 am. Garsdale shed (which was referred-to as 'Hawes Junction' by the NER) was officially closed on 1st May, 1939, and operations were, thereafter, transferred to Leyburn.

The shed at Leyburn was, like that at Garsdale, a small stone-built structure, and it usually held one or two engines for shunting or for use on general duties; these included local passenger workings, for which two

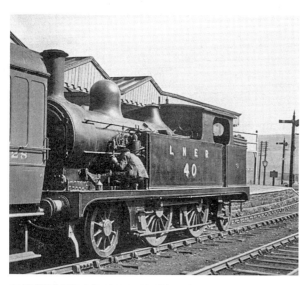

'F8' class 2–4–2T No. 40, seen at Garsdale while working a local service on 7th July, 1935.   *H.C. Casserley*

A freight train hauled by MR '3F' 0–6–0 locomotive No. 3731 running into Hawes Junction on the same day.   *H.C. Casserley*

crews were provided to work morning and afternoon shifts. (There had, in earlier days, been a small sub-shed at Leeming, but this had fallen into disuse by the 1870s.)

These arrangements varied, at different times throughout the line's history, one of the most significant changes being in 1915, when Leyburn shed was closed as an economy measure. In 1939, however, the latter shed was re-opened following the withdrawal of the branch engine from Garsdale.

The Grouping and After

In 1923 the independent life of the Midland and the North Eastern railways was brought to an end, for the Government had decided (as an alternative to nationalisation in the changed economic conditions following World War I) that the main line railway companies would be grouped into four large regional organisations. The necessary Act of Parliament was obtained in 1921, and on 1st January, 1923 the North Eastern Railway was merged with the Great Northern, Great Central, Great Eastern, North British, Great North of Scotland (and other companies) to form the aptly-named London & North Eastern Railway. The Midland, meanwhile, was merged with the London & North Western, Highland and Caledonian railways to form the London Midland & Scottish Railway,[16] and the operation of the Garsdale –Hawes–Northallerton route thereby passed into the hands of the LNER and LMS companies.

In the short term the 1923 Grouping produced few immediate changes, and the Wensleydale line continued to operate much as it had done in North Eastern Railway days. In the ensuing months, however, the LNER introduced its own liveries, and the local branch trains – which had hitherto been painted in NER plum red livery – started to appear in a sombre overall brown colour scheme. In theory, the LNER coach colour was 'varnished teak', but it was very hard to remove the paint from coaches that had been painted dark red in NER days, and in practice most LNER passenger vehicles were painted brown. Some main line stock received a 'scrumbled' or simulated wood finish, but the vast majority of local branch coaches were turned out in an unadorned mid-brown livery that did little to enhance their external appearance.[17]

It was a similar story in terms of locomotives. The attractive light green NER livery was replaced by a utilitarian black colour scheme – only engines with wheels larger than 6 ft 6 in. being considered important enough to carry LNER apple green livery. Former Midland Railway locomotives retained their traditional red livery for a few years, but by the 1930s the LMS decided that red liveries would be carried only by important main line engines, and thereafter the engines used on LMS services to Hawes were also painted in a plain black colour scheme.

Apart from these new liveries, the Grouping produced an entirely new system of class notation for LNER engines. This new system was both logical and simple in that 4–6–2s became 'As', 4–6–0s became 'Bs', 4–4–2s became 'Cs', 4–4–0s became 'Ds' and so on. As there was usually more than one type of engine with a particular wheel arrangement these basic notations were further subdivided by the addition of a numerical suffix. Thus the old Bogie Tank Passenger 0–4–4Ts became LNER class 'G6', while the former North Eastern class 'A' 2–4–2Ts became LNER class 'F8'. Both of these classes remained at work on the Wensleydale line during the immediate post-Grouping period, together with the ubiquitous Worsdell 'J21' 0–6–0s, which worked both goods and (occasionally) passenger trains.

Motive Power in the 1930s

The usual branch passenger engines, around 1930, were the 'F8' 2–4–2Ts, but these were replaced by former North Eastern Railway 'G5' class 0−4−4Ts in the next few years. Designed by Wilson Worsdell, the 'G5's had been built (as NER class 'O') between 1894 and 1901. One hundred and ten of these engines were built, and like the earlier 'G6's, they were used on branch line duties throughout the former NER system. Nos. 439 and 2089 arrived at Northallerton around 1929, followed by sister engine No. 435 some two years later. The 'G5' 0−4−4Ts eventually became the standard Wensleydale branch locomotive type, though they were helped on occasions by 'J21' or 'J25' 0−6−0s, and also by former main line 4−4−0s.

The 'G5' 0−4−4Ts were visually similar to the Worsdell 'F8' class 2−4−2Ts, both types being of similar size and weight, with standardised cabs and boiler fittings. The 'G5's had 18 in. × 24 in. cylinders and 5 ft 1½ in. coupled wheels; they carried 1,360 gallons of water and three tons of coal, and their weight in working order was a little over 51 tons.

Another former North Eastern Railway tank engine class used on the Wensleydale branch − albeit on a less regular basis − was the 'N8' class 0−6−2T. Introduced in 1886, the 'N8's were a mixed traffic design, intended for use on both passenger and goods duties. Designed by T.W. Worsdell, they had 18 in. × 24 in. cylinders and 5 ft 1¼ in. coupled wheels; some of the engines were originally compounds (NER class 'B') but the whole class was later converted into ordinary simple expansion engines (NER class 'B1'). There was usually one 0−6−2T based at Northallerton whereas there could be up to five 'G5' 0−4−4Ts at any one time, and it follows that the solitary 0−6−2T appeared less regularly than its 0−4−4T companions.

While on the subject of NER engines, it is of interest to record that the large tender engines appeared on the Wensleydale route on a number of occasions, unusually in connection with excursions, military specials or other special workings. In this context it is worth mentioning that there were no restrictions between Northallerton and Askrigg − engines of route availability groups '8' and '9' being allowed subject to a 30 mph speed restriction. From Askrigg to Hawes the route was considered suitable for all engines up to and including LNER group '7', with the addition of classes 'D49' and 'K3'. There was an overall speed limit of 45 mph, and sidings were restricted to engines in group '6' (and below).

It is likely that small engines were the norm prior to World War II, although former main line locomotives of classes 'D17' and 'B16' certainly appeared during the 1920s and 1930s. Other classes, including 'V2' 2−6−2s, 'USA' 2−8−0s and 'K1' 2−6−0s worked over the line on a regular basis during the 1939−45 war, and these workings will be mentioned in greater detail below.

Turntables were available at Northallerton, Leyburn and at Garsdale, but photographic evidence suggests that tank engines usually ran with their chimneys facing towards Garsdale. This ensured that they were facing the 'right' way in relation to the unremitting gradients between Bedale and Garsdale − though the real reason why the 'G5's were not turned probably reflected the awkward position of the turntable at Garsdale. This table was sited on the far side of the Settle & Carlisle main line, and it was not always possible for branch engines to cross the main running lines until connecting

LMS services had departed. The turntable was, moreover, manually-operated, and crews may have been reluctant to turn their engines when bunker-first running presented little discomfort (where tender engines were concerned the position was, of course, less clear cut!)

A further reason for the appearance of locomotives running bunker-first in the up direction stemmed from the operation of some train services to and from Hawes – there was no turntable at the latter station, and in these circumstances bunker-first running could not be avoided.

Train Services in the 1930s

The basic pattern of operation changed very little during the LNER period, and, as in North Eastern days, there were still up to five trains each way over all or part of the route. There had, for many years, been four up and four down trains between Northallerton and Garsdale, together with an afternoon service from Northallerton to Hawes that connected with the LMS-worked 'Bonnyface' branch working.

With engine sheds at Northallerton and Garsdale, it was possible for locomotives and train crews to be based at each end of the line so that up and down workings could depart more or less simultaneously and pass at Leyburn (or other intermediate stations). This mode of operation persisted throughout the 1930s, with a Garsdale-based engine making two return trips to Northallerton and a Northallerton locomotive making two round trips to Garsdale; a Northallerton engine also worked the solitary return service to Hawes which connected with an LMS service from Garsdale, and thereby provided a fifth daily train for local travellers (albeit with an intermediate change at Hawes).

In 1939, in an attempt to achieve operating economies, the sub-shed at Garsdale was closed, and as we have seen the small shed at Leyburn was then re-activated. This, in turn, necessitated a minor unheaval in the branch timetable in that the first up working departed from Leyburn rather than Garsdale. At the same time, the number of through trains between North-allerton and Garsdale was cut to just two return workings – though the 'Bonnyface' service continued to provide an alternative service for travellers who were prepared to change.

In November 1939, the first working of the day left Northallerton at 6.45 am and reached Garsdale by 8.40. The first up service had, meanwhile, left Leyburn at 8.00 am, and this working arrived at Northallerton at 8.51 am. The first up service from Garsdale departed at 11.00 am, while the locomotive and train set that had earlier worked the 8.00 am from Leyburn left Northallerton at 11.28 am; these two services passed each other in the loop at Constable Burton. At 12.45 pm the up train reached Northallerton, while at 1.04 pm the down service reached Hawes, where it terminated. Unfortunate through travellers (if any) were then faced with a long and boring wait until the departure of the LMS 'Bonnyface' working at 4.25 pm. In the reverse direction, the eastbound 'Bonnyface' was better timed in relation to the LNER timetable; the up LMS local left Garsdale at 3.42 pm and reached Hawes at 3.54, in good time for travellers to catch the 4.00 pm LNER departure for Northallerton.

Returning excursionists throng Leyburn station platform, waiting for one of the many specials to take them home after witnessing the total eclipse of the sun on 29th June, 1927.
H.C. Casserley

Special water tenders and extra gas-tanks vehicles brought into Leyburn for servicing the many special trains that arrived for the eclipse of the sun on 29th June, 1927.
H.C. Casserley

At 4.08 pm, the next down service left Northallerton, and at 4.48 pm this eastbound working passed the 4.00 pm from Hawes in the crossing loop at Constable Burton; the 4.08 ex-Northallerton reached Garsdale at 6.03 pm, while the 4.00 from Hawes reached Northallerton by 5.35 pm. Finally, the last up and down trains of the day left Garsdale and Northallerton at 6.30 pm and 6.15 pm respectively; at 7.05 pm the down service terminated at Leyburn, and as the train crew moved the engine to its shed, the evening up working made its way towards Northallerton. Leyburn was reached at 7.20 pm (i.e. after the arrival of the down train), and having called at all intermediate stations the last train of the day reached its destination at 8.28 pm.

Sunday services were not advertised in the November 1939 public timetable, but in practice the line was still kept open to deal with milk traffic between Leyburn and Hawes.

Eclipse Specials and Other Excursions

In common with other cross-country lines, the Wensleydale route fulfilled a useful role as a diversionary route during wartime, or in times of emergency. It also featured in a variety of excursion programmes during the pre-grouping era, with outward trips to east coast resorts such as Scarborough and Saltburn or west coast destinations such as Morecambe. At the same time, the scenic attractions of Wensleydale ensured that the line was also traversed by a number of incoming excursions from industrial cities such as Leeds, York and Bradford, and these special workings enabled Edwardian day trippers to walk on the fells or enjoy 'pic-nic parties' beside the sparkling River Ure. For a time between the wars the route was included in a scenic excursion circuit encompassing the Wensleydale, Settle & Carlisle and Stainmore lines.

Excursions of a different kind were run on 29th June, 1927, when the LNER ran a number of long distance specials in connection with a total eclipse of the sun. Such eclipses are exceedingly rare – indeed, prior to 1927, the last total eclipse of the sun to be seen in England had occurred in 1724! The 1927 eclipse was thus regarded as a remarkable phenomenon, and the railway companies were quick to realise that this 'once in a lifetime' opportunity presented many possibilities in terms of special excursion traffic. It was calculated that the total eclipse would occur, for a few seconds, over a 30 mile wide belt of country extending across Wales and the North of England; the eclipse would begin at 6.23 am over Tremadoc Bay, and reach the North Sea coast near Saltburn at 6.25 am. The time for viewing would therefore be during the early morning, while hills and mountain tops were obviously favoured as ideal places from which to view the phenomenon.[18]

The LNER operating authorities decided that Leyburn and Richmond would be ideal locations from which to view the eclipse, and special trains were provided in order to transport thousands of people to the Yorkshire Dales. One of the Leyburn trains ran through from Kings Cross on the evening of 28th June, 1927, the engine used on the initial stage of the journey

A general view of Finghall Lane station. *K. Taylor Collection*

A special, slatted van provided to convey local milk traffic on the Wensleydale line; this vehicle was built in 1908, and numbered 125 in the NER fleet list.
K. Taylor Collection

being LNER 'Atlantic' No. 4442. At Doncaster, the big 4−4−2 was replaced by 2−6−0 No. 4690 and 'J6' 0−6−0 No. 3535, and after a run to Leeds, these two engines were themselves replaced by former North Eastern Railway 'S' class 4−6−0s Nos. 798 and 819, which took the train on to Leyburn. Other excursions were, meanwhile, en route to Leyburn from Leeds, Hull, Norwich, Colchester, Scarborough, Dewsbury and Nottingham, and on arrival these diverse workings presented a major problem for local railway staff.

To cope with this vast influx of trains and passengers, the LNER stationed a 'control coach' and two additional coaches at Leyburn to accommodate extra staff. One of these vehicles functioned as a mobile staff restaurant, and old locomotive tenders and cylindrical gas tank wagons were needed to maintain supplies of water and gas. As an added precaution, an engineer's inspection saloon, together with a locomotive in steam, was parked in the goods sidings to help deal with any unforeseen emergencies.[19]

As the moment of total eclipse drew nearer, people positioned themselves in vantage spots in and around the station – unfortunately, the sky was partially overcast, and many people saw nothing of the eclipse other than a brief darkening of the sky. Others were rewarded with an unimpeded view of the famed 'corona' effect, which lasted for a few seconds as the moon passed across the orb of the sun, extinguishing its brilliance but leaving a magical halo around the obtrusive shadow. (The best viewing conditions were, apparently, in neighbouring Giggleswick.)

The eclipse over, thousands of people converged on the station, and, one by one, the excursions set off back to their points of origin – allowing Leyburn to revert to its normal condition of tranquility.

Milk and Freight Traffic

Solar eclipses notwithstanding, the Wensleydale line was a particularly quiet line which existed to serve the needs of an isolated part of the country. Coal was, for many years, the most important source of bulk traffic, this commodity being purchased by local dealers who resold it to their customers in ready-bagged quantities. The local stations had coal wharves at which the coal was unloaded, and (as usual on NER lines) most goods yards were equipped with raised coal drops which greatly speeded the otherwise laborious process of unloading the coal.

Wensleydale was an agricultural area, and many local farmers kept small herds of dairy cows for milk production. Although Yorkshire could not hope to compete with the West of England as a specialised dairy farming region, appreciable quantities of milk and cheese were nevertheless produced, and this gave rise to a welcome source of traffic for the railway. Milk was, for many years, conveyed in ponderous metal churns, but in later years the introduction of special tanker wagons represented a great improvement for both farmers and the railway company.

On the LNER part of the line, milk was loaded into single six-wheeled milk vans at wayside stations, or in block train loads which were, of necessity, efficiently timed and operated. There was, around 1930, a 7.00 pm milk and parcels service from Hawes to York; this was headed by a special engine

– usually ex-North Eastern Railway 'D17' 4–4–0 No. 1636, which was sent out light from Northallerton to work the train each day. The train ran during the early 1930s, but had ceased running by 1933 – after which more milk traffic was conveyed by ordinary passenger workings.

On Sundays an empty stock train ran out from Northallerton to Hawes and returned in the afternoon or early evening as a milk and parcels working. In September 1926 the empty train left Northallerton at 11.55 am and returned from Hawes at 1.30 pm – though by the early 1930s the time of departure from Hawes had been put back to 6.00 pm.

The LMS was also very keen on milk traffic, and was involved in its movement seven days a week, with milk trains from Hawes to Garsdale at 9.00 am and 11.45 am. Similar trains also ran on Sundays, the engines required to work the Sunday milk trains being sent out light (or on empty stock workings).

Rail transport enabled farmers to produce milk for consumption in industrial towns and cities such as Newcastle, Bradford, Leeds and Halifax, and large amounts of Wensleydale milk was forwarded to these northern destinations. However, the speed and efficiency of rail travel meant that milk could also be despatched to more distant centres of population such as London, and at one time much of the milk produced in the area was sent to a large milk depot at Finsbury Park. The 7.00 pm milk and parcels train usually conveyed five milk vans, two of which originated at Hawes while the remaining vehicles were loaded with churns at Askrigg and Leyburn; all five vans were sent down the east coast main line to Finsbury Park – the North Eastern/Great Northern route to London being, in many ways, a natural outlet for milk traffic to the metropolis.

The amount of milk conveyed on the Wensleydale line grew steadily during the early years of the 20th century. In 1906, for example, over 500,000 gallons were despatched in cans from the Leyburn to Hawes section alone, while by 1911 759,763 gallons were being sent through Northallerton each year.[20] To put these figures into perspective it is worth noting that stations on the Leek & Manifold line handled approximately 220,000 gallons of milk a year during the early 1900s,[21] while in 1915 the Great Western branch from Yarnton to Fairford was dealing with an estimated 540,000 gallons a year.[22]

These figures suggest that milk traffic was of particular importance to the Wensleydale line, and in this context it is interesting to find that the North Eastern Railway encouraged local farmers to produce milk, cheese and butter by erecting dairies on NER land in close proximity to selected stations. One of these railway-owned dairies was provided at Redmire, and in May 1911 *The North Eastern Railway Magazine* printed the following short report:

> We are informed that the North Eastern Railway Co. are erecting a dairy and depot at Redmire in Wensleydale, which is to be leased to the Wensleydale Farmers' Association – a society which has recently been formed with the object of manufacturing Wensleydale cheeses under standard conditions.

The Wensleydale Farmers' Association was a co-operative with about 50 members, and it lasted until the early 1930s – by which time changes in the dairy industry had led to the introduction of centralised dairies at places such as Appleby (on the Settle & Carlisle main line) and Leyburn. The Leyburn dairy was opened in 1937, and this new facility soon became a focal point for the collection of milk from surrounding farms; milk was, thereafter, sent to the dairy by road transport, and having been properly treated the milk was then forwarded by rail to London in milk tank wagons.

Horses and livestock were also carried on the line, particularly to and from Leyburn – which was a well-known breeding and training centre for racehorses. Horse boxes were sometimes attached to convenient passenger trains, though at other times there was sufficient traffic to justify the provision of special trains to or from Leyburn. (In 1936, the LNER prepared plans for a 'washing area for motorised horse boxes' at Leyburn station.)

In addition to these sources of agricultural traffic the Wensleydale line also carried limestone from quarries in the Wensley, Redmire and Leyburn areas. The coming of the railway had enabled these quarries to be developed – not so much for building purposes but as a source of flux for use in the iron and steel furnaces on Teeside. In the long term, this flow of limestone between Wensleydale and Teeside was of immense importance in that it provided a source of bulk traffic which would sustain the railway into the age of mass motoring.

There were, in fact, several rail-served quarries along the route of the line, among them Ord & Maddison's Quarry between Leyburn and Wensley, Harmby Limestone Quarry between Leyburn and Spennithorne, and the Redmire Quarry at Redmire. At list of rail-served quarries or quarry sidings is shown in *Table Two*, which reflects the ownership of these facilities in 1938.

Redmire, Leyburn and the other intermediate stations were equipped with loading docks, cattle pens and other facilities, although the type of accommodation provided varied considerably. Some of the smaller stations, for example, had no cattle pens or end-loading docks, while only the larger stations had fixed yard cranes.

The following table (compiled with the aid of the 1938 *Railway Clearing House Handbook of Stations*) will give some idea of the range of goods facilities available on the Wensleydale line. It should, be added, perhaps, that the presence of the letters 'F' or 'C' in the table shows that the stations concerned had end-loading docks suitable for the shipment of heavy machinery, furniture or motor vehicles; as a general rule, the absence of these letters would suggest that no end-loading bays were available.

A British Railways dog ticket issued at Leeming Bar, from the collection of J.M. Strange.

Table Two

STATION ACCOMMODATION & PRIVATE SIDINGS IN 1938

Station	Facilities						Crane	Private Sidings
Northallerton	G	P	F	L	H	C	5 ton	Cow & Gate Siding / Shell Mex & BP depot
Ainderby	G	P		L	H		—	Yafforth Siding
Scruton	G	P		L	H		—	—
Leeming Bar	G	P	F	L	H	C	15 cwt	Vale of Mowbray Bacon Factory
Bedale	G	P	F	L	H	C	1 ton	Anglo American Oil Co Siding
Crakehall		P					—	—
Jervaulx	G	P		L	H	C	—	—
Finghall Lane	G	P					—	—
Constable Burton	G	P		L	H		10 ton	—
Spennithorne		P					—	—
Leyburn	G	P	F	L	H	C	5 ton	Harmby Limestone Quarry / Ord & Maddison's Siding
Wensley	G	P					—	Wensley Quarry Company
Redmire	G	P	F	L	H	C	1 ton	Redmire Limestone Company
Aysgarth	G	P	F	L	H	C	2 ton	—
Askrigg	G	P	F	L	H	C	2 ton	—
Hawes	G	P	F	L	H	C	1 ton 10 cwt	—
Garsdale	G	P		L	H	C	—	—

G = Goods; P = Passengers; F = Furniture Vans, Motor Cars etc; L = Livestock;
H = Horses & Prize Cattle; C = Carriages, Motor Cars

The types of goods vehicle seen on the line reflected the traffic carried, wooden-bodied open wagons, cattle wagons and horse boxes being much in evidence. Photographic evidence shows that the North Eastern's characteristic wooden hopper wagons were widely used, these vehicles being specially-suited for use in conjunction with the company's raised coal drops. The NER had several types of hopper wagon, though the large, 20 ton hopper was probably the most distinctive type. The wagons were built with tapering sides to help the gravity unloading process, and their end pillars were extended downwards to form butting timbers for use when the wagons were shunted with old fashioned 'chaldron' wagons in the north-eastern coal fields.

As most of the stations between Northallerton and Hawes were equipped with raised coal drops, NER 20-ton wooden hopper wagons (and the older 10½-ton and 12-ton varieties) could usually be seen in the local goods yards. Ordinary high or low-sided open wagons were used to transport hay, building materials or general merchandise, and these vehicles could, if necessary, be sheeted-over to protect vulnerable loads.

Agricultural machinery or other heavy types of equipment could be carried in drop-sided open wagons, but in 1910 the NER introduced some specially designed flat-bedded steel vehicles, and these enabled portable engines, motor vehicles (or other wheeled loads) to be simply and easily loaded in end-loading docks. Timber, drain pipes and other extra-long consignments were loaded onto bolster wagons – some of which ran in permanently-coupled twin sets.

Photographs of stations and goods yards suggest that NER wagons pre-dominated between Northallerton and Hawes, although Hawes goods yard was usually full of Midland Railway vehicles. Through loads from beyond the confines of the North Eastern system might bring London & North Western or Lancashire & Yorkshire rolling stock onto the branch, but the overwhelming impression is of a line which (prior to 1923) was operated by goods vehicles from the parent NER company. Pooling arrangements may have modified this picture in later years, but it would appear that, even in LNER days, most pick-up goods trains were composed primarily of local wagons or covered vans.

Before leaving the subject of rolling stock, one might add that the six-wheeled milk vans used to convey milk churns were parcels-type vehicles with prominent louvred side panels to assist cooling and ventilation; at least one of the vans (LNER No. 125) was used by a local co-operative known as the Wensleydale Pure Milk Society, and this name was carried along its sides. These vehicles were rendered obsolete by the introduction of glass-lined milk tank wagons in the 1930s, and by the end of the LNER period most local milk traffic was being carried in tankers which were collected from the dairy at Leyburn; Leyburn thereby became the centre of local milk production, its goods yard being the collection point for loaded tank wagons.

Camping Coaches

The London & North Eastern Railway was the poorest of the 'Big Four' companies created as a result of the 1923 Grouping, yet it comes as a surprise to discover that this impoverished, and somewhat ramshackle undertaking was frequently an innovator. Its advertising policies, for example, were both innovative and imaginative, while the company was the very first to introduce so-called 'camping coaches' as a means of encouraging summer tourist traffic.

In August 1933 *The Railway Magazine* announced that the LNER was adapting a number of old passenger vehicles for use as 'complete holiday homes ... in sites in the dales of Northumberland, the Esk Valley, the Pennines, the Cheviots, and other favourite spots'. The coaches involved in this conversion were 10 former Great Northern Railway six-wheelers, and the conversion was effected by the simple expedient of removing some of the internal partitions to form an open living room and dining area – the end compartments being retained as sleeping cabins. These old vehicles were then sent out to selected stations in the North Eastern area, one of the lines concerned being the Wensleydale route.

Camping coaches were soon established at Wensley, Aysgarth and Askrigg, and these were soon attracting customers throughout the summer months. Each coach could accommodate up to six people, and the rent (during the mid-1930s) was £2 10s. per week during the summer, and £2 at the beginning and end of the holiday season. Towels, bed linen, cutlery and other essentials were provided by the railway company, but people staying in the coaches had to use the nearby station buildings for toilet and washing facilities.

It is believed that, when first installed on the Wensleydale line, the camping coaches retained their ordinary teak brown livery, but the LNER's attractive green and cream 'tourist' livery was later applied in an effort to brighten-up their appearance.

The introduction of camping coaches was part of a general movement towards camping, hiking and other forms of outdoor holidaymaking during the 1930s. With war clouds looming in the east, young (and even not-so-young) walkers, hikers and ramblers took to the hills and fells in increasing numbers – the castles, abbeys and beauty spots of Wensleydale being particularly popular at this time. Ironically, these healthy outdoor activities were being mirrored in Nazi Germany – with the important difference that, whereas in England camping and hiking were seen as innocent (even eccentric) pastimes, in Germany the sinister 'strength through joy' movement was controlled by an aggressive, militaristic one-party state. Although many people chose to ignore the German threat, it was clear that, by 1939, a major war could no longer be avoided.

World War II

On Sunday, 3rd September, 1939 a period of growing international tension prompted by the Nazi invasion of Poland culminated in the outbreak of war between Germany and the British Empire. For the second time in a little over 20 years, the British people found themselves engaged in a major European conflict – and nothing would ever be the same again.

The first months of the war were strangely uneventful, and despite initial fears of massive aerial attack, the first stages of the 1939–45 war were so quiet that people began to speak of a 'Phoney War'. The sudden and unexpected collapse of French resistance in May and June 1940 dispelled any illusions about the gravity of the situation, and in fear of imminent invasion the government ordered that all road signs and station nameboards should be taken down. Blackout regulations were rigorously enforced, and in an attempt to hinder enemy bomber pilots, platform lamps and street lights were no longer lit; for this reason white lines were hastily painted along platform edges to prevent unwary travellers from falling onto the darkened lines.

The threat of air attack was, in fact, taken very seriously. Zeppelin and aeroplane raids in World War I had given some indication of likely casualty figures in a modern conflict, and armed with this existing data government 'experts' predicted that the *Luftwaffe* would drop about 950 tons of bombs a day, resulting in two million casualties in the first six months of war. It was felt that there was no defence against the coming onslaught and that 'the bomber would always get through'; whole cities were expected to be wiped out in a series of so-called 'knock-out blows', while the railways were thought to be prime targets for the coldly-efficient Teutonic airmen.

Faced with this dreadful scenario (which was so appalling that it was withheld from public scrutiny) the British military authorities identified a number of vulnerable locations on the vital supply routes between industrial centres, Channel ports and naval bases such as Scapa Flow, and the railways were asked to install a number of emergency junctions or connections in order that supply trains could avoid potential trouble spots. In this situation, the complex British railway system emerged as a tremendous national asset. The competing routes laid down by Victorian capitalists enabled countless alternative routes to be identified – one of these, of course, being the Wensleydale branch, which could have functioned as a vital trans-Pennine link if other, more important routes had been knocked out by precision bombing.

In a slightly different context, Northallerton was considered to be a potential target because it was a nodal point for several diverging routes. A few expertly placed bombs would hinder operations on all of these lines while, perhaps more importantly, the vital routes from Leeds to Stockton passed beneath the east coast main line at one obvious target point. Plans were therefore drawn up for a new connection to be installed along the west side of the station, the idea being that traffic to or from Leeds would be routed well clear of the east coast main line to rejoin the latter route beyond the station. A double track connection was accordingly built between Boroughbridge Road signal box and the original Bedale branch junction at Castle Hills, this emergency link being ready for use in November 1941.

The new connection enabled trains between Leeds to Newcastle to avoid the station entirely, while at the same time it was possible for trains from London or York to diverge from the main line at the south end of the station and rejoin it at Castle Hills. Temporary platforms were installed on a low level site to the west of the main high level station, and in the event of a major raid on the main line, these emergency platforms could have been rapidly brought into use.

The most interesting feature of the wartime connection concerned the way in which it passed beneath the Wensleydale branch between Northallerton High and Northallerton West junctions. There was insufficient room for the wartime link to burrow beneath the branch, and an opening bridge had therefore been designed so that, in the event of the emergency line being needed, the obtrusive bridge girders could be rolled out of the way. When opened, the moving bridge created a gap in the Wensleydale line, and in these circumstances it was expected that branch trains would be diverted around the northern arm of the triangle via Northallerton West and Castle Hills Junction (in effect a reversion to the original, pre-1882 mode of operation!)

The bridge itself was a twin-span structure with two 17 ft girder spans, the latter being mounted on guide rails so that each span could be wheeled out of the way on platelayers' bogies. The rails across the bridge spans were secured by fishplates in the usual way, and these had to be unbolted before the structure could be moved. There was an interlocking arrangement between the bridge and the signalling system, and this ensured that the avoiding line could not be brought into use until the bridge spans were locked safely out of the way (conversely, the southern curve between Northallerton High and Northallerton West could not be used once the branch was severed.)[23]

Happily, pre-war estimates of likely wartime bomb damage were wildly inaccurate, and although, at certain periods during the war, the *Luftwaffe* did indeed turn its full attention onto London or other British cities, it emerged that the destructive power of the Nazi airforce had been greatly over-estimated. None of the wartime rail links were ever needed, and no rail centre was ever knocked-out in the way that had been feared.

Ironically, at a later stage in the war the RAF and allied bomber forces were able to inflict massive damage on German military and civilian targets, the employment of heavy, four-engined bombers such as the Lancaster being used to devastating effect in cataclysmic raids on cities such as Hamburg and Dresden. This gigantic air offensive called for an unprecedented expansion of the Royal Air Force, and by 1944 much of lowland Britain was covered by a dense network of aerodromes. Many of these airfields were sited in and around the plain of York, and although the elevated terrain around upper Wensleydale was not suitable for aircraft operations, the Wensleydale line became involved in the air war through the presence of an important Bomber Command aerodrome at Leeming.

Situated on level ground to the south of the railway, RAF Leeming was a front line Bomber Command station which, as part of '6 Group', was operated by the Royal Canadian Air Force. In 1944, Leeming housed two RCAF squadrons (Nos. 427 and 429) and its aircraft allocation consisted of Halifax four-engined heavy bombers.[24]

Wartime activity reached its peak in the weeks and months preceding the invasion of Europe in June 1944, and in addition to carrying men and equipment to RAF Leeming, the Wensleydale line served several army camps and supply dumps throughout the area – the most important military locations being in and around Catterick. In these months of hectic preparation for D-Day, branch trains were packed with servicemen and women from around the world, and the line was called upon to handle a variety of military specials, some of which brought unusual motive power onto the route.

The ordinary branch passenger services were merely a continuation of those provided during the 1930s. There was an up departure from Leyburn to Northallerton at 7.40 am and a return working in the down direction at 9.50 am. An earlier train had, meanwhile, left Northallerton at 7.05 am, and this down working reached Garsdale by 9.04 am. At 10.45 am, the same train returned to Northallerton, the latter station being reached at 12.35 pm. There were, by this time, two trains in operation on the branch, one having started its operations at Leyburn while the other had worked a return trip from Northallerton to Garsdale. These two trains continued their respective duties throughout the afternoon and evening, the Northallerton-based engine working a return trip to Garsdale at 4.08 pm, with a down working from Garsdale to Northallerton at 6.30 pm.

At the western end of the line, the train that had earlier left Northallerton at 9.50 am worked a return service from Garsdale to Leyburn at 12.45 pm; the balancing down working left Leyburn at 2.15 pm, and this service ran only as far as Hawes. After providing a connection with the LMS service from Garsdale, the LNER train then returned from Hawes to Northallerton at 3.57 pm. Finally, at 7.32, the locomotive and train set set off back to its point of origin at Leyburn.

Careful study of the above-mentioned times will reveal that the branch passenger service was worked by two trains, one of which performed two return trips between Northallerton and Garsdale while the other worked a complex diagram involving one journey between Northallerton and Garsdale, one trip from Garsdale to Leyburn, one trip from Leyburn to Hawes, one trip from Leyburn to Northallerton and one evening journey from Northallerton to Leyburn.

The 'G5' 0–4–4Ts still worked many local train services, though other ex-NER classes also appeared – among them 'N8' 0–6–2T No. 267 and (on a less regular basis) 'D20' 4–4–0s Nos. 476 and 2030. An article in the May/June 1943 *Railway Magazine* mentioned that the engines seen on these duties were 'generally an 'N8' 0–6–2 tank or a 'G5' 0–4–4T', and the writer added that 'the solitary LMS passenger service from Skipton to Garsdale and Hawes was usually headed by an LMS class '2' 4–4–0. (He made no mention of 'D20' 4–4–0s being used on local passenger work at that time, though it is known that these ex-main line locomotives were occasionally used at the start of the 1939–45 war.)

The *Railway Magazine* article also mentioned that freight traffic on the Wensleydale line was hauled by standard ex-North Eastern Railway 0–8–0s, while shunting duties at Leyburn were performed by four-wheeled Sentinel 'Y3' class locomotive No. 196. Other engines used on the branch during World War II included 'J21' 0–6–0s, 'K1' 2–6–0s, 'V2' 2–6–2s and 'USA' class 2–8–0s. These large tender engines worked through freight trains and military specials, double-heading being resorted to in the case of particularly heavy trains.

The war ended in 1945, but austerity conditions continued for many months thereafter, and the railways were unable to return to their pre-war patterns of operation. National recovery was impeded, in 1947, by one of the worst winters in living memory, and with the country's road transport in complete chaos, railways became vital lifelines for remote communities such as Aysgarth and Hawes. The great freeze lasted until March 1947, and a few months later, on 31st December, 1947 the British railway system was nationalised by Mr Attlee's post-war Labour government, and the LNER era was thereby brought to a close.

As we shall see, nationalisation had little obvious impact on the Wensleydale branch, though it would be convenient to mention here that in September 1948 (nine months after nationalisation came into effect) the entire line from Northallerton to Garsdale became part of British Railways North Eastern Region – the boundary between North Eastern and London Midland Region territory being moved westwards from Hawes to the junction at Garsdale.

Having taken the story of the Wensleydale line up to the start of the British Railways period it would now be appropriate to examine the stations and route of the railway in greater detail, and the next two chapters will take readers on an imaginary guided tour of the branch from Northallerton to Garsdale. Generally speaking, the topographical details will be correct for the later LNER period around 1930, although it should be stressed that the line did not change in any major way between the early 1900s and the withdrawal of passenger services in 1954.

NORTHALLERTON and HAWES and GARSDALE—Weekdays

	DOWN		1	2	3	4	5	6	7	8	9	10	11	12	13
Distance from Northallerton			B Mineral	PASSENGER			PASSENGER	B Goods	D Goods		EXPRESS PASSENGER	PASSENGER			
							TO				WThSO				
			arr. dep.	arr. dep.			arr. dep.	arr. dep.	arr. dep.		arr. dep.	arr. dep.			
M.C.			a.m. a.m.	a.m. a.m.			a.m. a.m.	S a.m. a.m.	a.m. a.m.		a.m. a.m.	J a.m. a.m.			
....	NORTHALLERTON ....✝		— —	— 7 5			— —	— 8 10	— —		— 9 53	— 10 48			
0 53	Northallerton West ⊕		.. ..	7 8			—	.. ..	.. ..		.. ..	10 51			
2 76	Ainderby ....⊕			7 13			—	.. ..	✱		.. ..	P ..			
4 33	Scruton	Middlesbro' lock 4.30 a.m. p.309	..	7 17			—	.. ..	✱		.. ..	.. ..			
5 70	Leeming Bar ......⊕		...	7 21			—	✱	✱		...	10 59			
7 42	Bedale .. .. ⊕			7 25 7 27			—	.. ..	✱		10 7 10 8	11 3 11 4			
9 57	Crakehall			7 33 7 34			—	.. ..	—						
11 41	Jervaulx .. .. ⊕			7 38 7 41			—	Darlington dep. 7.35 a.m. p. 60	✱		Not after 4th September	11 12			
13 20	Finghall Lane			7 45			—		✱						
14 26	Constable Burton .. ⊕			7 49			—		✱			11 17			
15 67	Spennithorne			7 53			—	.. ..	✱						
....	Harmby Quarry ..						—	.. ..	—						
17 44	Leyburn ....⊕		.... ✱	7 59 8 2			—	✱	DD		10 24 10 32	11 24 11 33			
....	Ord & Maddison's Q'ry		✱	✱			—	.. ..	—						
19 72	Wensley ....⊕		DD	8 8 8 11			—	✱	—		... 10 38	11 39			
21 78	Redmire .. .. ⊕		—	8 16			—	✱	—		... 10 43	11 44			
24 75	Aysgarth ....⊕		—	8 23			—	✱	—		10 50 10 55	11 51			
29 51	Askrigg .. .. ⊕		—	8 32			—	✱	—		.. 11 4	12 0			
33 73	Hawes............⊕		—	8 41 8 C44			9 46 DD	—	—		11 13 —	12 9 12c11			
39 68	Garsdale .. .. ⊕		—	8 58			10 1	—	—		—	12 25			

	DOWN	15	16	17	18	19	20	22	23	24	1	2	3	4	6	8
			PASSENGER	L.M.S. PASSENGER		D L.M.S. Goods	PASSENGER	PASSENGER					NO. 1 EXPRESS PARCELS		Engine and Van	
						SX										
			arr. dep.				arr. dep.	arr. dep.					arr. dep.			
			p.m. p.m.	p.m.		p.m.	F p.m. p.m	p.m. p.m.					a.m. a.m.		p.m.	
	NORTHALLERTON ....✝		— 1 35	—		—	4 9	— 7 20					— 8 24		3 45	
	Northallerton West .. ⊕		1 38			—	4 12	7 23		Sundays			S 27		3 45	
	Ainderby .... ⊕		...	1 45		—	4 17	7 27							..	
	Scruton		...			—	4 21	7 31					.. ..		..	
	Leeming Bar .... ⊕		...	1 49		—	4 25 4 28 7 35	7 36					.. ..		..	
	Bedale .. .. ⊕		1 53 1 54			—	4 32 4 33 7c40	7 42					.. ..		4	
	Crakehall		... A			—	4 39	7 48					8 45 8 47		..	
	Jervaulx .. .. ⊕		.. 2 3			—	4 43 7 52	7 55					.. ..		..	
	Finghall Lane		A			—	4 47 4 48	7 59					.. ..		..	
	Constable Burton .. ⊕		.. 2 10			—	4 52	8 3					.. ..		..	
	Spennithorne		..			—	4 55	V							..	
	Harmby Quarry					—										
	Leyburn ....⊕		2 17 2 23			—	5 1 5 5 8 9	8 14					9 W6 9 10		4 23	
	Ord & Maddison's Quarry		.. ..			—									—	
	Wensley .. .. ⊕		2 29			—	5 11	8 20					9 15 9 16		—	
	Redmire .. .. .. ⊕		2 34			—	5 16 5 21 8 25	8 28					9 30 —		—	
	Aysgarth .. .. ⊕		2 41			—	5 28 5 29	8 35					.. ..		—	
	Askrigg .. .. ⊕		2 50			—	5 38 5 39	8 44					.. ..		—	
	Hawes............⊕		2 59	4 25		4 45	5 48 5C50 8C53	8 55					.. ..		—	
	Garsdale .. .. ⊕		—	4 39		5 5	6 4 —	9 9					— —		—	

A—Calls on Tuesdays and Saturdays. Time allowed for stops.
F—"HC" to or from intermediate stations except—(a) for Bedale (b) from the Darlington mart for Hawes on Mondays and (c) racehorses for Leyburn when a special cannot be justified.
J—"HC" except by prior arrangement with D.P.M.

P—Stops on Tuesdays only.
S—Class D from Leyburn. On Fridays conveys live stock from Bedale and Jervaulx for Leyburn Mart.
V—Stops (SOQ) to set down.
t—Collect Jervaulx and Finghall Lane tickets.
‡—Low Yard.

The LNER Working Timetable for the branch for September 1937.

GARSDALE and HAWES and NORTHALLERTON—Weekdays

Distance from Garsdale	UP	1	2	3	4	5	6	7	8	9	10	11 B Mineral	12	13	17 D Goods
			PASSENGER			PASSENGER					PASSENGER			PASSENGER	
						TO									
		arr. dep.				arr.					arr. dep.	arr. dep.		arr. dep.	arr. dep.
M.C.		F a.m. a.m.				a.m.					a.m. a.m.	p.m. p.m.		p.m. p.m.	P p.m.
	Garsdale	— 6C23				9 16					— 10c23			— 1C26	
5 75	**Hawes** .. .. ⊕	6 34 6 36				9 27					10 34 10 37	Return of No. 1 Down		1 37 1 38	U
10 17	Askrigg ...... ⊕	6 44 6 45				—					.... 10 45			.. 1 46	*
14 73	Aysgarth .. .. ⊕	6 53 6 54				—					.. 10 54			.. 1 55	*
17 70	Redmire ...... ⊕	7 0 7 1				—					11 0 11 4			2 2 2 4	*
19 76	Wensley .. .. ⊕	7 6 7 7				—					.. 11 9	U		.. 2 9	*
	Ord & Maddison's Q'ry					—						*			*
22 24	**Leyburn** .. .. ⊕	7 12 7 17				—					11 14 11 27	*		2 14 2 19	*
	Harmby Quarry					—									
24 1	Spennithorne .. –	7 21 7 22				—					.. 11 32	.. ..		.. 2 24	
25 42	Constable Burton....⊕	7 26 7 27				—					.. 11 36	.. ..		2 29 2 30	
26 48	Finghall Lane	.. 7 30				—					.. 11 40	.. ..		.. 2 33	
28 27	Jervaulx .. .. ⊕	7 33 7 40				—					11 43 11 41	To Newport P. 304		.. 2 37	*
30 11	Crakehall	7 44 7 46				—					.. 11 43			.. 2 41	
32 26	**Bedale** .... ⊕	7 51 7 53				—					11 53 11 54	b		2 47 2 49	*
33 78	Leeming Bar – ⊕	7 58 8 1				—					11 59 12 0			2 54 2 56	
35 35	Scruton	.. 8 6				—					.. 12 4			.. 3 0	
36 72	Ainderby .. .. ⊕	.. 8 10				—					.. 12 8			.. 3 4	
39 15	*Northallerton West* ⊕	8 15				—					12 12			3 10	*
39 68	**NORTHALLERTON** .. ✝	8 18 —				—					12 15 —	— —		3 13 —	DD‡

UP	18	21 D L.M.S. Goods	22	23 D L.M.S. PASSENGER	24 D Goods	25	26 PASSENGER	27 EXPRESS PASSENGER	28	1	2	4 NO. 1 EXPRESS PARCELS	5	6 NO. 1 EXPRESS PARCELS
	PASSENGER													
		SX						WThSO						
	arr. dep.				arr. dep.		arr. dep.	arr. dep.				arr. dep.		
	p.m. p.m.	p.m.		p.m.	p.m.		p.m. p.m.	p.m. p.m.				a.m. a.m.		p.m.
Garsdale...............	—	3 20		4 0			— 6C40					— —		—
Hawes .. .. ⊕	— 3 17	3 40		4 12			6 51 6 54	7 35				— —		—
Askrigg .. .. ⊕	— 3 25	—		—	Return of No. 6 Down		7 2 7 3	7 43				— —		—
Aysgarth .. .. ⊕	3 33 3 34	—		—			7 11 7 12	7 52				— 9 53		—
Redmire .. .. ⊕	.. 3 40	—		—			7 18 7 19	7 59				9 59 10 6		—
Wensley .. .. ⊕	.. 3 45	—		—			.. 7 24	8 5				10 11 10 14		—
Ord & Maddison's Quarry		—		—	Detaches South and East wagons at Castle Hills.			Not after 4th September						
Leyburn .. .. ⊕	3 50 3 55	—		—	U *		7 29 7 37	8 10 8 15		Sundays		10 19 10 24		4 38
Harmby Quarry		—		—										
Spennithorne .. –	.. 4 0	—		—	*		.. ..	8 22				10 34 10 35		..
Constable Burton ...... ⊕	.. 4 4	—		—	*		.. 7 44					10 39 10 42		—
Finghall Lane	.. 4 7	—		—	*		.. M					10 45 10 46		—
Jervaulx .. .. ⊕	.. 4 11	—		—	*		7 51 7 54	8 27				10 49 10 52		—
Crakehall	.. 4 15	—		—	To Darlington p. 48		.. ..					10 57 10 59		—
Bedale .... ⊕	4 20 4 21	—		—	*		8 2 8 4	8 32 8 33				.. ..		5 3
Leeming Bar .. .. ⊕	4 26 4 27	—		—	*		8 9 8 16					.. 11 6		..
Scruton	.. 4 31	—		—	*		.. 8 20					.. ..		..
Ainderby .. .. ⊕	.. 4 35	—		—	*		.. 8 24					.. ..		5 19
Northallerton West ⊕	4 39	—		—	*		8 29	8 46				11 13		..
NORTHALLERTON .. ✝	4 42 —	—		—	*		8 33 —	8 49 —				11 16 —		5 23

F—"HC" to or from intermediate stations except from Leyburn, Bedale, and Leeming Bar. and to take up milk traffic. tickets. 1—Low Yard.   P—Class B from Leyburn.   b—Brakes.   M—Stops to set down only.   t—Collect Jervaulx and Finghall Lane.

The attractive garden between Northallerton station and the adjacent low level lines (looking north) can be seen in this poor quality 1950s photograph.

Courtesy K. Taylor Collection

A general view of the low level platforms at Northallerton. Built on the site of an earlier 1850s station, these emergency wartime platforms were occasionally used when the main lines were closed for engineering purposes.

Courtesy K. Taylor Collection

Chapter Four

The Stations and Route:
Northallerton to Leyburn

The east coast main line was, and indeed still is, one of the most important and fastest routes in the country, the section north of York up to Darlington having for long been regarded as a 'racing stretch' on which the old NER locomotives with their large driving wheels could show their paces.

Northallerton

Northallerton station occupied a strategic position on the ECML at the point where the original Great North of England line crossed over the Leeds Northern route from Harrogate, Ripon and Melmerby to Stockton and north-east coastal towns. The crossing was a gentle trailing one, and it was possible to run trains along the Leeds Northern line to the west of the station, passing beneath the Darlington line under a long bridge. Two connections – namely the Cordio loop from the south and the Northallerton loop to the north-east, enabled Leeds Northern trains to call as required. An additional burrowing junction (known as the Longlands loop) at the south end of the station enabled goods trains to come off the slow line and take the westerly Leeds Northern avoiding route and vice versa.

As first built, the Great North of England station had been little more than a wayside station, with staggered platforms and an ornate, Tudor-style station building on the up side. There were no physical connections between the main line and the Leeds Northern route until 1856, but in that year a spur was opened on the east side of the station. Later, in 1911, improved connections were installed on the west side of the station, and as part of these improvements, the main down platform was rebuilt as an island, with through lines on either side and a terminal bay for the Hawes branch trains. At the same time, the original up platform was extended and remodelled, an entirely new bay being provided for the benefit of local services to and from Harrogate.

In its rebuilt form, the station was provided with five platforms, the main station buildings being on the up side, together with the usual offices and a refreshment room as a sort of wooden addition. Extensive platform canopies were provided on both sides, and the platforms were further protected by wood and glass screens which prevented wind and rain from sweeping across the otherwise exposed station during inclement weather.

The platforms were numbered consecutively from one to five, platform one (the up side bay) being on the eastern side of the station while Nos. two and three (the up and down main lines) occupied the centre part of the station. The outer platform on the western side of the station was designated platform five, while platform four – the Garsdale branch bay – occupied the space between platforms three and five.

There were, in addition, two makeshift platforms on the low level Leeds Northern line which passed along the western side of the main line. These had originated in the 1850s, but they became more or less redundant when the Leeds Northern line was linked to the former Great North of England

71

route in 1856. In 1941, the low level platforms were reinstated for use in connection with the emergency wartime link, and they were, thereafter, occasionally used by passenger trains when the main line station was closed for engineering work.

The up and down sides of the station were linked by a subway connection, and it is interesting to note that this featured a means of access to the low level platforms – a door being provided in the subway wall so that, if necessary, travellers could have walked through to the Leeds Northern side of the station.

Architecturally, Northallerton exhibited several periods of construction. The original Great North of England station building (designed by the Newcastle architects John & Benjamin Green) remained *in situ* on the up side, though its Tudor details were largely hidden by various later additions. The building was a split-level design, and passengers walked upstairs to reach the high level platforms. Nearby, a small but attractive station master's house served as a further reminder of the Great North of England Railway and the early days of railway operation at this busy junction station.

In its Edwardian heyday the station provided a wide range of facilities for the travelling public, the up and down sides being fully equipped with booking offices, public toilets, staff accommodation, and separate waiting rooms for first and third class passengers. In later years, some of these lavish facilities were abolished; the down side booking office, for example, was adapted for a new lease of life as a buffet, while luxuries such as the first class gentlemen's waiting room were abandoned – leaving, however, separate waiting rooms for first class ladies.

Northallerton's goods traffic was handled in two yards – this apparent extravagance being (presumably) a legacy of the very early days when the town was served by the Great North of England (later York Newcastle & Berwick) and Leeds Northern railways. Both yards were on the east side of the line, the High Yard being immediately north-east of the passenger station while the Low Yard was sited further north on the Leeds Northern route to Stockton.

The High Yard contained an array of parallel sidings, some of which served commodious horse and carriage docks; four of the sidings were for coal traffic, and each of these was equipped with a 14-cell NER-style coal drop for use in conjunction with the company's wooden hopper wagons. The Low Yard was similarly equipped with coal drops, loading docks, and a range of other facilities including an extensive goods shed.

There were two private sidings at the station. One of these, in the Low Yard, served a Shell-Mex & BP fuel depot whereas the other – on the down side, and to the west of the passenger station – served the former Wensleydale Pure Milk Society's dairy. The dairy was actually built on NER land under a scheme whereby the railway company provided the facilities needed to foster dairy traffic, and farmers' associations or co-operatives then rented the property from the NER (as mentioned in Chapter Three, a similar scheme was initiated at Redmire in 1911). Sadly, the Wensleydale Pure Milk Society went out of business during the 1930s depression, and the dairy was later sold to the Cow & Gate Company.

A general (1969) view of the Wensleydale branch bay at the north end of Northallerton down platforms. Platform 3 (the down main line) is to the left and the staggered up platform can be glimpsed in the distance. *Courtesy K. Taylor Collection*

An unidentified 'D20' class 4−4−0 stands in the sunshine outside Northallerton engine shed during the early British Railways period. Four D20s were allocated to Northallerton around 1951, typical Nos. being 62347, 62359, 62373 and 62391. *Courtesy K. Taylor Collection*

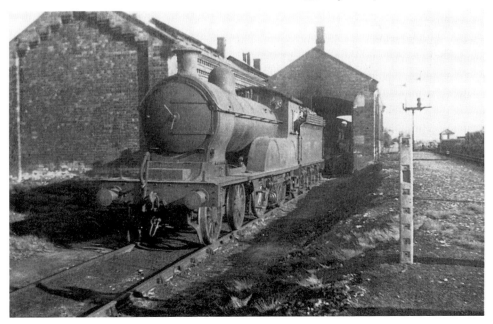

Northallerton engine shed was situated between the main line and the Leeds Northern route on the west side of the passenger station. Of brick construction, it was a two-road structure, the main entrance being at the south end. The right hand side of the shed (when viewed from the south) contained a dead-end line, but the left hand portion of the building spanned a through line that extended beyond the north gable to form additional stabling space for locomotives or loco coal wagons. Primitive coaling facilities and a 42 ft turntable were available near the shed, but these facilities were inconveniently-sited on the up side of the main line near the entrance to the High Yard.

As mentioned earlier, Northallerton's allocation typically included four or five 0–4–4T or 2–4–2T engines, together with one or two 0–6–0s or 0–6–2Ts for local goods or passenger work. In 1947 the allocation included three 'D20' 4–4–0s (Nos. 2388, 2391 and 2397), four 'J25' 0–6–0s (Nos. 5645, 5658, 5674 and 5693), two 'G5' 0–4–4Ts (Nos. 7324 and 7344), one 'N10' 0–6–2T (No. 9101) one 'J71' 0–6–0T (No. 8301) and Sentinel 'Y1' four-wheeled shunter No. 8159.

By 1950 the allocation had been slightly amended to include four 'D20' 4–4–0s, three 'J25' 0–6–0s, one 'J21' 0–6–0, three 'G5' 0–4–4Ts, one 'N10' 0–6–2T and a 'Y3' class Sentinel geared shunter. In general, the locally-based engines were usually former North Eastern Railway engines, though it is interesting to note that former Great Northern Railway 'N2' 0–6–2T No. 4724 was shedded at Northallerton for a short period during World War II.

In LNER days the line from York to Northallerton was regarded as something of a bottleneck, and to eradicate this problem the east coast main line was widened between York and Northallerton, new colour light signalling being installed at Northallerton and elsewhere. As a result of this resignalling, Northallerton signal box became one of the most modern of its kind after Hull Paragon. This electrically-operated box had a Teutonic look about it – as did many of the structures which were products of the 1930s. Considering the heavy wartime traffic through the junction, the new installation here must have been one of the most timely and useful investments ever indulged in by a railway. The three storeyed cabin was sited just north of the up platform, replacing an older version which was almost opposite on the down side.

The system of interlocking was similar to that at Hull, and up to 129 possible routes could be set up. The coverage of the visual line occupation on the track diagram included Cowton station to the south (about six miles) and the two miles north to Wiske Moor.[25]

Northallerton was regarded by many to have been the most potentially vulnerable spot on the LNER during the war, and all because of its modern signal box and the fact that two vitally important routes crossed each other to the north of it. There is no doubt that one bomb could have caused acute embarrassment to the war effort, severing supplies of coal, war materials and other vital commodities to and from Scotland and the north-eastern industrial areas.

The new power box and colour light signalling system enabled the LNER

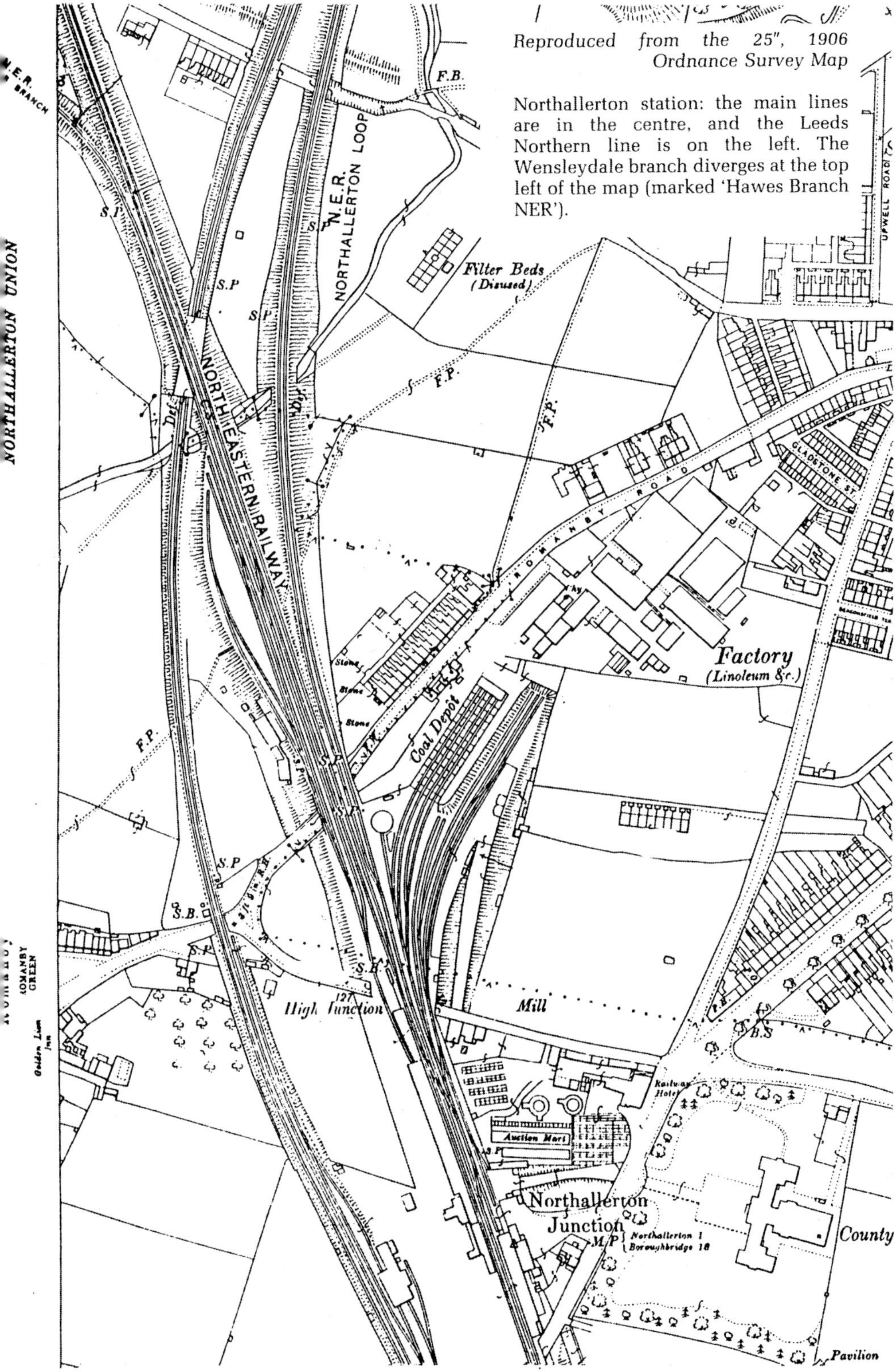

Reproduced from the 25″, 1906 Ordnance Survey Map

Northallerton station: the main lines are in the centre, and the Leeds Northern line is on the left. The Wensleydale branch diverges at the top left of the map (marked 'Hawes Branch NER').

N.E.R. BRANCH

NORTHALLERTON LOOP

N.E.R.

F.B.

NORTHALLERTON UNION

NORTH EASTERN RAILWAY

Filter Beds (Disused)

F.P.

F.P.

F.P.

S.P.

S.P.

S.P.

S.P.

ROMANBY ROAD

GLADSTONE ST.

UPWELL ROAD

Factory (Linoleum &c.)

Coal Depot

Stone

Stone

Stone

S.B.

S.P.

S.P.

ROMANBY GREEN

Golden Lion Inn

High Junction

Mill

B.S.

Railway Hotel

Auction Mart

Northallerton Junction

M.P.

Northallerton 1
Boroughbridge 18

County

Pavilion

A busy scene at Northallerton as class 'J21' 0–6–0 No. 65038 awaits the 'right away' in the branch bay while a British Railways Standard class '3MT' 2–6–0 hauling a stopping train stands alongside in platform 5. The swan-necked NER water crane is seen to great advantage.　　　　　　　　　　　　　　　　*N. Stead Collection*

Class 'G5' 0–4–4T No. 67312 leaves Northallerton with a two-coach train. The formation consists of a brake composite and a brake third, both vehicles being panelled coaches in BR maroon livery.　　　　　　　　　　　　　　　*N. Stead Collection*

to eliminate several older boxes including those at Northallerton West, Northallerton Low, Northallerton High, Cordio and Longlands. However, two traditional cabins remained in operation as gate boxes on the low level line. The cabins concerned were Boroughbridge Gates and Romanby Gates boxes, both of which were sited to the west of the station. Romanby Gates box was a particularly attractive design featuring a curious semi-hipped roof with a projecting gabled portion; it was further distinguished by the addition of a projecting porch and an ornate flared chimney pot. (Semaphore signals were retained in places on the low level line.)

The high level platforms were unsuitable for garden cultivation, but a large open space between the high and low level lines was beautifully landscaped by John Miller, the NE Area Civil Engineer, with wide lawns, flower beds, and a number of ornamental trees and shrubs.

Other features of interest at Northallerton included two ornate water columns at the north end of the platforms. These were of typical North Eastern design, their long, rotating booms having boldly curved 'swan's necks'; the cylindrical lower columns were adorned by the addition of large, tapered finials which, in turn, provided an anchoring point for wire stays. Flexible hoses enabled locomotives to replenish their tanks, and integral coal-fired braziers were available for use in the depths of winter, when unheated water supplies would have frozen solid.

A drip tank was provided near one of the columns and, amusingly, this contained a collection of large-goldfish, which lived quite happily in their unusual home! It is unclear how these fish got into the tank in the first place (or who put them there!) but at least two of them lived for several years during the 1950s.

Northallerton's status as a busy junction station necessitated a large labour force encompassing not only locomotive, goods and passenger staff, but also a variety of other railway employees in the permanent way, signal & telegraph, and clerical departments. Those employed at this thriving NER station in the early 1900s included ticket collector J. Wells, station inspector F.J. Teale, signalmen Charles Pinder and O.P. Ellis, goods clerks D.W. Fulton, L.P. Cooper J. Rucklidge and W. Crosby, ticket collector G. Brockhill, porter A. Richardson, labourers J. Blanchard, J. Fowler and B. Robson, platelayer I. Newton, timekeeper L.A. Atkinson, painter C. Braithwaite, joiner Joe Gibson and engine cleaner N. Fowler.[26] Some of these men had worked at the station for many years – one of the local ticket collectors, for example, remained at the station for almost half a century (see below)!

Obviously, the station master at a station such as Northallerton was an important figure with considerable managerial responsibility, and for this reason many station masters (particularly those who had started their careers as porters or other uniformed grades) would have regarded a posting to such a station as the pinacle of success. The station master here in the years preceding World War I was Thomas Beechcroft, but he retired in 1913 and was succeeded by Mr R. Chape. Northallerton was, at that time, considered important enough to have an 'assistant station master', and the latter position was filled, around 1915, by J.S. Ashmore. A much later station master, during the 1950s, was Mr Sanderson.

The pages of the monthly North Eastern Railway Magazine provide a fascinating insight into the everyday life of stations such as Northallerton during the pre-grouping era, and it would be useful to quote one or two extracts relating to locally-employed NER staff. In February 1919, for instance, the magazine reported a presentation that had recently made to long-serving railwayman Mr J. Walker on the occasion of his retirement after nearly half a century spent at Northallerton:

> Mr J. Walker, ticket collector, Northallerton, retired on December 31st 1918, after 48 years service. He had been at Northallerton during nearly the whole of that time, and was well known to the numerous passengers who regularly change trains there. He was presented by the staff with a testimonial as a mark of esteem.

Mr Walker was not the only long-serving employee at Northallerton, and a year or two previously, in the summer of 1914, *The North Eastern Railway Magazine* had reported a similar presentation that had been made to traffic agent J. Crossling:

> On July 2nd, a presentation was made to Mr J. Crossling by the staff at the Northallerton goods station on the occasion of his retirement from the position of Traffic Agent, which he had held for 38 years. Prior to his appointment to Northallerton he was engaged at Leyburn, the total length of his service with the Company being 45 years.
>
> The gift, which consisted of a marble clock, was handed over by M.H.T. Spink, at a meeting presided over by M.E.R. Sharpe. Both Mr Spink and Mr Sharpe spoke in kindly terms of the agent, as did also Messrs W. Hall, Stockdale, Farrell and Pickersgill.
>
> Mr Crossling thanked them all for their kindness, and said he will treasure their beautiful gift as long as he lived.

In the same year, the magazine also referred to a presentation that had recently been made to a newly-married railway clerk:

> At the Railway Hotel Northallerton, on July 23rd, a gathering of the passenger staff was held at which Mr W.B. Innes was presented with a set of cutlery and spoons on the occasion of his marriage. Mr H. Bartlitt, chief clerk, presided, and the gift was made, on behalf of the subscribers, by Mr R. Chape, Station Master.
>
> Afterwards there was a 'smoker', which was contributed to by Mr R. Chape, Mr H. Bartlitt, Mr Innes, Mr Shaw, Mr F.H. Pearson, Mr Brown, Mr Croft, Mr Dunning and Mr Feestenby. Mr H.A. Shaw acted as accompanist.

The picture that emerges from these glimpses of life on the NER is of a large, but happy family; one notes, for example, that station master Chape and head clerk H. Bartlitt both took part in the men-only smoking concert held after the above-mentioned presentation – and we can perhaps imagine the scene as these old time railwaymen sang their songs or recited their monologues to the accompaniment of Mr Shaw on the piano!

Sadly, the settled pattern of life and work at Northallerton was rudely shattered by the outbreak of World War I in August 1914. Railwaymen were exempt from conscription when that measure was introduced in 1916, but many NER employees were members of the reserve forces, while large numbers of other railwaymen enlisted as volunteers. Indeed, railwaymen in non-operational grades were encouraged to enlist, and by 1916, it was reported that '19 out of every 20 eligible men had enlisted'. At the end of the year, the North Eastern Railway could justifiably boast that almost 30 per

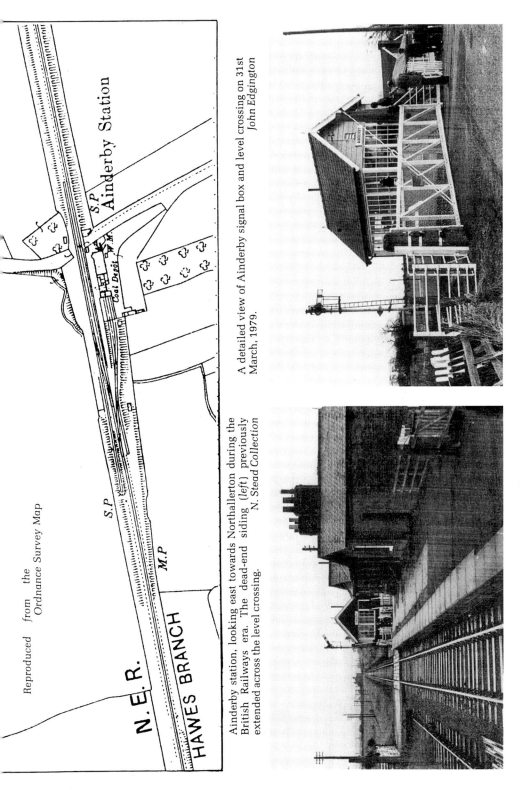

Reproduced from the Ordnance Survey Map

N.E.R.

HAWES BRANCH

S.P

M.P

S.P

S.P

Coal Depot

Ainderby Station

Ainderby station, looking east towards Northallerton during the British Railways era. The dead-end siding (left) previously extended across the level crossing.
N. Stead Collection

A detailed view of Ainderby signal box and level crossing on 31st March, 1979.
John Edgington

cent of its pre-war labour force was serving in HM forces.

Men were encouraged to join their local regiments, and it was not uncommon for groups of young men to join en masse. Something of this nature evidently took place at Northallerton, and it seems that this particular station contributed a proportionately-greater quota of volunteers than any of the smaller stations along the line to Garsdale (perhaps because Northallerton's work force included a greater number of 'eligible men').

With many men serving at the Front, the railways were obliged to employ female staff in jobs that had hitherto been regarded as 'men's work', and in this capacity at least three ladies were employed at Northallerton. The ladies in question were Miss Hancock, Miss Dunford and Miss Bailes – all of whom worked in the booking office in place of three male booking clerks who had joined the army.[27]

Meanwhile, as great land battles raged on the Western Front, the human cost of the war began to mount alarmingly, and several Northallerton railwaymen gave their lives. Sergeant J.R. Ellis, for example, was killed on 23rd April, 1917, while N. Fowler was reported 'missing presumed dead' on 30th November, 1917. In civilian life Mr Ellis had been a joiner in the locomotive department, and Mr Fowler had been an engine cleaner; he was 21 years old, and had worked on the NER for one and a half years.[28]

On 10th October, 1917, A. Richardson, formerly a porter, was reported missing, and on 30th April, 1918, Lance-corporal J.Y. Light, RE, formerly an NER mason, was killed in action; on 5th June, 1918, former time clerk L.A. Atkinson was killed while serving with the Royal Army Medical Corps. Other casualties included Lance-corporal D.N. Rose of Northallerton goods depot, who died of wounds on 9th October, 1916, and J.W. Hartley of the 2nd West Yorkshire Regiment, who died in Germany in December 1918 having been a prisoner-of-war; Mr Hartley had formerly been an engine cleaner at Northallerton locomotive shed.[29]

The ultimate cost of victory had been appalling, not only in financial but also in human terms; no town or village had been spared, but one feels that Northallerton station lost more than its fair share of men in the Great War of 1914–18.

Ainderby

From Northallerton the branch diverged westwards, and having crossed the Leeds Northern line, Hawes trains rattled over the pointwork at Northallerton West Junction. Here, the north-to-west arm of a triangular junction converged from the right. Until 1939 the junction was controlled from West Junction cabin, but thereafter the converging lines were worked from a ground frame on the north side of the line.

The easternmost extremity of the branch was, for many years, worked by train staff and ticket between Northallerton High and Northallerton West, but in later years the route was controlled by tokenless electrical interlocking as far as Ainderby at 2 miles 76 chains, and the section was unrelieved by anything apart from the level crossings at Yafforth and Ainderby, and by the Yafforth or Johnson Siding ground frame at less than a mile from Northallerton West. This siding lay to the south of the line and had a connection facing to trains in the down direction.

Ex-NER class 'J21' 0–6–0 No. 65038 drifts into Ainderby station at the head of a two-coach train. The wooden signal box has recently been re-erected (on a brick base) at Alston, in conjunction with the South Tynedale Railway Society. *N. Stead Collection*

The driver of class 'G5' 0–4–0T No. 67312 collects the single line tablet from the signalman at Ainderby station. *N. Stead Collection*

A rear view of the substantial brick-built station building at Ainderby. Although taken long after closure, this 1976 view clearly shows the split-level arrangement whereby the waiting rooms and other facilities were at first-floor level. *John Edgington*

An early (but poor quality) view of Ainderby station with station staff posing for the camera. *Lens of Sutton*

AINDERBY. N.ER.

Ainderby, the first intermediate stopping place for passenger trains, was one of the smaller stations *en route* to Hawes. Only one platform was provided, and the station was not a passing place. In operational terms, however, it had some significance in that after the abolition of Northallerton West box in 1939 Ainderby became the point at which tokenless electrical interlocking was replaced by electric train tablet operation (prior to 1939, the Northallerton West to Ainderby section had been worked by electric tablet).

Ainderby village was situated immediately to the south of the railway on the main Northallerton to Bedale road, and just west of it was the village of Morton-on-Swale, which also straddled the road and was in fact nearest the station.

Ainderby station was situated on an embankment, and this elevated position enabled coal drops to be provided in the small, two siding goods yard on the down (south) side of the line behind the passenger platform. Another siding was provided on the up side, all sidings being facing to up trains.

The station building, designed by G.T. Andrews, was of considerable interest in that it was a split-level design, with the main offices, etc. on the first floor. Like many early railway buildings, this brick-built structure was of dignified, classical appearance, with low pitched roofs and small-paned 'Georgian' style sash windows. When viewed from the rear, it looked rather like a stylish, early Victorian town house, with a main block and two gabled cross wings. The gables lacked barge boards, and for this reason the ends of the purlins could be clearly seen. The main exterior walls were built of brickwork, and the roofing material was slate; on the platform-facing side, the otherwise severe facade was enlivened by the addition of a bay window at the east end of the building, while an array of relatively tall brick chimney stacks added further character to this pleasant, country station building.

The single-storey, wooden signal cabin, with 20 levers, was sited on the down side of the line, and there was a level crossing at the eastern end of the station. Large crossing gates were needed here because the roadway crossed over both the running line and the adjacent siding – there were, therefore, two lines at this point, although the station had only one platform. Other facilities at Ainderby included a cattle dock and a weigh-house in the compact goods yard.

The station master at the turn-of-the-century was Mr R. Gill, but he moved to Tollerton, on the North Eastern main line, in 1911, and Mr G.M. Wood came from Bubwith (near Selby) to replace him. Country station masters often remained for many years at one station, with the result that they became familiar figures to generations of travellers. In earlier days, these local railway officials enjoyed a somewhat privileged position in the village hierarchy, being (in the eyes of ordinary folk) somewhere in importance between the squire, the Anglican vicar and the National schoolmaster. In these circumstances the retirement or promotion of a local station master was an event in itself, and it was usual for travellers and railway staff to show their appreciation of the departing official by organising a 'presentation' at which money or gifts would be handed over. Something of this nature took place on the departure of Mr Gill, who had served at Ainderby

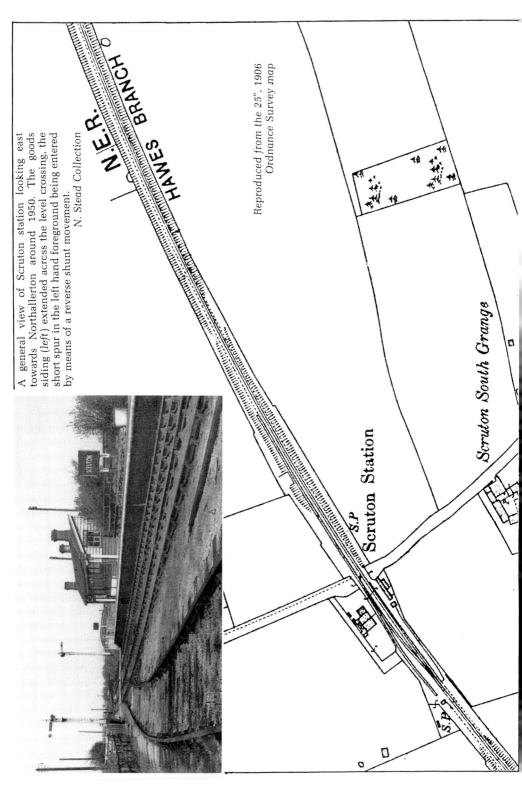

N.E.R.

HAWES BRANCH

A general view of Scruton station looking east towards Northallerton around 1950. The goods siding (*left*) extended across the level crossing, the short spur in the left hand foreground being entered by means of a reverse shunt movement.

N. Stead Collection

Reproduced from the 25", 1906 Ordnance Survey map

S.P.
Scruton Station

Scruton South Grange

S.P.

for over 20 years, and the resulting ceremony was reported as follows in *The North Eastern Railway Magazine* on 14th February, 1911:

> On December 23rd Mr R. Gill, who had been station master at Ainderby for 22 years, was presented with a testimonial by his friends at Ainderby Steeple (as the village served by the station is called) on the occasion of his promotion to the position of station master at Tollerton.
>
> The gifts consisted of a silver tea service, an oak tray, and a silver cake basket for Mrs Gill. The chairman of the gathering was Mr T. Gibson, who spoke of Mr Gill as 'a good man who had always done his duty'.

In Mr Gill's day stations such as Ainderby would have employed about half a dozen men as porters, signalmen or booking clerks, a typical staff complement, during the early 1900s, being one station master, two signalmen, one senior booking clerk, one junior clerk, and one porter. There might, in addition, have been a locally-based permanent way gang with responsibility for maintenance of a specific section of track; at Ainderby, for instance, William Armstrong worked as a 'ganger' in charge of a group of platelayers until his retirement in 1920.

Scruton

Between Ainderby and the next station at Scruton, the single line crossed the sluggish River Swale on a low, plate girder bridge with four spans resting on stone piers. Scruton, 4 miles 33 chains from Northallerton, was originally known as Scruton Lane. It was not a block post, but a siding was available on the north side of the line – the associated connection being released by the single line tablet.

There was a single platform on the down side, with a level crossing immediately to the east. The station building was a brick and timber structure incorporating a booking office, male and female toilets, and a large, glass-fronted waiting room.

The adjacent signal cabin was a wooden building with a single-pitch roof and a brick base; it contained 10 levers, but there was no mechanism for working the level crossing – the gates were opened and shut by hand, and locked by key.

In North Eastern days, even very small stations such as Scruton were fully staffed, with their own station master and perhaps one or two porters. At Scruton, for example, the station master from 1906 until his death in 1915 was Mr Francis Johnson, who had earlier served as station master at Spennithorne. An obituary notice, published in *The North Eastern Railway Magazine* on May 1916, contains a useful insight into the career of a typical NER station master, and this brief note is worth printing in full:

> We regret to hear of the death, on April 11th, 1915, of Mr Francis Johnson, station master at Scruton. Mr Johnson entered the service of the North Eastern Railway 36 years ago, at North Grimston, near Malton, and was subsequently employed at Honingham and Thirsk. From the position of ticket collector at Thirsk he was promoted, in 1903, to that of station master at Spennithorne, and after being three years at that station he was appointed to the position which he held at the time of his death.
>
> Mr Johnson took great pride in the beautifying of his station. During the years 1907 to 1913 he obtained three first class and four second class prizes for the

A North Eastern Railway signal at Scruton, still in position when photographed on 31st March, 1979.

John Edgington

Station master Francis Johnson, who served at both Spennithorne and Scruton. *Courtesy NER Magazine*

A summer day at Scruton. This *circa* 1910 photograph shows station master Francis Johnson (*centre*) flanked by two porter-signalmen. Mr Johnson was a keen gardener and close examination of the picture reveals that the station has been filled with potted plants and shrubs.   *K. Taylor Collection*

Another glimpse of Scruton station during the Edwardian era; the station clock stands at 4.35 pm on an obviously pleasant summer's afternoon.   *Lens of Sutton*

best-kept wayside stations. Mr Johnson's two sons, it may be mentioned, are both serving with the colours, one in the 32nd Northumberland Fusiliers (NER) at Newcastle, and the other with the Mechanical Transport at Salonika.

The reference to the 'best kept wayside station' competition is a reminder that, in 1895, the NER Directors agreed that small prizes would be awarded for the most attractive gardens at country stations. This idea was immensely popular, and for several years the gardens at Scruton were among the best on the Wensleydale line – thanks, mainly to Mr Johnson's tireless efforts. A later station master, at this North Eastern Railway outpost, was Mr H. Hutchinson who, until his promotion to Scruton around 1918, had been a telegraphist at York.

Leeming Bar

A straight run to the south-west brought the line, through shallow cuttings, to Leeming Bar. Here, the railway crossed the busy A1 Great North Road on the level, the 'bar' referred-to in the station name being a former toll gate. There were in fact two Leemings – Leeming Bar near the station, and Leeming proper to the south; both were on the Great North Road which had (in the days before railways) been a major stage coach route between London and the North.

Leeming Bar station (5 miles 70 chains) was more impressive than neighbouring Ainderby or Scruton. It featured a passing loop, with up and down platforms on both sides and a substantial brick-built station building on the down (westbound) side. The latter structure contained the usual facilities for passenger and parcels traffic, including waiting rooms, toilets and a booking office.

Like Ainderby, Leeming Bar station was of classical proportions, with a low pitched, slated roof and small-paned Georgian-style windows. The main block was two stories high, whereas an extension at the eastern end was a single storey structure; both parts of the building were of similar architectural design, and this suggests that they had been erected at around the same time. Unusually (for a country station) the building sported a pillared portico at its eastern end, and this ostentatious feature contributed an element of unexpected grandeur to the whole station. The architect was again G.T. Andrews.

The signal cabin was a two-storey design with a brick base and a glazed upper floor. Internally, it contained a 5 in. pitch McKenzie & Holland 36-lever frame with several white-painted 'spares'. The box, which dated from 1908, was sited on the up side beside the busy level crossing at the eastern end of the platforms. It had a pitched, slated roof, and the brick-built lower storey was constructed of bricks laid in a simplified form of 'English Bond' in which one course of bricks laid in a simplified form of 'English Bond' in which one course of bricks laid side-to-side) was laid above every three courses of 'stretchers' (bricks laid lengthways).

Until 1908 Leeming Bar had been a single platform station, but in that year the North Eastern Railway completed a programme of improvements, as a result of which it became a passing place for passenger trains. The necessary remodelling of trackwork and signalling was carried out in 1907, and in January 1908 the new works were inspected by Colonel Von Donop of the

A glimpse of Leeming Bar station buildings, seen on 28th August, 1974 after closure. The unusual portico at the east-end of the building is clearly seen.

K. Taylor Collection

Another glimpse of the elaborate entrance at the east end of Leeming Bar station on 31st March, 1979.
John Edgington

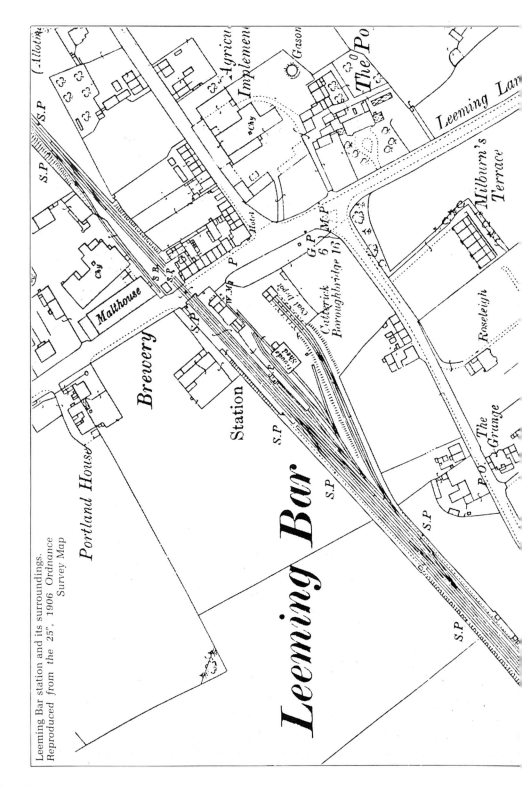

Leeming Bar station and its surroundings.
Reproduced from the 25", 1906 Ordnance
Survey Map

A useful view of Leeming signal box; the Vale of Mowbray Bacon Factory (formerly a Brewery) can be seen at the rear. The photograph was taken on 31st March, 1979. The box was equipped with a 5 in. pitch McKenzie and Holland, 36-lever frame.

John Edgington

Class 'G5' 0−4−4T No. 67314 pauses in the down platform at Leeming with a west-bound milk train. The curiously elongated chimneys of the station building can be glimpsed in the background.

N. Stead Collection

A panoramic view of Leeming Bar station and goods yard from the west. The hip-roofed goods shed is visible in the centre of the picture, while the NER styled coal-drops can be seen to the right. The siding on the extreme left was used as a refuge line.   *N. Stead Collection*

A close-up look at the 'Georgian' style two-storey buildings at Leeming Bar, captured on film on 31st March, 1979, long after the withdrawal of passenger services. The station was built in brick, laid in a simplified form of English Bond' with three courses of stretchers to every course of headers.   *J. Edgington*

Board of Trade. His inspection report, dated 20th January, 1908, provides a useful, first hand description of the new platform and signal box:

Sir,

I have the honour to report, for the information of the Board of Trade, that in compliance with the instructions contained in your minute of 9th December, 1907, I have inspected the new works at Leeming Bar station, on the Bedale branch of the North Eastern Railway.

This station has now been made into a passing place on the single line, a new up platform and up platform line having been provided; the new platform is 280 ft long, 3 ft high, and of ample width, and it is provided with waiting rooms, shelter and all necessary accommodation.

The only requirement noted was that the station names are required on the platform lamps.

The points and signals are worked from a new signal box, containing a frame of 37 levers, 6 spare. The interlocking is correct, and the arrangements are satisfactory, so I can recommend the Board of Trade to sanction the new works being brought into use.

I have the honour, etc.,
P.G. Von Donop[30]

On a footnote, it may be worth noting that Colonel Von Donop's description of a 'frame of 37 levers' seems to be a mistake, in that there were in fact 36 levers and a wheel for operation of the crossing gates.

The goods yard was fully equipped with raised coal drops, a hip-roofed goods shed, loading docks, cattle pens, and a small (15 cwt) hand crane. There were, in all, six relatively long sidings, together with a short end-loading bay; the coal sidings were sited on the southern side of the yard and the goods shed was sited in the centre. All of these sidings were sited on the down side of the running lines.

There was, in addition, a privately-owned siding on the up side, giving access to the nearby Vale of Mowbray Bacon Factory. The factory, on the north side of the line near the level crossing, was an impressive Victorian industrial building that had originally been used as a brewery by Messrs Plews & Sons; it was then known as the Vale of Mowbray Brewery and, perhaps for this reason, the 'Vale of Mowbray' title was retained when the premises were adapted for use as a bacon factory during the 1930s.

In staffing terms, Leeming Bar was more important than neighbouring Scruton or Ainderby, and those employed at the station during the Edwardian period included booking clerks W. Richardson, J. Routledge, H.R. Duffit, D.B. Ward and L. Tindill.

Although some men were content to remain at one station for all or most of their working lives other, perhaps more ambitious employees moved from place to place in a constant search for promotion. Clerical grades, in particular, were encouraged to apply for higher posts after serving a sort of 'apprenticeship' as juniors, and for this reason the turnover of junior clerks was surprisingly high. The pages of The North Eastern Railway Magazine record the names of many of these transient staff – in 1911, for example, L. Tindill moved from Leeming to Flamborough, while in 1915 D.B. Ward moved to Selby.

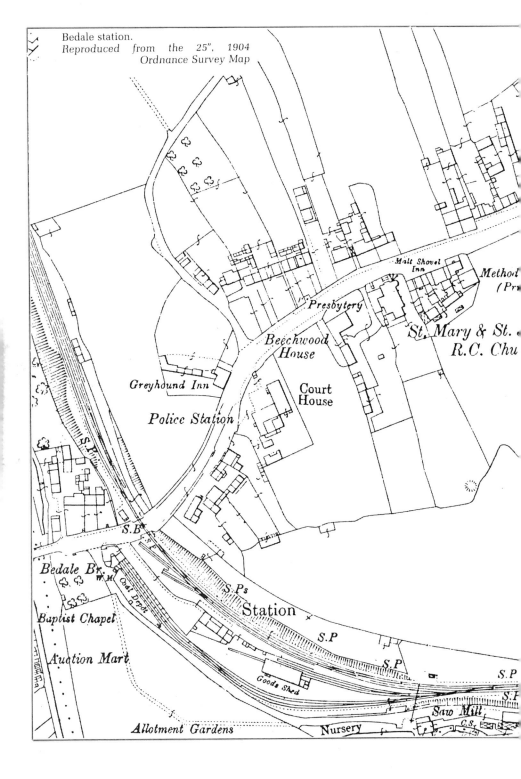

Bedale station.
Reproduced from the 25″, 1904
Ordnance Survey Map

Malt Shovel Inn

Methodi
(Pri

Presbytery

St. Mary & St.
R.C. Chu

Beechwood
House

Court
House

Greyhound Inn

Police Station

S.P

S.B.

Bedale Br.

Coal Depôt

S.Ps

Baptist Chapel

Station

S.P

Auction Mart

S.P

S.P

Goods Shed

S.P

Saw Mill

C.S.

Allotment Gardens

Nursery

BEDALE STATION. YORKS.

A platform scene at Bedale station during the Edwardian period; note that the platform canopy had not then been erected. *K. Taylor Collection*

A further, more detailed view of Bedale station, this time the scene includes the platform canopy, the short spur loading bay and a distinct assortment of signal posts and signals. *N. Stead Collection*

Other employees, during and after World War I, included booking clerks S.L. Dunford, D. Charlton, C.H. Watson and C.H. Walker, and goods clerks J.H. Dobson, A.J. Crossling and A. Limbert. C.H. Walker was one of the 17,000 NER railwaymen who served in HM Forces during World War I, and in this context it is interesting to record that he was commissioned as a 2nd Lieutenant in the Northumberland Fusiliers, and received a severe wound to the hand towards the end of the 1914–18 conflict.

The station master here, around 1920 and at the time of the grouping, was Mr R. Newton, who had previously served as station master at West Auckland. In earlier years, during the 1890s, the station master had been Mr George Atley.

For railway archaeologists, Leeming contained many points of interest, including a water tank and column that survived as relics of the days when trains had started or finished their journeys at this country station. Minor details included the usual collection of stores, huts and platelayers' sheds, together with a small wood and glass waiting room on the up platform. At night, the platforms were illuminated by simple oil lamps in traditional glass lanterns, while other platform furniture included some typical NER seats formed from two wooden planks bolted to angled iron legs; the name 'LEEMING BAR' was displayed on the back of each seat, and on prominent wooden nameboards affixed to the post-and-rail platform fencing.

As we have seen, Leeming had originally been the terminus of the line from Northallerton – its strategic position on the Great North Road making it an ideal railhead for the surrounding area; until 1902, the station had been called 'Leeming Lane', but it was renamed 'Leeming Bar' with effect from 1st July of that year.

Beyond Leeming Bar the route continued, as a double track line, towards the south-west. At Aiskew crossing trains crossed the main A684 road on the level, a small wooden signal cabin being provided as a gate box. This box, which had a 10-lever frame, was on the north side of the line, and like many rural signal boxes it was lit only by oil lamps. Amusingly, Aiskew crossing was indeed 'on the skew', the intersection of road and rail being effected at an awkward angle that posed many a hazard for cyclists and other road users!

Bedale

Beyond, trains continued through hillier terrain, and having passed around the village of Aiskew in a great curve, the line entered Bedale (7 miles 42 chains) in a westerly direction.

Serving a small town of a little over one thousand people, Bedale was one of the prettiest stations on the Wensleydale line. There was an attractive station building, and in summer time the single platform was graced by some fine floral displays. The layout here was somewhat curious in that, although trains approached the station on a double line the route became single before it reached the passenger station. Confusingly, there was a goods loop beside the main running line through the station but, because only one platform was provided, passenger trains were routed onto the southern line (which was signalled for two-way working).

The 'Three Dales Railtour' (double-headed) rounds the curve into Bedale station on Saturday 20th May, 1967. Note the brick-built NER signal box in the distance (*left*) and the short loading dock spur (*foreground*) with a disused second loading dock in front of the signal box. *N. Stead Collection*

A further view of the 'Three Dales Railtour', this time on the outward journey as it eases round the tight curve at Bedale station hauled by Class 'K1' 2−6−0 No. 62005. *N. Stead Collection*

Class 'G5' 0–4–4T No. 67345 leaves the curved platform at Bedale with an eastbound working. Tender engines were usually turned at the end of each journey, but tank locomotives ran bunker first in the up direction.   *N. Stead Collection*

Class 'BTP' 0–4–4T No. 465 is winched upright after the fatal accident at Bedale in December 1901; a class 'A' 2–4–2T can be seen on the extreme right.
          K. Taylor Collection

This method of operation was perfectly safe, but to minimise the risk of accidents, when up and down passenger trains had to pass here the two trains were worked into the station in the following way: the up (eastbound) working was allowed into the platform first, the down (westbound) service being held at the down outer home signal while passengers embarked or disembarked from the up working. The up train was then allowed to proceed onto the double track section at the east end of the station, and only then was the down service permitted to pass the down outer home signal.

Bedale's goods facilities consisted of a small goods yard on the down side of the line, and this contained a range of facilities including coal drops, a weigh-house, and a goods shed; additional facilities, including a cattle loading dock, were available on the up side, at the western end of the station. The goods yard sidings were worked from a ground frame on the up side, entry to and from the yard being via a trailing connection with the up main line that crossed the down line on the level.

There was a level crossing at the west of the passenger station and, nearby, a tall, NER Southern Division-type brick signal cabin stood sentinel on the down side of the line. The box contained a 31-lever frame, most of the levers being in action due to the generous provision of home, starting and shunting signals at this relatively small station.

The level crossing was wide enough to accommodate two lines of rails, although the line was single at this point. There was, however, a long refuge siding on the western side of the crossing, and it would have been a comparatively easy matter for this siding to have been linked-up to the nearby goods loop – thereby creating an extension of the double track through the station and over the crossing (presumably, the traffic requirements on this modest line did not justify such a modification).

Bedale was the site of an accident in December 1901 when Fletcher 'Bogie Tank Passenger' 0–4–4T No. 465 was derailed after floodwater had undermined a section of the line; sadly, the locomotive was overturned, and its unfortunate fireman was trapped and killed. The engine tumbled down the undermined bank, and this made its subsequent recovery a particularly difficult operation. After some thought, the engineers rigged up a block and tackle system and, using three locomotives, No. 465 was unceremoniously pulled upright; one of the engines used in this operation was an 'A' class 2–4–2T, which was used as a sort of 'anchor' while the two other locomotives moved slowly away from one another as they hauled the derailed engine back onto its wheels. Having righted the casualty, it was then a relatively simple matter for the rescuing engines to pull No. 465 up a specially-constructed wooden ramp, and by this means it was able to reach rail level for final re-railing.

Like neighbouring Leeming Bar, Bedale seems to have been used as a sort of training school for junior clerks, and there was, for this reason, a high staff turnover during the period from 1900 until 1923. Those employed in the booking office around 1911–15 included A.C. Carr, H.M. Whitton and H.E. Driffield, while the goods clerks at that time included F. Dobby, S.G. Robinson, and G.H. Wells. Another NER employee, around 1914–18 was platelayer George Gowland. F. Doddy was transferred to Jervaulx in 1912,

Class 'G5' 0–4–4T No. 67318 gathers speed as it leaves Bedale station with a down branch train. The lattice post signal is of interest.　　　　　*N. Stead Collection*

A loaded stone train approaches Bedale level crossing behind class '37' Co-Cos Nos. 37515 and 37517 on 27th July, 1989. The classic NER 'Southern Division' signal box is now the last one on the branch – although it has now been reduced to 'gate box' status.
　　　　　N. Stead Collection

and he served in the Royal Engineers during World War I – eventually becoming a sergeant; sadly, Sergeant Doddy was killed in the war on 25th April, 1918, and he thereby became one of the 7,000 NER railwaymen who lost their lives in the Great War.[31]

Other NER employees known to have served at Bedale during the early years of the century included goods clerks C. Potter and H.C. Wilkinson, and passenger clerk H. Pardoe. The station master at the turn-of-the-century was Mr William Pearson.

Bedale had of course been the planned terminus of the original branch from Northallerton, but as recounted in Chapter One, Hudson's fall from power and the simultaneous ending of the Railway Mania meant that the line was cut short at Leeming Bar. Interestingly, Bedale station building superficially resembled those at Ainderby and Leeming, being a two-storey classical structure. It was built of brick, with a low-pitched slated roof; the main block was 'L'-shaped, though the original structure was partially hidden by an accretion of single-storey additions and extensions. The platform frontage was protected by a fairly substantial canopy, and this further obscured the original appearance of the building. (The fact that the station did not have a Bedale & Leyburn-style building would suggest that the York Newcastle & Berwick Railway had built the station before work on the Leeming to Bedale line was suspended in the late 1840s.)

A further point that might be made in relation to Bedale concerns its track layout. The entire station was built on a relatively sharp curve, and while this may not have mattered greatly if the station had been opened as a branch terminus, it created minor problems when the railway was later extended westwards to Leyburn. The extension had to be aligned north-westwards along the east bank of the Bedale Beck, and this resulted in an even greater curve at the western end of the station. Lack of space dictated that two loading docks that were needed at the Leyburn end of the passenger platform could only be served by tangental sidings, while the goods shed (to the east of the station building) was also aligned at a tangent to the boldly-curved running line. The fact that these goods sidings were relatively straight served to emphasise the curving main line, and to casual observers the tightness of the curve was made even more apparent!

Before leaving Bedale it is necessary to add that the station was signalled with an interesting assortment of semaphore signals, many of which were typical ex-North Eastern Railway slotted-post lower quadrant arms. In later years, some of these NER specimens were replaced by modern upper quadrants signals, but a number of slotted post signals remained in use until the diesel era. Lattice post signals were also employed – the up home, with its bracketed siding arm, being a striking example.

Crakehall

Bedale was, in many ways, the gateway to lower Wensleydale. The first part of the line ran through level, pastoral countryside, but at Bedale the branch entered hillier terrain, and the first real gradients were situated to the west of the station – indeed, the route climbed steadily from Bedale to

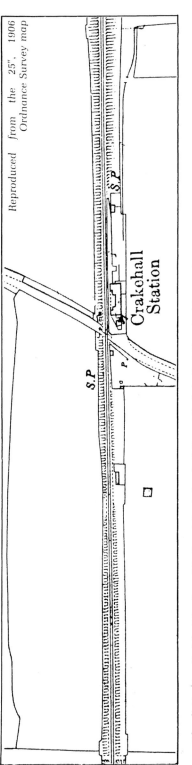

Reproduced from the 25", 1906 Ordnance Survey map

S.P.

S.P.

S.P.

Crakehall Station

The distinctive Bedale & Leyburn Rly Co.-style station building at Crakehall station, looking west towards Garsdale. In 1854 the inhabitants of the district petitioned the Bedale & Leyburn Rly Co. Directors for a station to be provided here.

George Potter, the station master at Crakehall from 1899 until his tragic death in 1915. *Courtesy NER Magazine*

N. Stead Collection

CRAKEHALL.

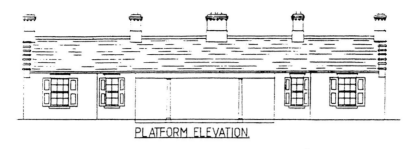

PLATFORM ELEVATION.

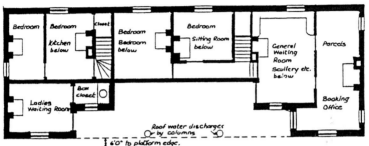

Bedroom	Bedroom	Closet	Bedroom		Bedroom			
	Kitchen below		Bedroom below		Sitting Room below		General Waiting Room	Parcels
							Scullery etc. below	
Ladies Waiting Room	Box closet							Booking Office

Roof water discharges
by columns

6'0" to platform edge.

PLAN AT PLATFORM LEVEL

APPROACH ELEVATION.

Scale Feet

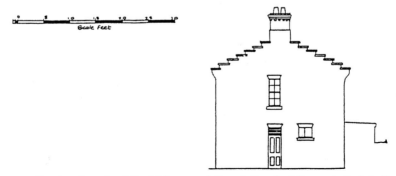

Diagrammatic drawings by J.F. Addyman of the station buildings at Crakehall designed by Thomas Prosser for the Bedale & Leyburn section of the NER; this building was probably erected around 1860, replacing temporary wooden structures provided at the time of opening.

Leyburn, the rising gradients being as steep as 1 in 77 (though the ruling gradient was around 1 in 100).

From Bedale the line was single as far as Leyburn, and having left Bedale in a north-westerly direction, the route ran chiefly westwards through a landscape of rolling hills which barely rose above 300 ft. The surrounding countryside was well-wooded, while the character of the line also changed perceptibly – this being the Bedale & Leyburn Railway, which had its own style of NER-derived architecture, with distinctive brick station buildings designed by Thomas Prosser, the North Eastern Railway architect.

Crakehall, the first station on the Bedale & Leyburn section, was a simple, passenger-only stopping place with a single platform on the down (south) side of the line. No goods facilities were provided, and there were no sidings or other connections. The station was 9 miles 57 chains from Northallerton.

The station building was a long, split level brick-built structure with stepped end gables, five squat chimney stacks, and an open loggia in lieu of a canopy; the main office accommodation was situated at the west end beside a minor road which crossed the line on the level. Nearby, a small signal cabin was situated on the down side, and to the west of the level crossing; this was, in effect, merely a gate box, and although four signals were provided Crakehall was not a block post.

In the days before mass motor transport Crakehall had served a number of small villages and hamlets, including Great Crakehall and Little Crakehall to the north of the railway and Kirkbridge to the north-east. To the south, the minor road that crossed the line led eventually to Thornton Watlass, some three miles from the station. None of these places generated much traffic for the railway, and, perhaps for this reason, Crakehall was one of the NER stations closed as a wartime economy measure from 1st March, 1917 until 6th February, 1922.

The staffing arrangements at Crakehall echoed those at Scruton. In North Eastern days the station had its own station master who supervised one or possibly two porter-signalmen, and at the turn-of-the-century this position was filled by Mr George Potter; later, during the early 1920s, the local station master was Mr J.E. Wells.

Sadly, Mr Potter died in the Rutson Hospital, Northallerton on 24th September, 1915, after an accident that had recently taken place at his station. This accident had occurred because Mr Potter and a porter bumped into each other on the platform while both men were checking the doors of a departing train. By a tragic stroke of misfortune, the hapless station master then fell under the train and sustained multiple injuries. A suitable obituary was published in *The North Eastern Railway Magazine* in February 1916, and this extract reveals that the deceased station master had been associated with the Wensleydale branch for many years:

> After signalling a passenger train away, he hurried towards one of the carriages in the rear, apparently under the impression that a door was not properly secured. Unhappily, he came into contact with a porter who was walking in the opposite direction and fell between the train and platform.
>
> Mr Potter, who was popular and well respected, was born on June 5th, 1851, and joined the NER service at Arthington in May, 1873. In July, 1874, he was transferred to Leyburn as assistant guard and, in 1875, became guard at Thirsk. In 1887, he

Newton le Willows

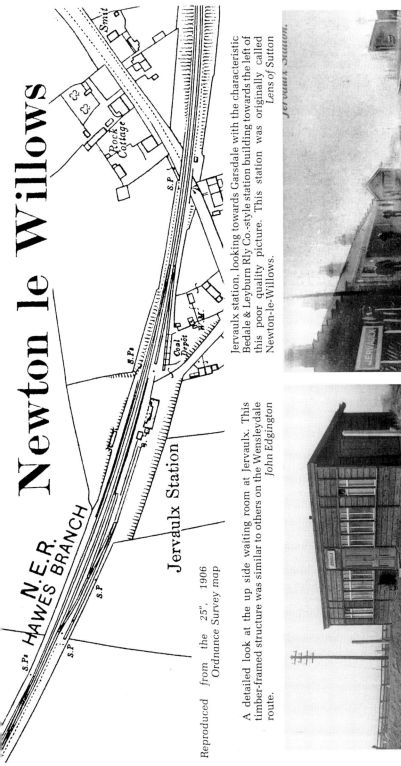

Reproduced from the 25", 1906 Ordnance Survey map

N.E.R. HAWES BRANCH

Jervaulx Station

Jervaulx station, looking towards Garsdale with the characteristic Bedale & Leyburn Rly Co.-style station building towards the left of this poor quality picture. This station was originally called Newton-le-Willows.

Lens of Sutton

A detailed look at the up side waiting room at Jervaulx. This timber-framed structure was similar to others on the Wensleydale route.

John Edgington

Jervaulx Station.

returned to Leyburn, still as guard, and on October 17th, 1899, was appointed station master at Crakehall, the position he held at the time of his tragic death.

Judging from the many expressions of sympathy following the occurrence, it is apparent that he was held in affectionate regard by all those who travel on the Wensleydale branch. He was of an energetic nature and, being fond of gardening, did much to beautify his station.

Leaving the scene of this long-forgotten tragedy, westbound trains continued their ascent towards the picturesque, upper parts of Wensleydale. The view from the carriage windows was still predominantly pastoral, and appreciative travellers were treated to an ever-changing panorama of rural English scenery at its best as their train tackled the rising gradient between Crakehall and Jervaulx.

Jervaulx

The single line followed a low ridge as it climbed towards 300 ft, and trains passed through a series of small cuttings before coming to rest in the slightly curved platforms at Jervaulx, some 11 miles 41 chains from Northallerton. A passing place, Jervaulx had up and down platforms, the main station building being on the down side. Sidings were situated at each end of the down platform, and their connections were (as might be expected) trailing in relation to down trains.

The station building was clearly in the same architectural 'family' as that at Crakehall; it was another brick-built structure with distinctive stepped gables, small-paned windows and squat chimney stacks. Internally, the building contained the usual booking office and waiting room facilities, together with toilets for male and female passengers. The nearby signal box – also on the down platform – had 25 levers, while the up side station building was a simple wooden shelter like the one at Leeming Bar.

The station served a neighbouring village called Newton-le-Willows, and it bore this name until 1877 when, to avoid confusion with the London & North Western Railway station between Liverpool and Manchester, it was renamed. Faced with the need to find a new name for the station the NER called it 'Jervaulx' after the famous Cistercian Abbey which was sited some four miles to the south-west over indifferent roads. (The abbey could also be reached from the neighbouring NER station at Masham, which was around five miles from the ruins along somewhat better roads.)

Jervaulx was unknown as an archaeological site until about 1805 when the owner of the land carried out excavations into a pile of ruins which had been used as a dump from which farmers could obtain cheap stone. The ground plan of the church, founded by the monks of Byland, reveals that it was one of the biggest to be found anywhere, being 270 ft long and 125 ft across the transepts.

In its heyday, Jervaulx station gave employment to over half a dozen railwaymen, among them goods clerks A. Robinson and B.H. Hugill, platelayer William Walker, lengthman William Firby and ganger J. Rountree – all of whom worked locally during the period 1915–20. Mr Hugill moved to Askrigg in 1915, while Mr Rountree retired in 1921.

Two close-up views of the atmospheric, two storey-station buildings at Finghall Lane station. The projecting portions formed a support for a covered loggia for waiting travellers, while the extension on the side of the building (*lower photograph*) housed the gentlemen's toilet. Note the two slotted-post NER signals.   *N. Stead Collection*

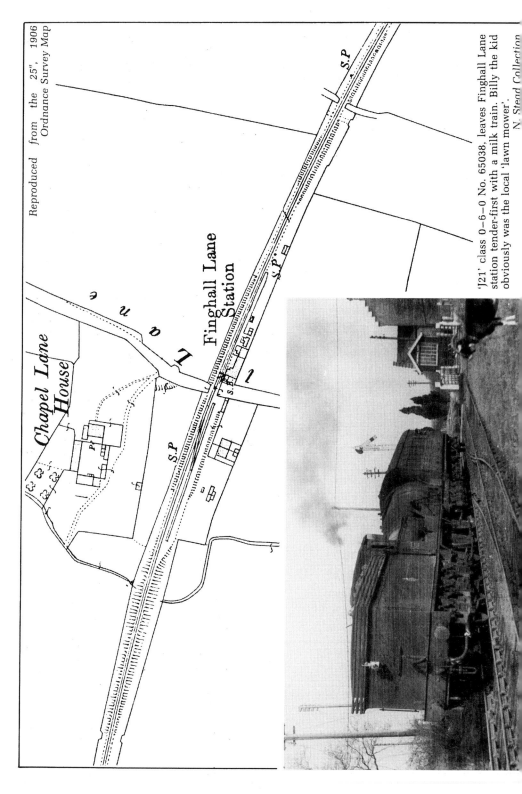

Reproduced from the 25", 1906 Ordnance Survey Map

Chapel Lane House

Finghall Lane Station

S.P

S.P.

S.P

S.P

'J21' class 0–6–0 No. 65038, leaves Finghall Lane station tender-first with a milk train. Billy the kid obviously was the local 'lawn mower'.

N. Stead Collection

Constable Burton
Station

P.O.

Crane

Constable Burton station with a local two-coach train waiting to leave behind 'G5' class 0–4–4T No. 67314.   N. Stead Collection

Finghall Lane

Having changed the single line tablet at Jervaulx, down workings proceeded westwards along a north-facing scarp slope which became steeper as
the railway entered a deepish cutting on a rising gradient of 1 in 77.

Finghall Lane, the next stopping place (13 miles 20 chains), was one of the
smaller intermediate stations. Serving the nearby village of Finghall, it had
just one platform on the down side. The impressive, two-storey station
building featured NER-style 'stepped' end gables, together with a recessed
loggia and no less than five chimney stacks. There was no crossing loop,
though a signal box was needed to control a public level crossing at the west
end of the station.

The box, which was not a block post, contained seven levers to control the
gates, signals, and a single siding on the west-side of the level crossing; the
latter had a connection facing for down (westbound) trains, and it was used
mainly for coal and other wagon load traffic.

Constable Burton

Running westwards through increasingly-hilly terrain, the route continued to the picturesque country station at Constable Burton. Situated
barely one mile from Finghall Lane, at 14 miles 26 chains, Constable Burton
was a passing place with up and down platforms and a small goods yard on
the down side. The station building, on the up platform, sported a centrally-
placed stepped gable, while the signal box – at the eastern end of the up
platform – was a timber structure containing a 28-lever frame.

The station was over a mile from the village that it purported to serve, and
potential travellers were obliged to walk along a winding country lane in
order to catch their trains. On the other hand, the remote and isolated
position of the station contributed to an atmosphere of rural seclusion – an
atmosphere that was further enhanced by the surrounding trees and foliage
that effectively hid the station from the outside world.

In contrast to most of the other stations between Northallerton and Hawes,
Constable Burton had no level crossing – instead, the relatively hilly surroundings had enabled the 19th century railway builders to provide an
underbridge beneath the line.

The two platforms at Constable Burton were widely staggered, the down
platform being much further east than the up side platform and station
buildings. It was, for this reason, possible for the goods yard to be sited on
levelled ground to the south of the up platform; the yard had two sidings,
one of which extended westwards from the end of the crossing loop as a sort
of headshunt, while the other, slightly longer, siding diverged via a facing
connection on the down side. The yard was equipped with a 10-ton hand
crane (later removed), but no goods shed was ever provided.

Spennithorne

The next station westwards from Constable Burton was at Spennithorne,
at 15 miles 67 chains, to reach which the single line had to thread its way

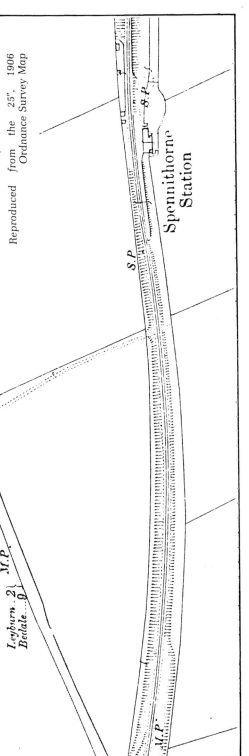

Reproduced from the 25", 1906 Ordnance Survey Map

Spennithorne Station

S.P

S.P

S.P

M.P

M.P

Leyburn 2

Bedale 9

A very early view of Spennithorne station showing its relatively large buildings for such a small station in a remote area.
Lens of Sutton

uphill on a series of adverse gradients. Running on a section of embankment, down trains passed over a minor road by means of a small underline bridge, and with a long approach road running parallel on the south side, they then came to rest in the single platform station at Spennithorne.

The station building, with its distinctive stepped gables, was similar to that at Constable Burton – though here the likeness stopped as there were no sidings, loops or other connections at this very minor stopping place. A small frame controlled up and down stop signals, but otherwise, Spennithorne was the simplest, and least-important station en route to Hawes. There was, in fact, little need for a station here as the tiny village of Spennithorne was well over a mile to the south-east, and would, perhaps, have been as well served from nearby Leyburn station (over better access roads). To the north of the railway lay little more than a couple of isolated houses and the main A684 road, which crossed the line on a skew bridge to the west of the station.

Architecturally, Spennithorne was worthy of close study in that its brick station building was clearly a relic of the Bedale & Leyburn Railway. It was, in fact, one of five former Bedale & Leyburn stations, all of which exhibited the same style of architecture. However, it is of interest to note that each of these stations was different – the only real points of similarity being in the systematic use of stepped gables, decorative chimneys and other recurrent architectural motifs. At Spennithorne, the station proper was a single-storey structure, while the adjacent station master's house was of two full storeys. Both sections of the building exhibited the familiar Bedale & Leyburn stepped gables, and the building was further distinguished by the French-style shutters which adorned the lower floor windows.

As mentioned in Chapter One, the Bedale & Leyburn Railway had been built with 'every economy which the Directors could devise', and it is, for this reason, surprising that the line should have had such ornate station buildings. On the other hand, the stations concerned were quite simply constructed, and their distinctive appearance was achieved by imaginative use of standard brickwork – which was, after all, one of the cheapest materials available during the mid-19th century. There is also evidence to suggest that the stations were built at intervals – perhaps as more money became available after amalgamation with the NER in 1859.[32]

In its later years, Spennithorne was reduced to the status of an unstaffed halt, though it is interesting to note that this very minor stopping place had been fully staffed during the North Eastern Railway era. Indeed, it had been considered important enough to have its own station master, this position being filled, around the middle-1890s, by George Greyson. A subsequent station master, from 1903 until 1906, was Francis Johnson. As we have seen, Mr Johnson then moved to a new position at Scruton, and there were, thereafter, several other station masters at Spennithorne, among them Mark Lawson, who retired in 1918 after 44 years service with the NER, and Mr L. Liddel, who was in charge of the station during the early 1920s.

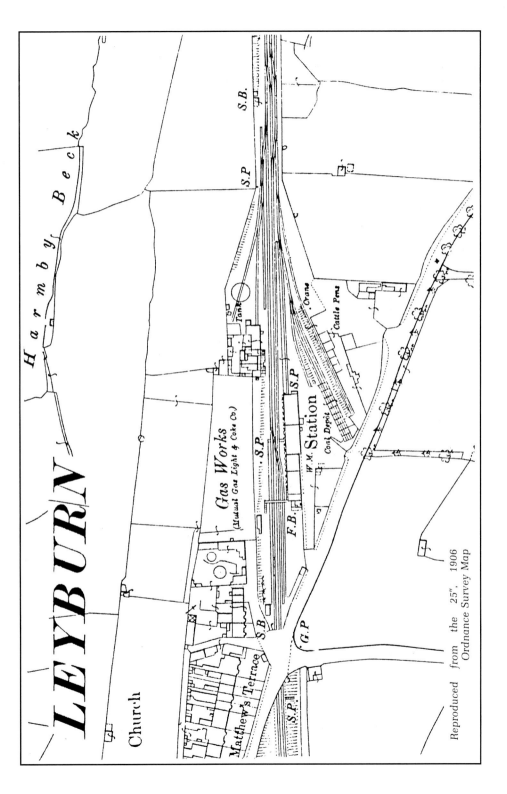

LEYBURN

Church

Harmby Beck

S.B.
S.P.

S.P.

Tank

Gas Works
(Mutual Gas Light & Coke Co.)

Crane

Cattle Pens

S.P.

S.P.

W.M. Station

Coal Depot

S.P.

F.B.

Matthew's Terrace

S.B.

G.P.

S.P.

Reproduced from the 25", 1906
Ordnance Survey Map

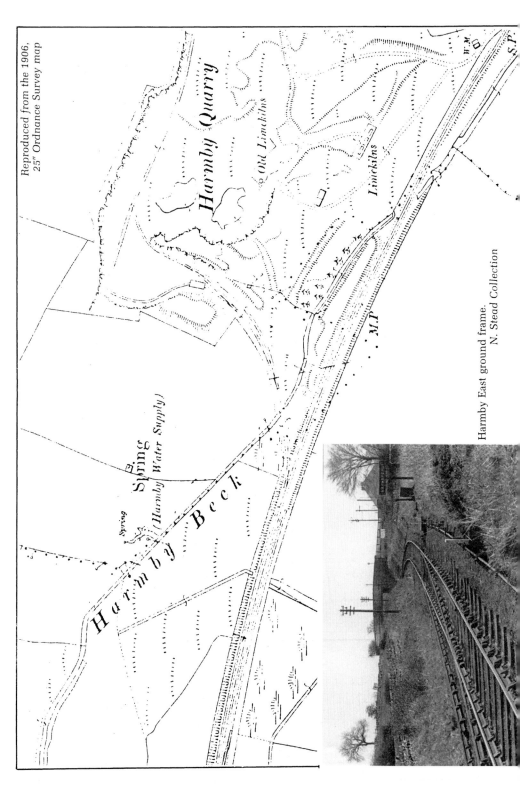

Reproduced from the 1906, 25″ Ordnance Survey map

Harmby East ground frame.
N. Stead Collection

Leyburn

Westwards, the line continued its relentless ascent, and having passed beneath the A684 road, trains soon reached an elevation of 500 ft. Running in a more or less straight line towards Leyburn and the picturesque scenery of Wensleydale, the railway entered a narrow valley, and with the River Ure now only a mile or so away, trains approached the important intermediate station at Leyburn, 17 miles 44 chains from Northallerton.

The track layout at Leyburn was quite extensive. Ground frames at the eastern end of the station complex gave access to Harmby Quarry siding, on the north side of the line. Two junctions, known as Harmby East and Harmby West, formed the lower part of a triangular connection, and beyond this, the main line doubled to form a lengthy passing loop through the station proper. Harmby quarry siding was first installed in 1908 when a connection was installed on the up side of the line for a siding to Siddall Brothers' quarry (in later years, the quarry was worked by the Harmby Limestone Quarry Company).

Board of Trade records reveal that 'the new siding provided in connection with Siddall's limestone quarry near Leyburn' was inspected by Colonel P.G. Von Donop on 18th July, 1911, and the BoT Inspector's report is worth quoting insofar as it contains a few further details of this little-recorded industrial siding:

18th July, 1911

Sir

I have the honour to report, for the information of the Board of Trade, in compliance with the instructions contained in your minute of 25th May, that I have inspected the new works near Leyburn, on the North Eastern Railway.

On the single line between Spennithorne and Leyburn, a new connection, which is facing to down trains, and which leads to a siding, has been provided.

The points and signals are worked from a ground frame of two levers, which is locked by the tablet of the section.

On account of the gradient, it is necessary that traffic to and from the siding should only be worked with the engine at the lower end of the trains, and this the Company has agreed to carry out.

The interlocking is correct, and the arrangements are satisfactory and, subject to the fulfilment of the above mentioned requirements, I can recommend the Board of Trade to sanction these new works being brought into use.

I have the honour, etc.,
P.G. Von Donop, Lt. Colonel, RE[33]

The Inspector's description of a connection leading 'to a siding' suggests that the newly-installed mineral line connected with the earlier line that entered Siddall's quarry via a connection facing to up trains. In later years the 1911 connection became Harmby East while the earlier ground frame at the west end of the quarry complex became Harmby West frame.

The rising gradient in the vicinity of Harmby West ground frame was 1 in 100, but as trains proceeded westwards the climb steepened to 1 in 79, then eased to 1 in 99 as the line neared Leyburn station.

Leyburn's passenger platforms were staggered, the up (eastbound) platform being further west than its counterpart on the down side of the line.

'F8' class 2−4−2T, No. 40 standing (on a local service) at Leyburn station on 7th June, 1935. *H.C. Casserley*

A 1960s view of the sturdy, two-storey station buildings at Leyburn station, photographed from the roadway. *Mowat Collection*

A very useful view of Leyburn station during the British Railways period showing the station buildings to full advantage. Note that the main station building was in fact situated on the goods loading platform – which was not (in normal circumstances) used for passenger traffic. The footbridge, visible in earlier views, has now been removed.   *K. Taylor Collection*

Leyburn station looking eastwards from the down platform, probably in the early 1920s. The combined station building and goods shed is visible to the right.

Lens of Sutton

The main station buildings and the extensive goods yard were on the down side, and there was, in addition, a goods loading platform which formed a sort of extension to the down platform. This goods platform was served by a separate goods line that was linked to both the up and down running lines by trailing connections; access to the goods line was controlled from two ground frames which were known (logically) as Leyburn 'A' and Leyburn 'B' ground frames.

The presence of the above-mentioned goods siding meant that there were three parallel lines through the western part of the passenger station, and this gave Leyburn an atmosphere of importance that was, perhaps, unusual at a branch line station. This air of importance was further accentuated by the apparent complexities of the layout at the eastern end of the station, where three parallel lines were again provided – the up and down running lines being flanked by a long goods loop on the down side. The goods loop continued eastwards to form a lengthy headshunt, and a similar headshunt extended due east from the crossing loop, the result being a triple track layout that extended as far as Harmby West ground frame (at which point the two sidings on the south side of the line were terminated by buffer stops).

The stone station buildings at Leyburn were both extensive and unusual. The main downside building was physically connected to the adjacent goods shed, the result being an extensive range of buildings that physically dominated the station. These buildings were, at least by Victorian standards, utterly plain, the goods shed being a simple, barn-like structure, while the adjoining station building was not unlike a farmhouse. With their grey stone walling and Georgian-type sash windows, these austerely-simple buildings recalled the kind of barrack-like stations erected in Ireland on lines such as the Midland Great Western Railway during the 1850s and 1860s (they were certainly unlike neighbouring ex-NER stations, which were often highly-decorated in Tudor or Jacobean style).

The western end of the station building was a two storey structure with a gabled roof. Moving eastwards, the centre part of the building was of just one storey, though the eastern block, which incorporated the goods shed, had a higher roof line. Curiously, the station building proper was situated on the part of the platform area used as a goods loading platform, and this unorthodox arrangement suggested that the goods platform had originally been used for passenger traffic (probably before the line was extended to Hawes in 1877). The slab-like façade of the station building/goods shed was rendered more pleasing by the addition of a lightweight sloping canopy that was attached to the main structure by curved metal brackets.

Facilities on the up platform consisted of a waiting shelter that resembled the simple glass-fronted shelters found at Leeming and at other two platform stations on the Wensleydale branch. The staggered up and down platforms were linked by a pedestrian footbridge (later removed), and the embankment behind the waiting shelter was attractively-landscaped.

The goods yard contained sidings for coal traffic and general merchandise, a five-ton crane being available for use when large or bulky loads were transferred from road to rail (or vice versa).

Leyburn's stone-built engine shed was sited on the up side of the running lines, access from the up main line being achieved via a trailing connection.

The single road shed was a simple, gable-roofed building, with a row of decrepit-looking smoke vents along its roof ridge and a large arched entrance for locomotives. Nearby, a 42 ft 4 in. diameter Bray & Waddington turntable was large enough to turn small or medium-sized branch locomotives.

A short dead-end siding enabled engines to be manually coaled from special 'loco coal' wagons, while a standard NER swan-necked water crane was conveniently-sited beside the up running line. Water was supplied from a raised metal tank on a stone-built base that formed a sort of extension to the east end of the locomotive shed. The tank, which dated from the 1850s, was given a second row of cast iron plates in 1911, and it could, thereafter, hold 6,800 gallons of water.

The lengthy passing loop through Leyburn station was, at one time, treated as a distinct block section, this mode of operation being necessitated by the provision of signal boxes at each end of the station, which were designated Leyburn East and Leyburn West boxes. In 1936, however, the West box was closed, and thereafter the station was signalled from the surviving East box – the latter being a single storey brick structure of NER Southern Division design.

Leyburn was the operational centre of the branch, and its importance was underlined by the presence of officials such as a 'Passenger Agent' and the local permanent way inspector, who were based here for administrative purposes. The station master was also a figure of importance, being responsible for a relatively large labour force of porters, clerks and signalmen. Guards were also stationed here, together with two sets of locomotive drivers and firemen (although, as we have seen, the engine shed was closed for several years during the 1920s and 1930s).

The station master here prior to 1913 was Mr J. Fairweather, while in the period from around 1915 until 1920 the station was supervised by Mr T. Horsley. Mr Horsley was then transferred to Market Weighton, his place at Leyburn being taken by Mr J. Lee – who had previously served at Redmire. The booking and parcels clerks, around 1916 included C. Hartley, J. Bowman and E.C. Potter, while the goods clerks included W. Chapleo, F. Peacock, P.F. Limbert, A. Robinson, J. Irving and J.W. Richardson. The senior goods clerk at the end of World War I was A.F. Sanderson, who had moved to Leyburn from Filey.[34]

Other locally-employed NER staff during the period 1910–20 were ganger Edmund Payne, permanent way inspector J. Coates, passenger guard Thomas Featherstone, platelayer W. James and local passenger agent H.B. Holliday.

Some of these individuals enjoyed a particularly long association with the Wensleydale branch, and in this context special mention must be made of J. Coates, who worked on the North Eastern Railway for almost half a century, and served as permanent way inspector on the Wensleydale line for no less than 38 years. Indeed, Mr Coates had worked on the Bedale & Leyburn section since its opening, and for this reason his retirement on 31st December, 1915, represented the end of an era. His retirement did not pass un-noticed, and in February 1915 *The North Eastern Railway Magazine* published the following note:

Mr J. Coates, who, on December 31st, retired from the position of Permanent Way Inspector at Leyburn, joined the service as timekeeper as long ago as January 1st, 1866. He held, until February 1877, a position under the District Permanent Way Inspector, Northallerton District, and was then appointed inspector on the Northallerton and Leyburn branch.

When the new line between Leyburn and Hawes was taken over from the contractor on December 8th, 1877, Mr Coates was given charge of that also, and the whole branch remained under his supervision up to the time of his retirement – a period of 38 years.

In May 1915 the magazine reported a retirement ceremony in which Mr Coates had been presented with a 'purse of gold', while his wife was given a tea service. The ceremony had been held in the Congregational schoolroom at Leyburn, and several local railwaymen turned up to hear station master Horsley speak in 'laudatory terms' of Mr Coates, and his long and honourable service on the Wensleydale branch.

It is, perhaps, easy to imagine the attractions of life as a permanent way inspector on a scenic line such as the Wensleydale route; Mr Coates clearly liked the healthy, open air work – though, sadly, he did not live long enough to enjoy a particularly happy retirement; he died in June 1921 at the age of 75, and with his passing a tangible link with the early days of the Bedale & Leyburn Railway was finally severed.

While on the subject of NER employees at Leyburn, it is interesting to note that Mr H.B. Holiday, who was appointed to the post of 'Local Passenger Agent' at Leyburn in 1911, was given responsibility for the entire Wensleydale, Swaledale and Teesdale districts, the idea being that he would be able to stimulate travel throughout this popular and highly picturesque area. The promotion of tourist traffic was clearly an important aspect of Mr Holiday's work, and a note in the North Eastern Railway Magazine in August 1911 reveals that this new NER official was a highly experienced man, who had worked in the Chief Goods Manager's Office at York before becoming a station master at Lartington in 1901. The North Eastern authorities evidently hoped that a lucrative tourist business could be developed in the Wensleydale area, but sadly, World War I intervened, and thereafter the development of road transport began to deprive the railway of this important source of leisure traffic.

Leyburn itself was a small, but busy township serving as a shopping and marketing centre for the surrounding area. Six or seven racehorse trainers lived locally, while dairy products also gave the station much revenue; in 1911, Leyburn booked a little under 24,000 passengers, making it the busiest station on the Wensleydale branch.

After the closure of Leyburn West signal box in 1936, it was possible for train crews to obtain a single line token which was electrically released at the down starting signal by the Leyburn East signalman (thereby saving a long and time-consuming walk back to the signal cabin). To facilitate this mode of operation an auxiliary key token instrument was installed at the down starting signal, and LNER working appendices contain the following instructions in connection with the Leyburn to Wensley single track section:

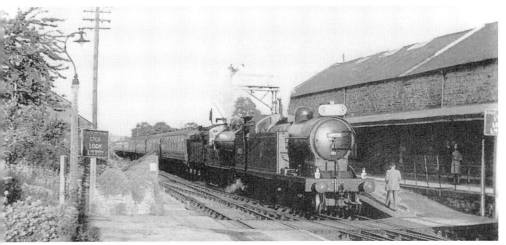

A double-headed SLS special waiting at Leyburn station on 4th September, 1955 (facing Northallerton). *R.M. Casserley*

LNER No. 1672 passing Leyburn West signal box on 7th June, 1935. *H.C. Casserley*

Former NER class 'G5' 0–4–4T No. 67345 on a local stopping service at Leyburn station on 20th March, 1954. *John Edgington*

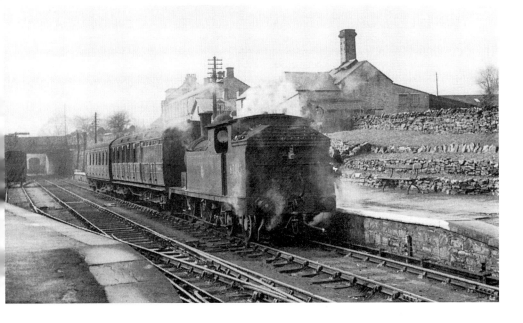

Instructions for single line working at Leyburn,
consequent on the closure of Leyburn West signal box.

The section between Leyburn and Wensley is worked in accordance with the Regulations for Train Signalling on Single Lines of Railway by the Electric Key Token Block System.

An auxiliary Key Token instrument is installed at Leyburn Down Starting Signal to enable drivers to obtain a token for the section.

When it is necessary for a driver to receive a token from the Auxiliary instrument the Signalman must, after obtaining permission from the Signalman at Wensley in the usual way, withdraw the special key from the instrument in the signal box, place it in the slot at the side of the token instrument, give it one half turn to the right and press the plunger which will cause the indicator on the Auxiliary instrument at the signal to show 'Free'.

When a train is about to depart the driver must, if not in possession of a token, proceed to the Auxiliary Token instrument referred to, and unless the indicator on the instrument shows Free, he must communicate with the Signalman by means of the telephone. When the indicator on the instrument shows Free a token must be extracted in accordance with the instructions shown on the brass plate fixed on the instrument which reads as under:

Wait until indicator shows Free.
Then lift a key token with web downwards into keyway.
Turn key token in anti-clockwise direction and withdraw it.

After token has been obtained from the instrument the driver must advise the signalman accordingly on the telephone and place the token in the usual leather pouch and the signalman must pass the special key by way of the slot into the token instrument. Tokens cannot be replaced in the Auxiliary instrument. Should it be necessary to cancel a token, which has been withdrawn from the Auxiliary instrument, this should be done by returning the token to the Signalman at Leyburn.

Accelerating away from Leyburn, down trains soon reached Ord & Maddison's extensive limestone quarry, which was less than a mile from the station at the end of a long cutting crossed by the A684 road. The quarry was served by another private siding, the connections for which were worked from a ground frame. To the north, a limestone ridge known as the Leyburn 'Shawl' rose boldly above the railway, its wooded slopes affording some superb views for intrepid walkers and tourists.

Ord & Maddison's quarry siding was installed around 1911, and in this respect it was roughly contemporary with neighbouring Harmby Quarry sidings. Unlike Harmby quarry, however, the Ord & Maddison quarry was situated in an elevated position above the railway, and an inclined tramway was therefore provided so that stone could be lowered down the Leyburn Shawl to the main line. Contemporary Ordnance Survey maps reveal that the tramway was about a quarter of a mile in length, and it ran in a dead straight line from Leyburn Quarry on the top of the Shawl, to the quarry sidings below. The tramway was double track with two closely-spaced lines of rails that were slewed apart at the very centre of the incline to provide an intermediate passing place.

There was one small overbridge at the top of the incline, and this carried a footpath across the line. At its lower end the tramway terminated in a loading dock beside the NER exchange sidings – the latter being arranged as a loop siding with access from the main line at either end. The tramway was probably worked by gravity on the continuous rope system whereby empty wagons were hauled up to the quarry by the weight of loaded vehicles on the other line.

Before finally leaving Leyburn one might add that the town and station was conveniently sited in relation to nearby Middleham Castle – one of the greatest Medieval strongholds in the north of England, and the childhood home of King Richard III. Situated on the southern side of the River Ure, the castle consisted of a massive square keep standing within a protective screen of later fortifications. The castle was one of a number of historic buildings within the area served by the Wensleydale line, and its presence enabled the NER and LNER companies to promote Wensleydale as an attractive venue for tourists (unlike neighbouring Jervaulx Abbey, Middleham Castle was an 'Ancient Monument' in state guardianship, and as such it is now in the care of English Heritage).

An interesting shed scene at Leyburn, as Sentinel 0–4–0 shunter No. 68182 simmers gently in the sunshine. The water tower stands behind the locomotive and part of the water crane can be glimpsed to the right. The wagon on the right is, somewhat surprisingly, a Western Region vehicle.   *N. Stead Collection*

Ivatt class '4MT' 2−6−0 No. 43101 passes Leyburn East signal box with an eastbound stone train. A down passenger train stands in the westbound platform and the entrance to Leyburn goods yard can be seen on the left. *N.E. Stead Collection*

'J21' class 0−6−0 No. 65038 stands in the down platform at Leyburn station with a westbound passenger train. The barn-like building behind the locomotive is Leyburn's single-track engine shed. *N.E. Stead Collection*

Ord & Maddison's quarry siding was situated to the west of Leyburn station; an inclined tramway linked the quarry to the NER main line.

Reproduced from the 1906, 25" Ordnance Survey map

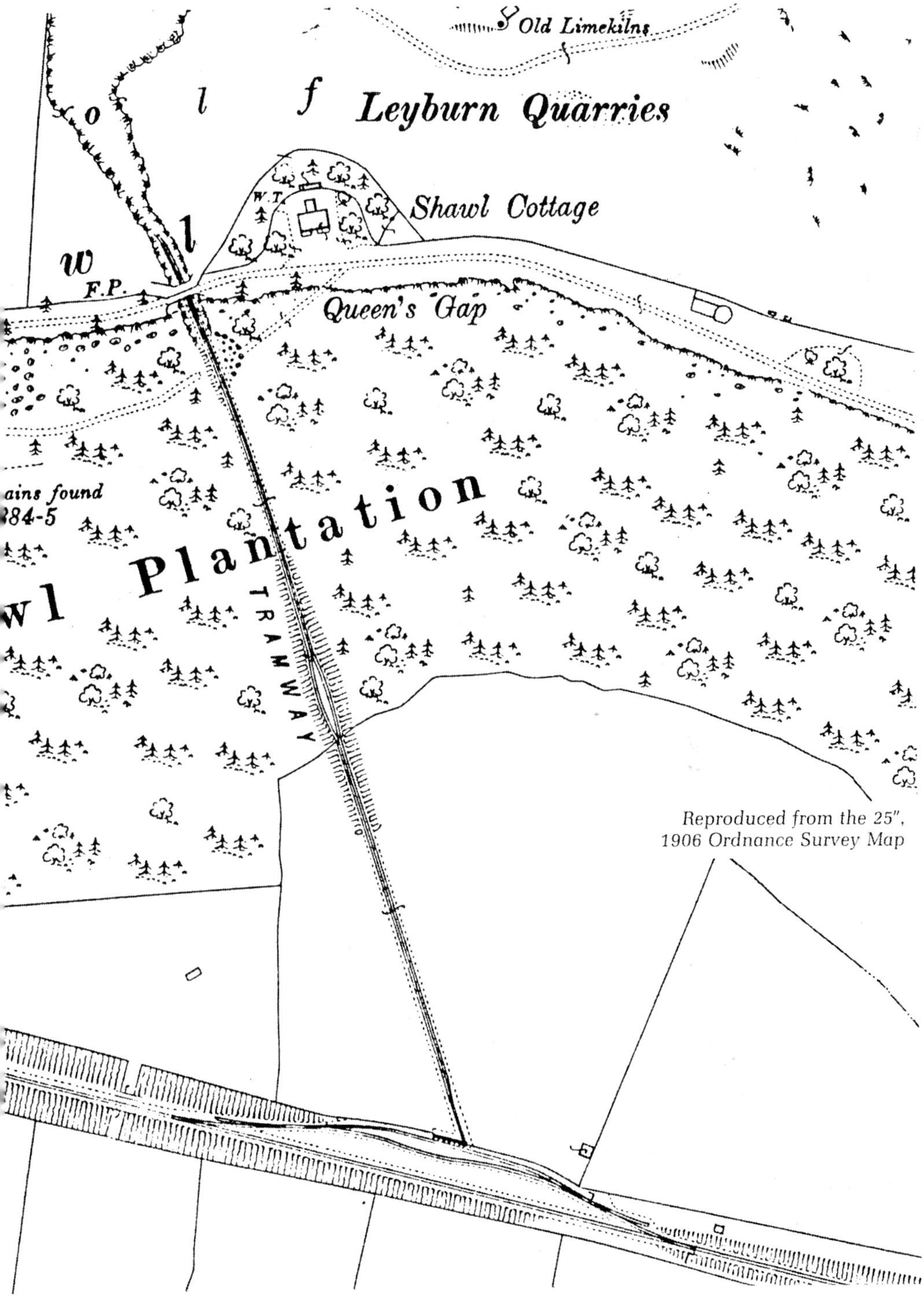

Old Limekilns

f **Leyburn Quarries**

Shawl Cottage

W.T.

w

F.P.

o l

l

Queen's Gap

ains found
84-5

wl **Plantation**

TRAMWAY

Reproduced from the 25",
1906 Ordnance Survey Map

A general view of Wensley station after closure, viewed from the north.
K. Taylor Collection

Wensley station buildings, again after closure. The left-hand wing housed the station master's office, whilst the centre portion contained the waiting room. The two-storey wing to the right contained the station master's house.
K. Taylor Collection

Wensley station, looking east towards Northallerton during the North Eastern Railway era. The staggered up and down platforms were bisected by a level crossing. *Lens of Sutton*

Two views of the Wensley Limestone Company's quarry sidings, installed in the
1920s.   *N. Stead Collection*

Wensley Quarry at Preston-under-Scar with Manning, Wardle No. 14 with a train of loaded tip wagons in 1954.   *R.B. Ledbetter/Alan Rimmer Collection*

A general view of Redmire station, showing the substantial stone station buildings. Note the raised coal drops (*centre*) and the small single-storey signal cabin (*right*).   *N. Stead Collection*

Chapter Five
The Stations and Route: Leyburn to Garsdale

With the Leyburn Shawl still prominent to the right, the line was carried westwards along a stretch of embankment that was pierced, at one point, by an underline occupation bridge connecting the fields on one side of the railway to those on the other. Beyond, westbound trains were faced with a series of moderate gradients as they climbed along the northern side of the valley at an average elevation of 600 ft.

Wensley

On either side, bare hills rose to over 1,000 ft, and on their scarred sides observant travellers could discern the signs of former mining and quarrying activities. Nearing Wensley (19 miles 72 chains), trains passed another rail-connected limestone quarry on the north side of the line; this quarry was worked by the Wensley Limestone Company, and the quarry siding was installed during the early 1920s.

Wensley station was a passing place with staggered up and down platforms. The station building and goods yard were on the down side, and there was a level crossing between the platforms; the signal box, with 34 levers (including many spares) was strategically-sited beside the crossing gates.

The goods yard was used mainly for coal and other wagon load traffic, and (in later years at least), there were no cattle docks, yard cranes or end-loading docks. The station was, on the other hand, one of those selected by the LNER as an ideal site for a camping coach, and this vehicle could usually be seen in the goods yard sidings.[35]

The station building at Wensley was built in a distinctive 'country cottage' style that incorporated a single-storey office portion and a two-storey station master's dwelling house, the two parts of the station being linked by a low, central structure to form an 'H'-shaped building with asymmetrical cross wings; the recessed, central portion of the building formed a small, but convenient, roofed waiting area for local travellers. An extension at one end of the building functioned as a gentlemen's urinal, and the whole building was constructed of irregularly coursed stonework, the large and smaller stones being laid in a decorative 'snecked' form of bonding.

This style of building was, in many ways, typical of the later Victorian period, and it was noticeable that Wensley station was entirely different in relation to the stations east of Leyburn (which had been built a few years earlier). Internally, the station building contained a booking office and general waiting room, together with male and female toilets, a ladies' waiting room, and a private waiting room for the exclusive use of Lord Bolton and his family.

Wensley's track plan was comparatively simple, the main point of interest being the connection to nearby Wensley limestone quarry. Access to this facility was arranged via a siding connection from a long headshunt that extended eastwards from the passing loop. The points were worked from a small ground frame.

On a minor point of detail, it is worth adding that the quarry approach line was partially laid with second-hand London & South Western Railway

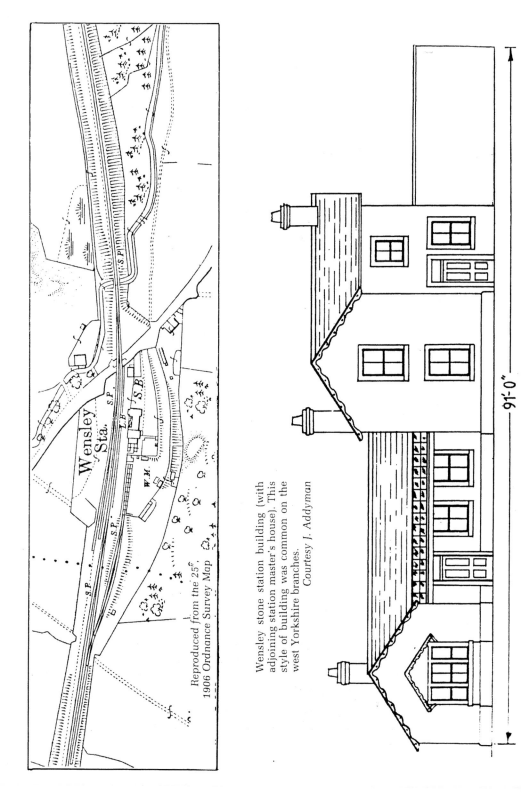

Reproduced from the 25", 1906 Ordnance Survey Map

Wensley stone station building (with adjoining station master's house). This style of building was common on the west Yorkshire branches.

Courtesy J. Addyman

91'-0"

chairs – though in practice it was not unusual for one company to acquire permanent way equipment from another (such transfers of material probably stemmed from the period of government control in World War I).

The up side building at Wensley was a simple timber structure with a glazed platform frontage, while the nearby signal cabin was another typical NER Southern Division design; it was built of coursed stonework and roofed in grey slate. As usual on former North Eastern lines, the goods yard was equipped with raised coal drops, though no goods shed was provided.

Although not a particularly large station Wensley was staffed by about eight or nine railwaymen. *Kelly's Directories of Yorkshire* show the names of local station masters such as Richard Kaye, who served here in 1893, and Mr C. Ward, who supervised the station during the early years of World War I. *The North Eastern Railway Magazine* furnishes the names of a succession of clerical workers, such as passenger clerk J.J. Lyll and goods clerk J.S. Irving; as usual, some of these individuals appear to have been highly mobile – Mr Irving moved from Sledmere & Fimber (on the Malton to Driffield line) in 1915, yet by 1916 he was working at Leyburn, having remained at Wensley for little more than a year!

Wensley was not a particularly busy station and its passenger bookings, even during the Edwardian heyday of railways, hovered around the 6,000 –7,000 mark. In view of this apparent lack of traffic, it is surprising that Wensley was one of the few stations on the line to have two platforms and a crossing loop.

Wensley itself was prettily situated around a village green, on one side of which was the lodge of Bolton Hall – the seat of the Bolton family, who had moved here in the 17th century. The village gave its name to Wensleydale and a large parish church survived as a tangible reminder of the days when Wensley had been more important than nearby Leyburn. In more recent times Wensley had been a centre of the local lead industry, the Keldheads mine and smelting mills being conveniently-sited to the north of the station. Sadly, lead mining was in decline by the 1870s, and the opening of the railway failed to revive this once-important Wensleydale industry.

Redmire

· From Wensley, the single line continued due west, and having passed beneath a minor road bridge trains soon reached Redmire, the next stopping place (22 miles 0 chains). Although only one platform was provided here for passenger traffic, Redmire was an important freight centre with a full range of facilities for the carriage of coal, minerals, livestock and general merchandise traffic.

The platform was situated on the north side of the line – in which position it was poorly-sited in relation to the inhabitants of Redmire, most of whom lived on the south side of the railway. The station building, designed by Thomas Prosser, was solidly-built of local stone, and like others on this section of the line it incorporated an 'H'-shaped layout, with two cross wings and a recessed loggia in lieu of a canopy. The eastern cross wing was a two-storey structure containing domestic accommodation for the station master and his family, and there was, in addition, a further two-storey extension at the easternmost end of the building. The western cross wing, in contrast, was one storey high – its most obvious feature being a projecting bay window which, in earlier days, had probably housed telegraph equipment; this part of the building contained the station master's office, while the waiting room was situated in the centre part of the structure, with direct access to the platform.

The building sported ornate, scalloped barge boards, and an array of tall, decorative chimneys added further character to this delightfully 'vernacular' structure.

There was a small, one-and-a-half storey signal cabin at the eastern end of the single platform, and this, too, was built of stone. In true LNER fashion, the box carried 'REDMIRE' name boards on each side rather than on the main facade. The box, which was of NER Southern Division design, had 30 levers.

The station was equipped with an interesting assortment of antiquated signals, many of which were genuine ex-NER slotted post semaphores complete with ornate finials; the bracketed starting signal beside the signal box was a particularly good example.

Other features of interest at Redmire included some raised coal drops behind the platform, and an elevated stone yard at the west end of the passenger station – the latter facility being operated by the Redmire Limestone Company. The goods yard was equipped with a one-ton fixed crane, and at night the station was lit by simple oil lamps resting in picturesque glass and iron lanterns – some of which were attached to the station building by ornate iron brackets. Entry to the limestone company's private siding was controlled by a ground frame at the western end of the station.

The most interesting feature in the Redmire area was probably Bolton Castle, which was situated in the nearby hamlet of Castle Bolton, to the north-west of the station. Hardly a thing of beauty, being both stark and square, this brooding Medieval fortress had been built by Lord Chancellor Scrope during the reign of Richard II. In the Tudor period Bolton Castle was, albeit briefly, a place of imprisonment for the unfortunate Mary Queen of Scots; she is said to have escaped at one stage, but having fled as far east as Leyburn she was quickly apprehended. Later, during the civil war of 1642–46, the castle was garrisoned by royalist forces until its surrender in the final year of the conflict.

Reverting to strictly railway matters, it is worth mentioning that Redmire's track layout was unusual in that, although a passing loop was provided, there were no 'up' and 'down' lines; instead, passenger trains were diverted onto the northern line while goods workings enjoyed a straight run through on the southernmost line. Both lines were signalled for two-way working, the southern line being used exclusively for goods traffic while passenger workings were always routed into the platform line.

Like other country stations, Redmire was supervised by a succession of station masters throughout the years, some of whom remained for only a few months, while others stayed in the area for much of their working lives. The station master here at the end of World War I was Mr J. Lee, but in 1920 Mr Lee moved to the more important station at Leyburn, his place at Redmire being taken by Mr J.H. Appleyard.

Redmire station seen from the west, showing the quarry sidings at the Garsdale end of the station. The slotted-post ex-NER signals can be seen to advantage. The cast-iron milepost (right) indicates 22 miles from Northallerton. *N. Stead Collection*

Class 'G5' 0−4−4T No. 67345 leaves Redmire station with an up branch train. The up starting signal (right) was a slotted-post semaphore with a subsidiary siding arm; a supporting post (left) provides support for a wire stay which (in turn) supports the signal. *N. Stead Collection*

A further view of Redmire quarry sidings showing the complicated pointwork and unevenness of the trackwork.   *N. Stead Collection*

Class 'K1' 2−6−0 No. 62005 stands at Redmire quarry sidings on the occasion of the 'Three Dales Railtour' on Saturday, 20th May, 1967.   *John Edgington*

A view of the overhead ropeway that brought the material from the quarry to the rail-head via the loading hopper.   N. *Stead Collection*

Class '47' diesel locomotive No. 47 361 *Wilton Endeavour* stands on a freight train alongside the rebuilt loading hopper at Redmire on 1st June, 1984. N. *Stead Collection*

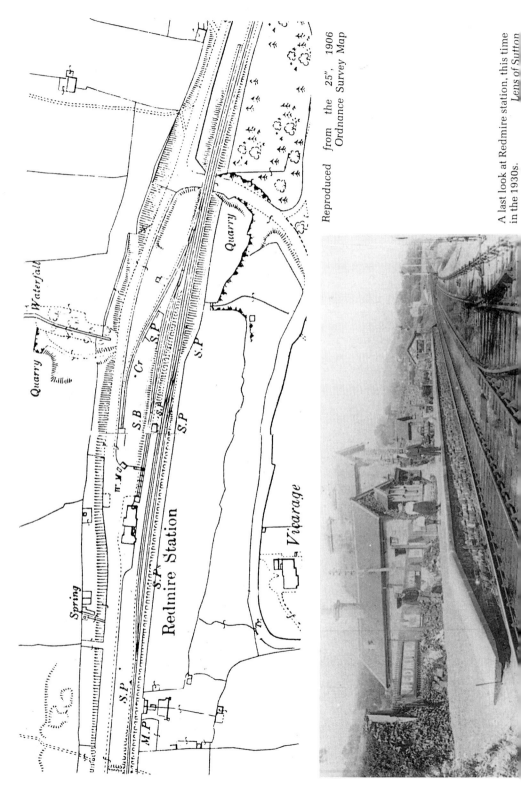

Reproduced from the 25", 1906 Ordnance Survey Map

Waterfall

Quarry

Spring

S.B. ·Cr

S.P.

S.P.

S.P.

S.P.

S.P.

Quarry

Redmire Station

Vicarage

S.P.

M.P.

A last look at Redmire station, this time in the 1930s.

Lens of Sutton

AYSGARTH. NER,

A group of Edwardian travellers wait on the platform at Aysgarth; the station building here was identical to those at Redmire and Wensley. *K. Taylor Collection*

Two six-wheeled NER coaches stand in the sidings at the south end of the station. (It is believed that these vehicles are the first camping coaches to be stationed at Aysgarth.) *N. Stead Collection*

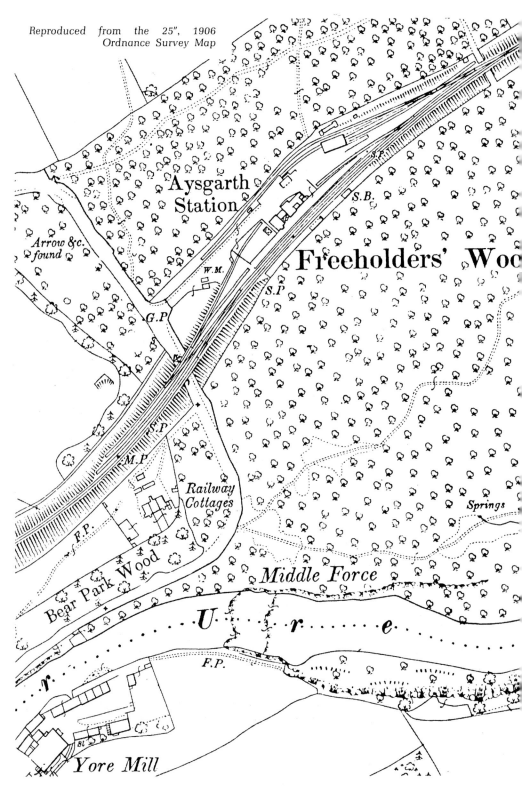

Reproduced from the 25", 1906
Ordnance Survey Map

Aysgarth
Station

Arrow &c.
found

Freeholders' Woo

S.P

S.B.

W.M.

S.P

G.P

S.P

M.P

Railway
Cottages

Springs

F.P.

Middle Force

Bear Park Wood

U . . . r . . . . e . . . .

r

F.P.

Yore Mill

Aysgarth

Departing from Redmire, down trains crossed over the tiny Apedale Beck on a small bridge, beyond which the single line passed beneath a minor road leading to Castle Bolton. Beyond, the route curved south-westwards, and after traversing a series of embankments trains rumbled over Beldon Beck on another small bridge.

Aysgarth, some 24 miles 75 chains from Northallerton, was situated at the point where the line turned through 90 degrees in order to take up a north-westerly heading. A passing place, Aysgarth boasted up and down passenger platforms, the station building and goods yard being on the up side.

The solid, stone-built station building was similar to those at Redmire and Wensley, being an 'H' plan structure with two cross wings, one of which was of two storeys. The signal box, with 20-levers, was equipped with a pair of detonator placers, while the goods yard was able to handle a variety of freight traffic, including, coal, livestock, horseboxes and general merchandise. A two-ton yard crane was provided, and there was also a camping coach.

Aysgarth's track plan consisted of a passing loop, with a number of sidings on the up side. The main goods yard was sited at the Northallerton end of the station, and its four dead-end sidings were entered via a trailing connection from the up running line. One of the sidings served a goods shed, while the others ran into side or end-loading docks. There was a cluster of additional sidings at the west end of the station, and these were entered from a headshunt connection at the west end of the passing loop.

Minor buildings at this station included a small weigh-house at the west end of the goods yard and a simple waiting room on the down platform. The latter building was a masonry structure that afforded rudimentary shelter for westbound travellers.

When first opened in February 1877 Aysgarth was provided with a crossing loop, a three-siding goods yard and a single-siding coal depot. The track layout had not yet been finalised, and it is conceivable that the station had been brought into use before its goods facilities were fully operational. Track laying and other work was evidently still under way during the summer of 1877, and in the following September Major-General Hutchinson was sent to Aysgarth in order to inspect a new siding on the up side of the line.

Maps prepared in conjunction with this inspection show that the newly-laid siding served a loading dock at the east end of the up platform. Further work was in progress in the coal yard at the western end of the station, where a second coal siding was being installed. This was, however, purely a goods line, and the following BoT report, dated 25th September, 1877, confines itself to the new siding connection from the up running line:

25th September, 1877

Sir,
    I have the honour to report, for the information of the Board of Trade, that in compliance with the instructions contained in your minute of 29th ultimo, I have

A fine elevated view of Askrigg station looking northwards, with the village in the background. The two cottages to the right of the station buildings provided domestic accommodation for local railway employees.　　Lens of Sutton

Reproduced from the 25″, 1906 Ordnance Survey Map

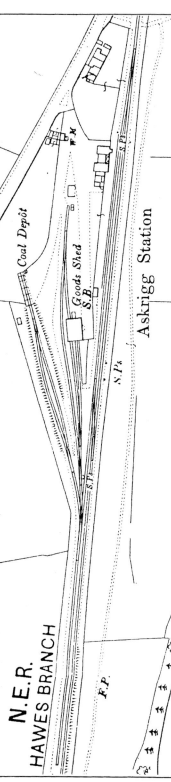

Coal Depôt

Goods Shed

S.B.

W.M.

S.P.

S.P.

S.P.

S.P's

N.E.R.
HAWES BRANCH

F.P.

Askrigg Station

inspected a new siding connection at Aysgarth station on the Leyburn and Hawes branch of the North Eastern Railway.

The siding joins the up line of the loop with trailing points. The points are interlocked only with the up station signal; they should also be interlocked with the up main and up distant signals.

Upon the Board of Trade being informed that these requirements have been done I can recommend that the use of this new siding connection can be not objected to.

I have the honour, etc.,
C.S. Hutchinson,
Major-General, RE[36]

The new siding brought the total number of sidings at the east end of the station to four, while the works under way at the west end of the station meant that there were now two sidings in the coal yard; there were, in addition, two longish headshunts at the Garsdale end of the station, and a third, much shorter shunting neck in the main goods yard (the latter was probably intended to serve as a 'safety point' to prevent runaway wagons from fouling the up running line). This extended track layout was controlled from the single-storey signal cabin at the east end of the down platform; the box had a 19-lever frame at the time of Major-General Hutchinson's September 1877 inspection, four of the levers being spares at that time.

One of the longest-serving station masters here was Mr Frederick Kitching, who was in charge of the station in the early 1890s and during the Edwardian era. Mr Kitching resigned (probably as a result of ill health) in 1911, his replacement being Mr T.H. Walls, who had previously worked as a night foreman at York. W. Chapleo, C.H. Mirfield, H. Houlding, G.R. Pearson and M. Hesleteine all worked at Aysgarth as booking clerks during the period from 1913 until 1918, while M. Percival – who retired in 1918 – was one of the locally employed platelayers.[37]

Aysgarth itself was situated to the west of the station. A noted beauty spot, the village was famous for its water falls which poured in spectacular fashion over a series of limestone steps. The River Ure was only yards from the railway, though the falls could not easily be seen from the train. It was, nevertheless, only a short walk from the station to the falls, and having left their trains tourists and visitors were able to proceed through attractively-wooded scenery towards the roaring cascades. Aysgarth was also the site of a large boarding school, and special trains were sometimes run in connection with this establishment.

Askrigg

Leaving Aysgarth, westbound trains continued generally north-westwards, with the sparkling River Ure visible to the left and the A684 motor road running parallel to the railway on the far side of the line. With 2000 ft hills such as Wether Fell (2015 ft) and Rogan's seat (2204 ft) rising in the distance, the railway climbed steadily through remote moorland countryside.

As trains neared Askrigg, they passed a fortified Medieval manor house known as Nappa Hall. Situated near the railway, on the north side of the line, the hall had been built in the reign of Richard III; it was once the home

A class 'G5' 0−4−4T runs bunker-first into Askrigg station with a two coach branch service. The loop at this station was signalled for two-way running, the left hand line being used for goods traffic, while passenger trains used the platform line. The modern, tubular-post signal on the right has replaced an original NER slotted-post semaphore. *N. Stead Collection*

A more detailed view of the west end of Askrigg station showing the single-storey signal cabin and the goods shed behind. *N. Stead Collection*

of the Metcalfe family who were said to have been the most prolific in England – though how many offspring were produced is not recorded!

Askrigg (29 miles 51 chains) was another single platform station, the passenger facilities being situated on the north side of the line. The substantial, stone-built station buildings here were a mirror image of those at Redmire; two cross-wings were again provided, the two-storey 'domestic' wing being at the west end while the single storey 'station' wing was to the east. The pierced and scalloped barge boards were, if anything, even more ornate than those at Redmire, but otherwise the station building clearly belonged to the same architectural 'family' as its neighbours at Redmire, Wensley and Aysgarth. All of these stations had been designed by Thomas Prosser, the NER architect who had also been responsible for the distinctive station buildings on the Bedale & Leyburn section.

Askrigg's goods facilities consisted of the usual coal sidings, cattle pens and weigh-house. There were five goods sidings, one of which ran into a substantial goods shed; the yard was equipped with a two-ton crane, and a camping coach was available for use by holidaymakers during the summer months.

The station could be pressed into use as a passing place if two freight trains (or one passenger and one goods working) had to pass, but it was unsuitable for crossing two passenger trains because of the absence of a second platform; the loop was signalled for two-way working, the northernmost line being the main running line while the southern line was used as a goods loop. The signal box, with 15 levers, was sited at the west end of the station.

Askrigg station served two small villages – Askrigg itself, which was to the north of the railway, and the nearby hamlet of Bainbridge, about one and a half miles to the south-west. Askrigg was a stone-built village with an old cross, a church and a Tudor manor house; at one time it was noted for clock making and knitting which was 'taken in' by the men as well as by the local women. Neighbouring Bainbridge was the site of a Roman fort, and also the starting point for some interesting walks across the surrounding fells. The fishing hereabouts was excellent, especially along the River Bain and on the nearby Semerwater – one of the few natural lakes in the Yorkshire Dales.

In the early 1890s, the station master at Askrigg was Mr Joseph Lee (who later served at Redmire before becoming station master at Leyburn in 1920). Mr Lee's immediate successors at Askrigg included Mr J. Thorpe and Mr T. Groves; Mr Thorpe was a long-serving NER railwayman whose career lasted from 1872 until his retirement in 1917. In June 1917 *The North Eastern Railway Magazine* printed the following brief account of Mr Thorpe's career:

> Mr J. Thorpe, who had been station master at Askrigg since 1898, retired from active service on March 31st. Altogether, he had been with the North Eastern Railway for 45 years, having started his railway career at Helmsley in 1872. In 1873 he was transferred to the booking office at Central station, Newcastle, where he remained until his appointment to Askrigg.
>
> On April 4th, at a gathering held at the Temperance Hall, Askrigg, Mr Thorpe was presented with a wallet containing treasury notes and a framed testimonial expressing the appreciation of the inhabitants of Askrigg, Bainbridge and low

A fine Edwardian view of Hawes railway station photographed from the road bridge on a summer's evening (the clock reads 6.30 pm). Note the MR and PO wagons in the sidings and the ornate glass in the station building. One horse-trap is unloading a quantity of milk churns for

Abbotside of his uniform kindness and courtesy during his period of office. Mr J. Leyland presided, and the gifts were handed over by Miss Lewis, of Urlay Nook. The Reverend F.M. Squibb, Vicar of Askrigg, and others, also spoke. Mr Thorpe, in expressing his thanks for the gifts, mentioned that he greatly loved country life as contrasted with life in the town, and he hoped to spend his last years in beautiful Wensleydale.

Mr T. Groves, who took over from Mr Thorpe, had earlier served at Raskelf, on the East Coast main line between York and Northallerton. The booking clerks, around 1913–16 included L. Ellerker, E.M. Whitton, C.W. Rogers and J.J. Metcalf; Mr Metcalf, who came to Askrigg in 1916 left two years later to take up a new post at Redcar. Two other employees at this time were goods clerk B.W.H. Hugill, who had also worked at Jervaulx, and porter Joe Foster.

The labour force needed to run a station such as Askrigg would have included porters, signalmen and permanent way men as well as clerical grades; Bill Wilkinson, for instance, worked in the Askrigg area as a lengthman during the early 1900s, while T.W. Bell was employed as a chargeman platelayer on the Askrigg to Hawes section. Like many old time railwaymen, Mr Bell was something of a 'character'. He was an enthusiastic goat keeper, and in World War I he emerged as a leading member of the North Eastern Railway Goat Club, which had been formed as a means of increasing milk and home-made cheese production during the 1914–18 emergency (many railwaymen also became allotment keepers at this time, potatoes and other vegetables being cultivated on lineside plots as a means of helping the national war effort).[38]

There were two signalmen during the Edwardian period, the signal box being manned on a two-shift basis by Tom Langdale and William Hugill. Mr Hugill worked at Askrigg for many years, having come to the station as a signalman in 1901, after previous service as a platelayer on other parts of the NER system; he lived in a railway cottage at a rent of 3s. 9d. a week, and was allowed three days holiday a year (as far as can be ascertained, William Hugill was not related to goods clerk B.W. Hugill).

The route from Northallerton to Askrigg was, at least by Pennine standards, a relatively easy one, and having reached the Askrigg area trains were still no higher than 700 ft above mean sea level (the Stainmore route, in contrast, climbed to a maximum elevation of 1,370 ft). Beyond Askrigg, the route climbed steadily towards its junction with the Settle & Carlisle line, though the earthworks on this part of the line were still reasonably modest.

Hawes

The line maintained a generally westerly heading, with the A684 still running more or less parallel to the south and a minor roading continuing in a similar direction on the north side of the railway. After about three miles the railway crossed from the north to the south bank of the River Ure on a 200 ft girder bridge, and having travelled westwards for a further mile, trains came to rest in the capacious passing loop at Hawes joint station, 33 miles 73 chains from Northallerton and about 800 ft above mean sea level.

Travellers with an eye for architectural detail would have noticed that

Hawes was a Midland-style station, its station buildings, goods shed and signal cabin being identical to those on the Settle & Carlisle Railway. Up and down platforms were provided, with the main station building on the down side and a smaller waiting room on the up platform. A spacious goods yard fanned out on the down side, and there was a large goods shed behind the station building, together with cattle docks and a weigh-house.

The station was, in many ways, better designed than the purely North Eastern stations further east – though this was, perhaps, to be expected when one remembers that the Hawes branch was built as an adjunct to the main Settle & Carlisle scheme. The main station building was a stone structure, measuring approximately 50 ft × 28 ft at ground level. Viewed from the platform, this characteristic Midland Railway building appeared to be a conventional 'H' plan structure incorporating a central booking hall and two gabled cross wings, but in fact the projecting gables were not true cross wings and there were no corresponding gables at the rear. Instead, the rear elevation featured a single, centrally-sited gable with a deeply-recessed window.

There was no rear access to the station building (though the rear gable could easily have been re-designed as a central porch). The gap between the two front gables was filled by a small wood and glass screen, behind which a pair of double doors gave access to the ticket office; to the right, another door allowed travellers to enter the general waiting room, while a similar door in the left hand wing gave access to the ladies' waiting room. At the left of the ladies' room (when viewed from the platform) a 25 ft long extension contained the gentlemen's urinal, and also provided additional storage space for coal, platform trolleys and other items.

Facilities on the up platform were somewhat simpler, and consisted of a small stone waiting room measuring roughly 40 ft × 12 ft 6 in. at ground level. The building was entered through a centrally-placed doorway, and there was a further door in the western gable, giving access to a gentlemen's toilet.

The nearby goods shed was built in the same architectural style as the station buildings; all of these structures exuded a faintly ecclesiastical air, and although there were few overtly gothic details, the presence of Medieval-style trefoil or quatrefoil mouldings high in their gables added further gothic atmosphere. These distinctive structures are believed to have been designed by I.H. Saunders, the Midland Railway architect – who would no doubt have worked in close conjunction with John Crossley (1812–1878), the Midland Railway Engineer with overall responsibility for the Settle & Carlisle Railway.

Other features of interest at Hawes included a small wooden weigh-house, a 1 ton 10 cwt yard crane, and a standard Midland Railway timber-built signal cabin. The latter structure was situated at the west end of the station on the down side of the line; it contained a 20-lever frame. The platforms were fenced with typical Midland Railway pale-and-space fencing, the wooden paling being angled at 45 degrees to the vertical to produce a simple, but highly effective decorative effect.

There had, at one time, been two signal boxes at Hawes – a second cabin, known as Hawes West, being situated at the west end of the crossing loop, on the down side of the line. The west box, however, had a very short life, and it had evidently been abolished by the turn of the century; in later years, 'Hawes West' became merely an open ground frame – this facility being sited at the west end of the down platform.

Although Hawes station was replete with classic Midland Railway architecture, it was staffed entirely by North Eastern Railway employees. Successive station masters here included Henry Smith, F. Raine and W. Milner; Henry Smith was in charge of the station during the 1890s, while Mr Raine served at Hawes between 1913 and 1918. He then moved to Hornsea, and Mr Milner came from Bolton-on-Deane as a replacement (coincidentally, Mr Raine had also worked at Bolton-on-Deane before transferring to Hawes!)[39]

People employed at the station in Pre-grouping days included passenger guard W. Little, booking clerks C.H. Fowler, J.S. Irving and J. Beaumont, goods clerks W. Airey, G.M. Lumley and J. Dinsdale, and porter J. Moore. J.S. Irving moved to Moorthorpe in 1913, but he later returned to the Wensleydale line as a goods clerk at Leyburn. Porter J. Moore had a somewhat more adventurous career, and having joined the 114th Field Artillery Brigade in World War I he was awarded the Military Medal for displaying conspicuous gallantry under heavy shell fire on 21st March, 1918.[40]

Hawes station was always staffed by North Eastern (later LNER) men, although the station and goods yard were regarded as joint property shared equally between the NER and Midland Railway companies; west of Hawes, however, the line became purely Midland property.

The station was well-sited in relation to the town, and visitors arriving at this popular tourist centre by train had only a short walk to the town centre. Although its population was less than 1000, Hawes was a surprisingly busy township, being the marketing centre for farms throughout upper Wensleydale.

Leaving Hawes, westbound trains passed beneath Brunt Acres Road, which was carried across the line on a triple-arched stone overbridge. Just beyond this, the line was carried across Gayle Beck on a three-span girder bridge supported on low stone piers; two spans crossed the stream while a third formed a small cattle creep. Westwards, the line reached a stretch of low embankment which was pierced by further small underbridges or cattle creeps through which farmers could pass from one side of the line to the other.

Garsdale

With Hawes receding into the distance, the bustling 'G5' 0–4–4Ts and their trains of veteran panelled coaches hurried along the single line, crossing further bridges as they approached the soaring stone viaduct at Appersett. This, the most impressive engineering feature on the Wensleydale route, was a multiple-arched structure with five masonry spans and a total length of 375 ft. The viaduct, which carried the railway across the valley of the Widdale Beck, was about 80 ft high at its centre point, and each of its semi-circular arches was of 25 ft radius. The stream passed beneath the centre arch, and the easternmost arch spanned a minor road running southwestwards from Appersett.

HAWES DOWN SIDE (MAIN) STATION BUILDING

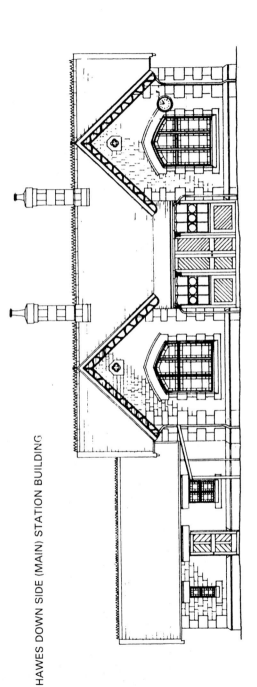

NORTH ELEVATION

The next few pages contain drawings of the buildings at Hawes, prepared by M.K. White and reproduced by kind permission of the *Model Railway Constructor*.

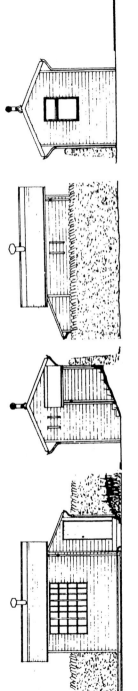

EAST ELEVATION

SOUTH ELEVATION

WEST ELEVATION

NORTH ELEVATION

HAWES STATION BUILDING

SOUTH ELEVATION

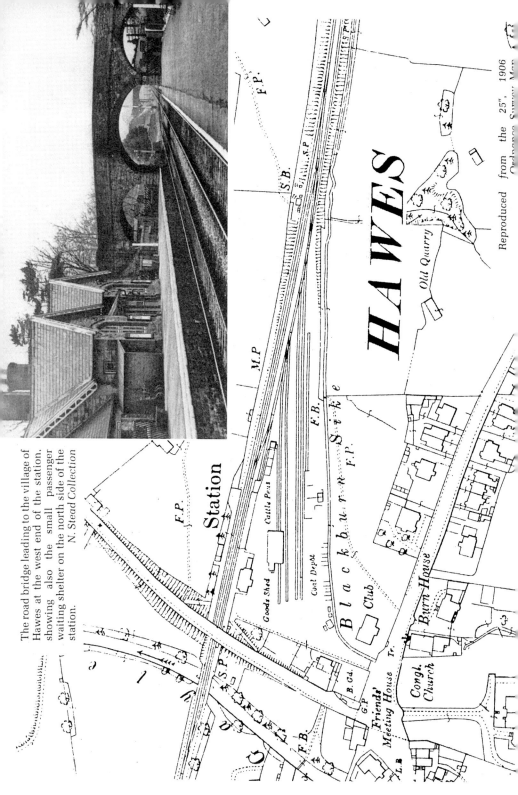

The road bridge leading to the village of Hawes at the west end of the station, showing also the small passenger waiting shelter on the north side of the station.
N. Stead Collection

Station

F.P.

F.P.

M.P

S.P

S.B.

S.B.

F.B.

F.P.

Good's Shed

Cattle Pens

Coal Depot

Blackburn Stile

Club

B. Gd.

G.P.

Friends' Meeting House

F.B.

L.B.

Burn House

Congl. Church

HAWES

Old Quarry

Reproduced from the 25", 1906
Ordnance Survey Map

A further look at Hawes with 'G5' class 0−4−4T No. 67345 waiting at Hawes signal box The box here was a two-storey wooden construction of typical Midland Railway design. *N. Stead Collection*

A close-up view of the timber weigh-house at Hawes yard. *K. Taylor Collection*

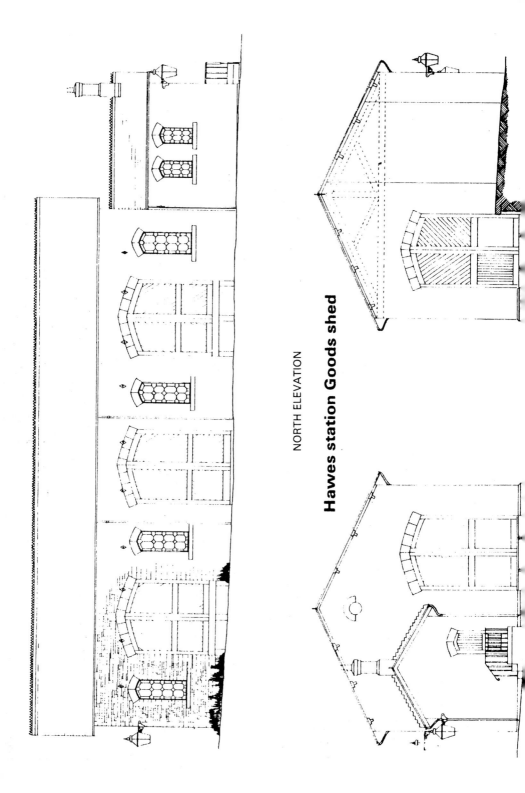

NORTH ELEVATION

Hawes station Goods shed

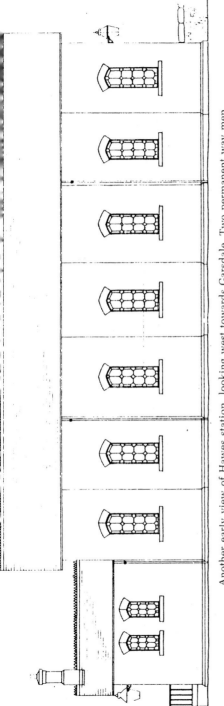

Another early view of Hawes station, looking west towards Garsdale. Two permanent way men stand beside a four-wheeled trolley – one of these (on the right) is possibly Bill Wilkinson.

Lens of Sutton

A general view of Hawes station from the road bridge.

HAWES UP SIDE STATION BUILDING

SOUTH ELEVATION

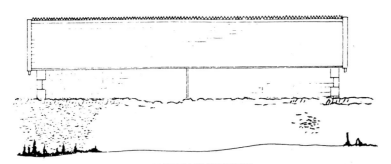

NORTH ELEVATION

EAST ELEVATION   WEST ELEVATION

Fairburn 2−6−4T No. 42132 stands in the down platform at Hawes in 1958, preparing to leave with the 4.25 pm departure for Garsdale.   *N. Stead Collection*

Ex-NER class 'B16/Z' 4−6−0 No. 61435 passes the skeletal remains of Hawes signal box with the 'North Yorkshireman' railtour on Saturday 25th April, 1964. This was the last train to work through from Northallerton to Garsdale.   *N. Stead Collection*

Worsdell 'J21' class 0−6−0 No. 65238 bursts-out into the daylight from the 245 yds-
long Mossdale Head Tunnel.   *N. Stead Collection*

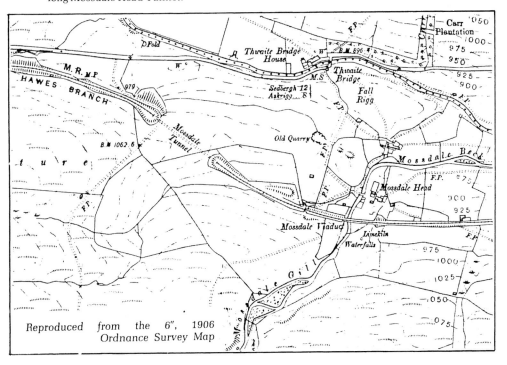

Reproduced from the 6″, 1906
Ordnance Survey Map

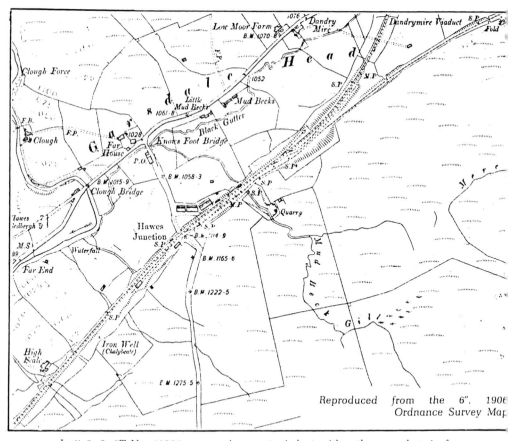

Ivatt 2–6–2T No. 41304 crosses Appersett viaduct with a three-coach train from
Hawes.   H.C. Casserley

A Wensleydale branch train hauled by class 'D20' 4−4−0 No. 62391 entering Garsdale (Hawes Junction) station on 30th May, 1951.   *H.C. Casserley*

An early view of Garsdale station, looking north towards Carlisle, with the Wensleydale branch bearing to the right and the branch platform in the foreground.
                    Lens of Sutton

Climbing at 1 in 150, the single line turned imperceptibly north-westwards as it wound between 2,000 ft fells. Keeping to the south side of a narrow valley the line passed through cuttings and then along embankments as it climbed towards Garsdale, and with the A684 running parallel to the right the route curved gradually westwards as it neared Mossdale Head. Here, the railway was carried across a tributary of the Ure on a four-arched stone viaduct.

Having reached an elevation of about 1,000 ft, the line plunged into the Stygian darkness of the 245 yds-long Mossdale Head Tunnel, beyond which the railway passed through a short cutting. A brief stretch of embankment followed, but this soon gave way to a much longer cutting that continued for about half a mile.

With its destination now in sight, the single line curved south-westwards in order to join the Settle & Carlisle line on the up side of Garsdale station. To the right, the main line emerged from Moorcock Tunnel and swung round in a great curve, crossing the towering Dandry Mire viaduct, and then running south-westwards into Garsdale station. Main line and branch continued parallel to each other for a short distance before the branch came to an end in its own platform on the eastern side of the main line.

Once known as Hawes Junction & Garsdale, this remote junction station was renamed Garsdale for Hawes in 1933. It was 61 miles 43 chains from Leeds and 39 miles 68 chains from Northallerton, and was of some interest in that it was the only junction station on the Settle & Carlisle line.

Three platform faces were provided here, the up platform being an island with tracks on either side, while the down side had just one platform face. The branch platform had its own run-round loop, and there were trailing and facing connections to the up main and down main lines; by crossing the up and down main lines incoming branch engines were able to reach sidings and a turntable on the west side of the running lines. There were additional sidings on the up side, the main goods and marshalling sidings being at the north end of the station. A further dead-end siding at the south end of the station marked the site of the former North Eastern Railway engine shed, which had been burned down in 1917 and officially closed in 1939.

In architectural terms, Garsdale was a typical Midland station, its up and down side buildings being similar in design to the subsidiary waiting room block on the up platform at Hawes. The up side buildings at Garsdale incorporated a transverse platform canopy that afforded at least some protection for travellers waiting on the exposed island platform. Both buildings were constructed of regularly-coursed stonework, with prominent quoins at each corner.

The signal box was sited on the down platform, and as might be expected, it was another standard Midland Railway design. It was built of prefabricated timber components, and measured approximately 39 ft × 14 ft. The external walls were clad in horizontal weather boarding, and the box had a hipped, grey slate roof with two prominent finials.

There was a large, Midland-style water tank near the site of the former NER engine shed; this structure was very substantially built with a stone lower storey and metal tank above. (The space below the tank was, at one

A last day scene at Garsdale station as class 'J21' 0–6–0 No. 65038 stands in the branch platform on Saturday 24th April, 1954. Note the funeral wreath adorning the top lamp bracket.   *N. Stead Collection*

The Garsdale 'stockade' built around the turntable to help keep it in service during the windy months of winter. Worsdell class 'J21' 0–6–0 No. 65038 is the locomotive being turned.   *Lens of Sutton*

time, used as a sort of social club by local railwaymen.) Nearby, on the down side of the line, a row of typical railway cottages provided accommodation for local railway staff, but otherwise there were few signs of habitation in the bleak landscape which surrounded this lonely railway outpost.

Much of Garsdale's importance stemmed from the Midland's policy of using small engines for all services; this meant that many northbound workings needed banking assistance on the long climb up from Settle Junction to Ais Gill summit, and having been detached at the summit the assisting engines were sent back to Garsdale for turning. In Midland Railway days Garsdale was thus a place of great activity, with large numbers of light engines awaiting turning, or running back towards Settle for their next turn of duty.

On 24th December, 1910, the need to keep these assisting engines clear of the main line led to an appalling accident when signalman Alfred Sutton allowed two light engines to proceed northwards in the path of a down express.[41] There were, on the night in question, no less than nine light engines in and around the station, including MR class '2' 4−4−0s Nos. 448 and 548, driven by drivers Edwin Scott and George Bath. Both men were eager to return to Carlisle after waiting for over an hour in the sidings at Garsdale, and perhaps for this reason neither bothered to carry out 'rule 55' (which stated that when a train was detained on a running line the guard, shunter or fireman should go to the signal box to remind the signalman of the position of the train).

While the two Carlisle enginemen waiting impatiently for an opportunity to proceed northwards, signalman Sutton attempted to find paths for a succession of up and down trains. Surrounded by no less than nine light engines, and worn out by fatigue at the end of his ten hour night shift, the signalman decided to accept an up express; the two Carlisle engines had, by that time, been shunted onto the down main line, and when the down main starting signals changed from red to green, the Carlisle drivers naturally assumed that they could proceed. The two 4−4−0s therefore set off into the gloom of a stormy Pennine morning; just three minutes later, at 5.47 am, the double-headed Scotch express swept through the station behind Kirtley 2−4−0 No. 48 (leading) and class '2' 4−4−0 No. 549.[42] When his relief came in a few minutes later, signalman Sutton uttered the memorable words *'I'm afraid I have wrecked the Scotch express'*.

The impact came at a point just to the north of Moorcock Tunnel; despite the poor visibility, the drivers of the Scotch express saw the red tail light at the rear of 4−4−0 No. 548, while at the same time the two light engines increased speed in an attempt to lessen the coming blow. This emergency action may, indeed, have prevented a worse catastrophe, though both express engines and one of the light engines were derailed by the violence of the collision. Unfortunately, the two leading carriages of the express were telescoped, the resulting destruction being worsened by the ignition of escaping Pintsch gas from the cylinders beneath the wrecked vehicles. Heroic efforts were made to save those trapped in the wreckage, but at least a dozen passengers (including a five month old baby girl) were killed in the disaster.

Identification of the bodies was understandably difficult, and an inquest opened at the nearby Moorcock Inn was subsequently continued at an adjourned inquiry in the market hall at Hawes on 29th December. When the inquest was completed, the unfortunate victims of the disaster were interred in the little churchyard at Hawes on that same afternoon.[43]

By a stroke of tragic misfortune, a further destructive collision took place near Garsdale Junction on 2nd September, 1913. On this occasion Deeley 4–4–0 No. 993 failed to keep time while heading the 1.35 am up express from Carlisle to St Pancras. This train, which had originated in Glasgow, was a heavy formation consisting of nine vehicles weighing 243 tons, and in normal circumstances such a load would have required double-heading. The 4–4–0 struggled to lift its heavy train over Ais Gill summit, but as luck would have it the tender had been filled with poor quality 'slack' and, unable to maintain sufficient steam pressure, No. 993 came to a stand short of the actual summit, and only two miles away from the site of the 1910 disaster.

Although standard regulations required that the stalled train should have been protected by detonators, the train crew neglected to carry out this simple precautionary measure, and although the stationary express was protected by the Mallerstang signals, the crew of a following train failed to reduce their speed or to take notice of a desperate hand signal from the signalman at Mallerstang. As a result of these mistakes, the speeding train – headed by rebuilt Johnson 4–4–0 No. 446 – ran into the back of the stalled express; No. 446 sliced through two coaches and came to rest amid the wreckage of a third class vehicle. Fire immediately broke out, and as in 1910, escaping gas ensured that the demolished coaches were transformed into a raging inferno. In retrospect, the disaster could have been far worse, but 14 innocent travellers were nevertheless killed in an accident which (in theory at least) should simply not have happened.[44]

Two accidents in roughly the same place (and within less than three years) gave Garsdale an unenviable reputation, and superstitious individuals may have wondered if the place was cursed. Incredibly, the station was the scene of a further mishap on 6th October, 1917 when fire consumed the single road engine shed on the up side of the running lines. There were no human casualties in this incident, though Fletcher 0–4–4T well tank No. 207 (which had been inside the shed at the time) was rendered totally unfit for service and had to be sent to Darlington Works for repairs and repainting.

An incident of a different kind is said to have taken place at Garsdale Junction when an engine was being turned on the turntable. By a freak of nature, the wind took charge of it and the locomotive was turned slowly round and round on its axis until somebody shovelled stones and cinders into the turntable pit! To prevent such incidents from happening again the turntable was given a protective stockade of old sleepers, and these acted both as a windshield and as a snow-screen during the depths of winter.[45]

Garsdale was, in many ways, an unusual 'terminus' for a railway, being situated in remote and desolate fell country at an elevation of more than 1,000 ft above mean sea level. Although there were scattered hill farms in the surrounding area, there were no towns, or even large villages – the railway was, indeed, the only reason that Garsdale existed. In this respect, the contrast between Northallerton and Garsdale could not have been greater; although Northallerton was not a large place, it was positively metropolitan in comparison with Garsdale Junction!

Amusingly, many of the farms around the station were painted in a red and cream colour scheme, and this gave rise to an intriguing local legend concerning a consignment of Midland Railway red paint, which is said to have been 'lost' from a train in the Garsdale area! In this context it may be worth adding that most 19th century buildings were painted green or brown, and these colours remained in common use until recent years; red paint was rarely used on external woodwork (certainly not on farm buildings) and one wonders when, in fact, local farmers started using this colour on their houses and barns (probably at some time in the 1930s, when cheap red paint would have been available for domestic use).

Garsdale station was (together with the nearby Moorcock Inn) one of the few public meeting places in the area, and for this reason its waiting room was once used for church services! The station could also boast a small library, which had been started through the generosity of two stranded travellers who donated a small collection of books for public use.

A view of Garsdale station looking south, the branch platform is on the left and the main line on the right; June 1954.   *H.C. Casserley*

Chapter Six

From Nationalisation to the Present Day

The nationalisation of railways on 1st January, 1948 made little difference to rural branch lines such as the Wensleydale route, and the later 1940s and early 1950s were, in most respects, merely a continuation of the LNER era. As on so many other lines, the only obvious change concerned the liveries of locomotives and rolling stock. The plain brown coach livery of the LNER was replaced by an overall maroon colour scheme, while 'mixed traffic' locomotives such as the 'G5' 0-4-4Ts were repainted in London & North Western Railway style lined black livery. There was also a change in locomotive numbering systems, the existing LNER four-figure numbers being extended by the addition of a two-figure prefix which (in the case of former LNER engines) began with a 6.

Post-Nationalisation Motive Power

These changes were, however, only cosmetic, and in terms of motive power the Wensleydale route remained a North Eastern Railway line - the ex-NER 'G5' 0-4-4Ts being much in evidence around 1950. The regular engines at this time included 'G5' 0-4-4Ts Nos. 67312, 67314, 67318, 67342, 67344 and 67345. (Interestingly, No. 67318 had originally worked on the line - as No. 2089 - as far back as the 1930s.) There were usually three or four 'G5's allocated to Northallerton at any one time, and one of these would be outshedded at Leyburn.

Other ex-North Eastern Railway classes used on the line during the early British Railways period included 'J21' or 'J25' 0-6-0 goods engines, together with former NER 'D20' class 4-4-0s, which were first allocated to Northallerton shed during the late 1930s. Dating back to 1899, the 'D20' class 4-4-0s - which had been NER class 'R' before the 1923 Grouping - were, in many ways, ideal locomotives for use on the Wensleydale route. As tender engines, they had ample coal and water capacity for the 80 mile round trip between Northallerton and Garsdale, while as relatively small engines they were not over-powered in relation to secondary duties on a rural line.

Several 'D20's worked on the line during the period 1948-54, typical numbers being Nos. 62347, 62359, 62373, 62388, 62391 and 62397. About four of these engines were allocated to Northallerton at any one time, and one would sometimes be out-stationed at Leyburn in place of the usual 'G5' 0-4-4T.

Excursions or other special workings brought 'B1' 4-6-0s, 'V2' 2-6-2s or other large tender engines onto the branch while, at the other end of the scale, a 'Sentinel' 0-4-0T was allocated to the sub-shed at Leyburn in order to assist with shunting duties; Nos. 68159 and 68182 were both outstationed at Leyburn at various times during the early 1950s. The following table shows some of the locomotive classes used on the line during the 20th century. For completeness, modern diesel types are also shown, together with sample numbers for the benefit of potential modellers.

Two bridges to be seen on the branch: *(top)* class 'G5' 0-4-4T No. 67345 hurries across the arched stone viaduct at Yafforth, during the early 1950s, whilst *(bottom)* class 'D20' 4-4-0 No. 62388 crosses the four-span viaduct over the River Swale between Ainderby and Scruton stations.   *N. Stead Collection*

Table 3
MOTIVE POWER USED ON THE WENSLEYDALE LINE 1900-2002

Class	Type	Typical Numbers
Fletcher 'G6'	0-4-4T	15/28/69/71/188/189/321/322/324/357/465/588
Worsdell 'G5'	0-4-4T	67312/67314/67318/67342/67344/67345/67347
Worsdell 'D20'	4-4-0	62347/62359/62372/62373/62388/62391/62397
Worsdell 'J21'	0-6-0	65038
Worsdell 'J25'	0-6-0	
Worsdell F8'	2-4-2T	40/279/418/420/423/469/1603
Worsdell 'S'	4-6-0	798/819
Worsdell 'D17'	4-4-0	1636
Thompson 'B1'	4-6-0	61216
Peppercorn 'K1'	2-6-0	62005/62044/62045/62063
Sentinel shunter	0-4-0	68159/68182
Worsdell 'N8'	0-6-2T	
Class '20'	Bo-Bo	20172/20173
Class '25'	Bo-Bo	D5169
Class '37'	Co-Co	37083/37116/37131/37227/37421/37514/37515/37517/37667/ 37668/37688/37714/37719/37884
Class '47'	Co-Co	47033/47051/47200/47218/47219/47287/47291/47303/47314/ 47361/47363/47365/47749/47766/47819/47820
Class '60'	Co-Co	60005/60008/60018/60022/60025/60029/60031/60038/60049/ 60086
Class '66'	Co-Co	66001/66011/66024/66098/66113/66208/66248
Ivatt class '2MT'	2-6-2T	41205/41206/41304
Ivatt class '2MT'	2-6-0	46475
Ivatt class '4MT'	2-6-0	43101
Fairburn '4MT'	2-6-4T	42051/42132
Fowler class '4F'	0-6-0	43893

The ex-LMS engines listed at the end of Table Three worked between Garsdale and Hawes on the local 'Bonnyface' service, though in later years Ivatt class '4MT' and other London Midland Region classes occasionally appeared on freight workings between Northallerton and Hawes.

The train service between Northallerton and Garsdale changed very little after 1948, and apart from minor alterations in times of arrival or departure

Ex-NER class 'G5' 0-4-4T No. 67312 enters Wensley station with a three-coach branch train during the early 1950s. The leading vehicle is an LNER corridor coach in red and cream livery.   *N. Stead Collection*

there were still just four or five trains each way over all or most of the route. In 1950, down workings left Northallerton at 7.15, 9.30 am, 4.10 and 9.15 pm - the 7.15 am and 4.10 pm departures being through workings to Garsdale, while the two remaining services terminated at Leyburn.

In the reverse direction, the corresponding up services left Garsdale at 10.15 am and 6.40 pm, Leyburn at 7.52 am, and Hawes at 4.00 pm - the latter service running in connection with the 3.16 pm London Midland train from Garsdale. The weekday (Monday to Friday) timetable in force in 1950 is shown below.

DOWN TRAINS		am	am	pm	pm	pm	pm
Northallerton	dep:	7.15	9.30			4.10	9.15
Ainderby	dep:	7.23	9.38			4.18	9.23
Scruton	dep:	7.27	9.42			4.22	9.27
Leeming Bar	dep:	7.32	9.46			4.26	9.31
Bedale	arr:	7.40	9.52			4.31	9.39
Crakehall	dep:	7.46	9.58			4.36	9.45
Jervaulx	dep:	7.50	10.02			4.40	9.49
Finghall Lane	dep:	7.54	10.06			4.44	9.53
Constable Burton	dep:	8.02	10.10			4.49	9.57
Spennithorne	dep:		10.14			4.53	
Leyburn	arr:	8.11	10.19			4.58	10.05
	dep:	8.17		3.00		5.04	
Wensley	dep:	8.23		3.05		5.09	
Redmire	dep:	8.29		3.10		5.14	
Aysgarth	dep:	8.36		3.17		5.21	
Askrigg	dep:	8.45		3.26		5.30	
Hawes	arr:	8.54		3.35		5.39	
	dep:	8.56			4.25	5.40	
Garsdale	arr:	9.10			4.39	5.44	

UP TRAINS		am	am	pm	pm	pm
Garsdale	dep:		10.15	3.16		6.40
Hawes	arr:		10.27	3.27		6.51
	dep:		10.30		4.00	6.53
Askrigg	dep:		10.38		4.08	7.01
Aysgarth	dep:		10.50		4.17	7.10
Redmire	dep:		10.56		4.23	7.16
Wensley	dep:		11.01		4.28	
Leyburn	arr:		11.06		4.33	7.25
	dep:	7.52	11.11		4.38	7.31
Spennithorne	dep:	7.57				
Constable Burton	dep:	8.01	11.18		4.45	7.38
Finghall Lane	dep:	8.04	11.21		4.53	7.41
Jervaulx	dep:	8.09	11.25		4.57	7.45
Crakehall	dep:	8.12	11.29		5.01	
Bedale	dep:	8.18	11.35		5.08	7.54
Leeming Bar	dep:	8.24	11.41		5.18	8.00
Scruton	dep:	8.28	11.45		5.22	
Ainderby	dep:	8.32	11.49		5.26	8.07
Northallerton	arr:	8.39	11.56		5.33	8.14

On Saturdays, the 9.30 am down service was extended to Garsdale and the 3.00 pm short distance working from Leyburn to Hawes was replaced by a 2.03 pm (SO) service from Northallerton to Hawes. In the up direction, an additional Saturday-only train ran from Garsdale to Northallerton at 2.55 pm. The Sunday service provided just one out and back service from Northallerton to Leyburn.

This basic pattern of operation persisted until the closure of the line in 1954, and the timetable in use at the very end of passenger services showed the following trains: 7.15 am Northallerton to Garsdale, 9.30 am (SX) Northallerton to Leyburn, 9.30 am (SO) Northallerton to Garsdale, 1.33 pm (SO) Northallerton to Leyburn, 2.30 pm Leyburn to Hawes, 4.25 pm Hawes to Garsdale, 4.10 pm Northallerton to Garsdale and 9.05 pm Northallerton to Leyburn.

In the up direction, the balancing eastbound services were: 7.35 am Leyburn to Northallerton, 10.27 (SO) Garsdale to Northallerton, 10.41 (SX) Garsdale to Northallerton, 12.55 pm (SO) Garsdale to Northallerton, 3.16 pm Garsdale to Hawes, 4.00 pm Hawes to Northallerton, and 6.40 pm Garsdale to Northallerton.

Goods services, in these final years, consisted of a pick-up freight working between Northallerton and Hawes, a Northallerton to Jervaulx return trip, and a stone train to Wensley or Redmire; additionally, the London Midland Region continued to provide an out and back goods trip from Hellifield to Hawes.

The passenger vehicles employed on the Wensleydale line during the early 1950s were of various kinds. Photographic evidence suggests that the usual formation consisted of two elliptical roof coaches, at least one of which would be a brake third. Panelled vehicles were the norm, and in addition to former North Eastern Railway stock, coaches from the Great Northern Railway (or other constituents of the LNER) also appeared. The London Midland Region, in contrast, provided steel-bodied 57 ft ex-LMS non-corridor stock for the local service to and from Hawes, and in the 1950s the 'Bonnyface' services were typically formed of three-coach sets with a brake third at each end.

Reasons for Decline

The Wensleydale line ran through an area of scattered rural communities that can never have produced much passenger traffic for the railway. Although stone traffic was of some importance, it is likely that the route had never been profitable in a strictly financial sense. Viewed in isolation from the rest of the North Eastern system, the line probably made a technical 'loss' for much of its life, but in practice companies such as the NER were willing to use profits from other, more profitable parts of the railway system to subsidise less profitable routes. This was, at least in part, because branch lines were seen as useful 'feeders' to the main line system, but at the same time the old time railway companies were aware that their monopoly position was both total and unassailable. As the only providers of public transport facilities in remote areas, the railway companies realised that they had a duty to the nation at large as well as to their shareholders, and if the cost of running unremunerative services did not become excessive, most railways were willing to let marginally profitable routes continue in operation.

Sadly, the insidious growth of road motor transport - first buses and lorries and later the private car - destroyed the monopoly position that had hitherto been enjoyed by the railways, and by the 1930s the threat of mass railway closures had, for the first time, become a reality. Faced by the threat of rival forms of transport, and hard-hit by the Great Depression, the 'Big Four' companies closed branch lines in increasing numbers during the 1930s (the Masham to Melmerby line, for example, had been closed at the end of 1930). Petrol rationing during and after World War II gave the railways some respite during this difficult period, but the lifting of rationing and the removal of all restrictions on private road transport during the early 1950s soon brought a further round of branch line closures.

The situation, as far as the Wensleydale line was concerned was especially bleak, the main problem being a lack of passenger traffic. The railway served no large centres of population, and many of the upland settlements served by the line contained no more than a few hundred people. Aysgarth, for instance, had a population of only 290, while Bainbridge (near Askrigg) was home to just 220 people during the late 1940s. Of the larger towns *en route* to Hawes, Leyburn had a population of about 6,000, though Hawes itself had only 900 people. Northallerton - the County Town - was even smaller than Leyburn, with a population of around 5,000.

Closure of the Line

It was clear that villages with populations as small as 200 could not provide sufficient traffic to sustain the railway, and although the line continued to fulfil a valuable role as a winter lifeline to isolated communities, BR decided that the Wensleydale line was no longer worth retaining in its entirety. Accordingly, in 1953, it was announced that the passenger service between Northallerton and Garsdale would be withdrawn. In support of this proposal a British Railways spokesman claimed that the line was being used by only 2½ per cent of the local community, and he added that the proposed closure would save up to £14,500 a year.

Although few local people used the railway, they objected most strongly when they learned that closure was being seriously considered; in 1953, railways were seen as a vital part of the national infrastructure, and it was assumed that the BR system would be maintained in perpetuity as a public service for rural communities throughout the land. Hill farmers, in particular, were concerned that lack of a railway would leave them at the mercy of winter snow storms - and in this context people remembered the appalling winter of 1947, when road transport had been unable to bring food and fuel to the upper dales.

Opposition to the proposed closure was intense, and a meeting of the North East Area Transport Users' Committee held in Newcastle on 14th December, 1953 was unable to reach a conclusion *vis-à-vis* closure or retention. The meeting was therefore adjourned pending the receipt of 'further information' from British Railways.

Regrettably, it was subsequently decided that the closure would be approved, and BR stated that the line would be closed on 29th March, 1954, leaving, however, a residual passenger service on the former Midland Railway section between Garsdale and Hawes. Crakehall and Finghall Lane stations would be closed completely, but Ainderby, Scruton, Leeming Bar, Bedale, Jervaulx, Constable Burton, Spennithorne, Leyburn, Wensley, Redmire, Aysgarth and Askrigg were to remain in operation for goods and parcels traffic.

In the event, the line could not be closed on 29th March because closure was dependent upon the provision of alternative bus services, and these could not be arranged until the bus company's application for new services had been heard by the Traffic Commissioners on 19th March.

The anti-closure protesters had in the meantime appealed to the Central Transport Users' Consultative Committee, and the resulting hearing was not due to take place until 13th April, 1954. However, the appeal was unsuccessful, and on Easter Monday it was announced that passenger services would be withdrawn between Northallerton and Hawes with effect from 26th April, 1954. As this was a Monday, the last trains would actually run on the preceding Sunday, while Saturday 24th April, 1954 would be the last full day of operation for passenger trains between Northallerton, Hawes and Garsdale.

The Last Trains

Many extra travellers turned out on the Saturday to ride on the last trains between Northallerton and Garsdale, and the normal branch two-coach sets were strengthened to accommodate these extra passengers. The final services were worked by 'D20' class 4-4-0 No. 62347 and 'J21' class 0-6-0 No. 65038, the 9.30 am morning train from Northallerton to Garsdale being headed by No. 65038 while No. 62347 worked the 1.33 pm departure. The latter train was delayed at Constable Burton while the branch mineral train was shunted, and there were further delays at Hawes in consequence of the 4-4-0 being sent light to Garsdale for turning.

The afternoon train to Garsdale left Northallerton at 4.10 pm behind 'J21' No. 65038. This working was the focus of much attention as it made its melancholy way towards Garsdale, and in recognition of the funereal nature of the occasion the locomotive carried a wreath of mourning on its top lamp bracket. At 6.40 pm, the return working set off from Garsdale, and there were further delays at the intermediate stations as local people turned out to see and photograph this last scheduled through service; the train was driven by driver R. May and fireman D. Appleby (both of Northallerton).

Meanwhile, 'D20' No. 62347 had left Hawes with the 4.00 pm up service, and having passed the 4.10 pm from Northallerton in the crossing loop at Constable Burton, the 4-4-0 reached its destination at 5.40 pm.

As the 'last day' drew to a close, the 'D20' was prepared for its final departure, and at 9.05 pm No. 62347 left Northallerton at the head of a four-coach train. The engine, which was driven by driver T. Hobbs and fireman A. Gaythorpe of Leyburn, was much photographed as it waited at Scruton, Leeming, and the other intermediate stations; well-wishers thronged the

darkened platforms, and as the brightly-lit train slowly made its way along
the doomed branch, people realised that an era was drawing inexorably to
a close. All too soon, the train reached Leyburn - the time of arrival being
ten minutes later than normal in consequence of the many delays *en route*
from Northallerton.

On the following day, 'G5' class 0-4-4T No. 67345 was rostered to work
the last scheduled passenger train between Northallerton and Leyburn. For
local enthusiasts, this very last Sunday train was something of an
anticlimax - after all, it did not traverse the entire length of the branch, and
for this reason Saturday 24th April had really been the last day of full
operation. Nevertheless, the Sunday evening up service from Leyburn to
Northallerton was undoubtedly the last train, and its arrival at
Northallerton at 6.00 pm on 25th April, 1954, marked the end of 100 years
of railway history for the eastern section of the Wensleydale line.

The 1954 closure did not mean the end of passenger services in their
entirety because a residual service of one train each way daily was still
maintained on the former Midland Railway section between Garsdale and
Hawes. There was, moreover, still a regular Northallerton to Leyburn
parcels working which left Northallerton at 7.25 am, while goods services
continued to operate throughout the 39¾ miles between Northallerton and
Hawes.

The Post-Closure Period

Occasional passenger trains still ran to and from Jervaulx in connection
with nearby Aysgarth school, while, so long as the line remained in being
as a freight-only route, it continued to function as a vital lifeline during the
severe snowstorms that sometimes paralysed road transport in the
Wensleydale area.

The continuing importance of the railway was vividly demonstrated in
January 1962, when a blizzard brought chaos to the dale. Snow lay a foot
deep in the valleys, while drifts of up to 15 ft blocked several local roads.
Motor vehicles were abandoned throughout the area, and farmers were
unable to transport their milk along exposed upland tracks. The problems
were particularly severe in the Redmire area and on the bleak hillsides of
upper Wensleydale, and in these crisis conditions an emergency passenger
service was hastily arranged on Monday 2nd January - 'K1' 2-6-0 No. 62044
being rostered at the head of a makeshift train.

The steam age was, by 1962, drawing rapidly to a close, but the old
fashioned railways - with their heavy locomotives and equipment - really
came into their own during the January 1962 emergency. Locomotives such as
'K1' class 2-6-0 No. 62044 were able to forge through minor snowdrifts
without assistance, though, to make doubly sure that the line would remain
unobstructed, snowplough-fitted '2MT' 2-6-0 No. 46475 was sent ahead of the
special passenger train. Railway staff, meanwhile, struggled to work so that
the emergency service could be maintained, and thanks to their efforts the
Wensleydale line was brought back to life, albeit briefly, at a time when road
transport revealed its pitiful deficiencies in relation to winter snow and ice.

On 6th January, 1962 *The Darlington & Stockton Times* printed a report of the recent weather crisis, and some of this information is worth quoting in full:

The snow blizzard on Saturday brought chaos to Wensleydale. It left a foot of snow in the valleys and up to 15 feet drifts blocking several main roads. Motor vehicles were abandoned in many parts of the dale, particularly on the Wensley to Redmire and Redmire to Carperby roads. And on the Bainbridge to Hawes road there were deep drifts at Cupples Hill, west of Bainbridge. Three milk lorries were abandoned on Saturday, but were dug out by Sunday night.

The villages of Redmire and Carperby were isolated. A road was made through to Redmire by Sunday evening, but Carperby was not opened out until Tuesday. Several farms were isolated, including Thoresby, where Mr Robert Foster accumulated four days' milk supply, using up all the containers on the farm. Milk churns were in short supply, but on Tuesday British Railways left milk churns from a passenger train going to Hawes and collected 22 full churns containing 240 gallons of milk on the train travelling from Hawes to Leyburn, where they were taken to the rail siding of the local dairy. In an interview Mr Foster said he had farmed there for 60 years and had never before been isolated; he expressed thanks to British Railways for the help given, and for the quantity of milk saved.

On Monday Coun. John Sunter, Chairman of Aysgarth Rural District Council, approached the Leyburn station master, Mr Norman Darby, seeking help with a passenger service which was granted in an emergency, and a snow plough, after having difficulty in entering Leeming Bar station as the gates were frozen, came to Leyburn and preceded a passenger train; the railway plough went through to Hawes and encountered drifts, particularly opposite Cams House Farm between Askrigg and Hawes. After its return, the passenger train left Leyburn with nine passengers. It stopped at closed stations *en route*, at Wensley, Redmire, Aysgarth and Askrigg. At Aysgarth, a further 16 passengers were entrained. Thirteen were from the Willerby County Secondary School at Hull.

On the return railway journey down Wensleydale the train stopped at stations and also opposite the home field of Thoresby farm, where Mr Marmaduke Foster and two farm men had brought the 22 milk churns to the line for entrainment. British Railways officials were again helpful in making another journey from Leyburn to Hawes and returning in the early evening. At Hawes on Tuesday market day, there was an important livestock auction mart sale, which was able to take place and which was the centre for stock from a wide area.

Mr Foster and many others praised the concessions British Railways had made, keeping a promise made before the passenger line was closed that if an emergency arose such as severe snowstorms they would meet it. It was chiefly brought about because the public bus service was suspended. It was continued from Northallerton to Leyburn and partly resumed later on Tuesday in the upper dale. The railway staff worked hard on the Leyburn to Hawes line to free the many signals and points; the fare from Leyburn was 7s. 3d. return (36p) to Hawes: the train was heated and what became known as 'the farmers' express' on that day did a really worthwhile job.

Some hope it may be the forerunner of a skeleton passenger service being resumed; they argue that as the line is much used for goods traffic, particularly the conveyance of thousands of tons of limestone from Wensleydale quarries to the Middlesbrough district blast furnaces, a service highly remunerative to British Railways, this might be considered, even though it might not be a fully profitable venture.

Sadly, the emergency service provided in January 1962 did not lead to a permanent reinstatement of passenger services between Northallerton and

Garsdale, and although the terrible winter of 1962-63 once again demonstrated that railways could keep running during the worst possible weather conditions, the pace of closure and retraction showed no sign of abating. The government of the day was openly hostile towards the state-owned railways, and with no political friends to argue their case, the railways fell victim to an even worse programme of cuts.

In 1963 the publication of Dr Richard Beeching's notorious report, The Reshaping of British Railways, recommended the withdrawal of passenger services from a further 5,000 miles of line and the closure of 2,363 of BR's 4,709 stations - the idea being that a much smaller railway system would concentrate on supposedly-profitable long distance passenger services, and on the carriage of bulk freight such as coal, oil and aggregates.

The Beeching proposals were rushed into effect, and although a change of government in October 1964 brought the mass closures to an end, the new Labour government did not entirely disagree with the Beeching philosophy; the surviving parts of the once-great Victorian railway system were now seen as a specialised bulk transport system, and there was no place for small passenger and goods stations handling modest amounts of traffic. As far as the Wensleydale line was concerned, the future was now clear; the route already carried lucrative bulk stone traffic from the quarries around Redmire, and it was envisaged that this traffic would be retained for the foreseeable future. The remaining local goods yards would, on the other hand, be closed.

The Run-down Continues

There had, in the meantime, been further withdrawals. The Garsdale to Hawes passenger service was withdrawn on Saturday 14th March, 1959 and the line was then closed completely between Garsdale and Hawes (exclusive). The final train from Garsdale at 2.56 pm and its return working from Hawes at 4.25 pm was worked by Fairburn class '4MT' 2-6-4T No. 42492. Scruton had lost its goods facilities in May 1956, while Jervaulx was closed to goods traffic in November 1963. Five months later, on 27th April, 1964, the line was closed completely between Redmire and Hawes, and Redmire then became the terminus of a 22 mile long goods-only branch from Northallerton.

Further retraction followed over the next few months as the piecemeal withdrawal of goods facilities continued. In November 1965, for example, Ainderby and Leeming Bar lost their surviving goods facilities, while in July 1967 Wensley was closed to all traffic. These withdrawals left Leyburn, Bedale and Redmire as the only stations on the branch, the main types of traffic being handled at this time being coal, fuel oil, sugar beet and of course limestone.

The progressive withdrawal of goods-handling facilities was accompanied by a gradual reduction in terms of signalling and other infrastructure. In the 1970s, the branch was still fully signalled, with signal cabins or gate boxes at a number of places including Ainderby, Scruton, Leeming Bar, Aiskew Crossing, Bedale, Leyburn and Wensley. This situation lasted until the early 1980s, but on 26th October, 1983, Leyburn signal box was closed and 'one train' operation was then extended all the way from Bedale to Redmire. The level crossings at Ainderby, Scruton, Crakehall, Finghall Lane and Wensley were operated by the train crews, and most signals had, by that time, been removed. As a result of this rationalisation, Bedale signal box became the only one on the line.

Freight Services in the 1970s and 1980s

The freight train services provided in recent years were 'conditional', workings that ran only as and when required. There was, in general, a Monday to Friday limestone working, together with a branch pick-up service which, in the early 1970s, usually left Tees Yard (Middlesbrough) at about 9.00 am. This service entered the branch at 10.30 am, and reached Redmire at 12.30 pm, having called *en route* at Bedale and Leyburn as required; the train carried both stone traffic and general goods traffic such as coal and fuel oil. It was scheduled to leave Redmire at 3.00 pm, and Leyburn and Bedale were again served on the return journey depending on the amount of traffic available.

The daily limestone working generally entered the branch at about 7.00 am, and having picked-up loaded hopper wagons at Redmire it arrived back at Northallerton before the arrival of the pick-up freight around 10.30 am.

This pattern of freight operation varied in relation to traffic conditions, and on occasions there was no traffic at all. Happily, demand for limestone was buoyant during the later 1980s, and in 1989 the branch was served by a bulk stone train that ran six days a week (including Saturdays) between Teeside and Redmire. The train left Redcar at around 9.00 am and reached Redmire by mid-day - double heading being necessary to handle 2,000 ton loads. At Redmire, the incoming working was split into three portions, each of which was then shunted into the elevated sidings at the west end of the former passenger station. From there the empties were fed, by gravity, to a nearby loading tower, after which they ran into reception sidings at the western end of the station. When each vehicle was fully loaded the train was reformed, ready for the return working to Teeside around 1.00 pm.

Motive Power Since the 1960s

Steam locomotives lasted in the Wensleydale line until the mid-1960s, the usual motive power, at the very end of steam operation, being a Peppercorn 'K1' class 2-6-0. The 'K1's were replaced by English Electric type '3' Co-Cos, one of the locos used on the line being No. D6776 (later 37076). The English Electric type '3's - which later became better- known as the class '37's - were themselves replaced by Thornaby-based class '47' Co-Cos during the later 1970s, and by 1983 the class '47's were handling most of the local stone services. Numerous members of the class appeared on the line, including Nos. 47223, 47287, 47291, 47303, 47361 and 47363.

In 1986, pairs of class '20' Bo-Bos started work on the route, and at the same time the stone trains were increased from 24 to 33 hopper wagons. To underline the firm links that now existed between BR and the Redmire

Class '37' Co-Co No. D6757 passes Aiskew Crossing with the daily stone train; a diesel brake tender is coupled behind the locomotive. *N. Stead Collection*

Double-headed class '20's Nos. 20172 and 20173 shunt the daily stone train at Redmire; the ruined castle can be seen in the background. *N. Stead*

quarries, two of these engines were given appropriate names - No. 20172 becoming *Redmire*, while sister engine No. 20173 was named *Wensleydale*.

The class '20's did not remain on the line for very long, and with train lengths increased from 33 to 36 vehicles, there was a sudden reversion to class '37' haulage. The engines worked in pairs, and typical numbers, around 1989-90, included Nos. 37083, 37227. 37514, 37515 and 37517.

In a further development, the heavy Redmire to Teeside limestone workings were taken over by newly-built class '60' Co-Cos at the end of 1990, and these 3,100 hp Brush-built locomotives were able to handle the trains without recourse to multiple heading. Among the first class '60's to be seen on the line were No. 60050 *Roseberry Topping* and No. 60029 *Ben Nevis*, which worked Redmire stone trains on 22nd March, 1991 and 23rd March, 1991 respectively. Another class '60' used on the branch around 1991 was No. 60022 *Ingleborough*; all of these locomotives were based at Thornaby for use on heavy freight duties such as the Corby-Lackenby steel trains and the Teeside-Redmire stone workings.

Visits by the Royal Train

It is interesting to note that the Royal Train has visited the Wensleydale branch on several occasions in connection with royal visits to nearby Catterick army camp. It was usual, in recent years, for the Royal Train to be berthed overnight at Bedale before being taken to Darlington for guests to alight. In May, 1970, for instance, HM the Queen spent the night aboard the train at Bedale, while on 31st October, 1978 HRH the Princess Royal was conveyed along the branch. A few months previous to this, HRH the Prince of Wales visited the North East by train, and the royal vehicles were again berthed at Bedale. These royal workings were usually hauled by spotless class '47' Co-Cos.

Steam and Diesel Specials

Growing interest in rural lines such as the Wensleydale route brought some interesting enthusiasts' specials to the area during the 1950s and 1960s. On 4th September, 1955, for example, the Stephenson Locomotive Society joined forces with the Manchester Locomotive Society to arrange the 'Northern Dales' tour of lines in northern England. The 'Northern Dales Railtour' consisted of seven centre gangway coaches, and it was hauled in stages by a range of locomotives including Ivatt class '2MT' 2-6-0 No. 46478, 'J21' 0-6-0 No. 65061, 'A8' 4-6-2T No. 69855, 'D20' 4-4-0 No. 62360 and Midland Compound 4-4-0 No. 41102.

The tour started at Manchester, from where the train proceeded through Blackburn and Hellifield to Ingleton and thence on to Tebay and Kirkby Stephen. Diverging eastwards onto the Stainmore route, the tour continued across the Pennines to Darlington and Eaglescliffe, from where the 'Northern Dales' excursion turned south-westwards to reach Northallerton and the Wensleydale line. Having traversed the Wensleydale route from east to west, the special regained the Settle & Carlisle route at Garsdale, and as dusk was falling it sprinted back to Manchester behind Compound 4-4-0 No. 41102.

Another, equally ambitious, tour was arranged by the Railway Correspondence & Travel Society on Saturday 25th April, 1964. On this occasion the special - known as 'The North Yorkshireman' - left Leeds City at 8.30 am and proceeded via Harrogate and Boroughbridge, thence along the Wensleydale line from Northallerton to Hawes. From there, the tour continued via Middleton-in-Teesdale, Darlington, York, and then back to Leeds. 'The North Yorkshireman' was hauled along the Wensleydale line by ex-NER 'B16/2' 4-6-0 No. 61435, and it is interesting to record that this RCTS special was the last passenger train to work through from Northallerton to Garsdale before the closure of the line between Redmire and Hawes just two days later.

Subsequent railtours were out-and-back trips from either Northallerton or Garsdale, but this did not deter trip organisers from planning a variety of special excursions. On Saturday 20th May, 1967, for example, the Stephenson Locomotive Society 'Three Dales Railtour' brought a double-headed excursion onto the branch, the motive power being provided by Peppercorn 'K1' class 2-6-0 No. 62005 in conjunction with a Type '2' Bo-Bo. This train, which had originated in Stockton-on-Tees, also visited the Richmond and Bishops Auckland branches.

The demise of steam power in 1968 meant that all later tours over the line were worked by diesel power, and on 23rd May, 1976 a four-car Metro-Cammell class '101' multiple unit worked through to Redmire with a ramblers' excursion. The unit returned to Northallerton as an empty stock working, but it travelled back to Redmire in the evening in order to collect the walkers for their homeward trip.

The 1976 ramblers' excursion was followed by a somewhat similar excursion in the Autumn of 1977 when the Yorkshire Dales National Park Committee organised a 'Dalesrail' special along the Wensleydale line. The Park Committee had already organised weekend passenger services along the Settle & Carlisle line, and as an extension of this venture it was decided that a day trip would be organised from Redmire to Durham and Newcastle on Saturday 17th September, 1977. Buses were chartered to convey excursionists to and from Redmire or Leyburn stations. and over 300 people willingly paid £2 for their specially printed tickets.

The success of the 1977 'Dalesrail' excursion encouraged the Park Committee to arrange a similar excursion on Saturday 17th June, 1978. On this occasion, an eight-car multiple unit formation ran from York to Redmire, enabling visitors from York to ride through to Wensleydale, while people of the Dales were able to spend an interesting day in York. The stock provided for this excursion included Metro-Cammell, Birmingham Carriage & Wagon and Derby vehicles - the leading set (on the outward journey) being a class '101' unit in white livery.

A further York to Redmire excursion was run by BR on 16th September, 1978. This working left York at 9.30 am and arrived at Redmire by 11.20 am. A second service was run from Northallerton to Redmire and back at 1.30 pm, the fare from York being £2.50 for the round trip. These trains were worked by a six-car dmu formation and, as on previous trips, Metro-Cammell class '101' stock was well represented.

Various other special passenger trains worked over the line during the 1980s and early 1990s. The motive power, on these occasions, encompassed multiple units and a range of locomotive types - including class '20's, class '37's and class '47's. On 18th February, 1990, Hertfordshire Rail Tours arranged a tour involving a strengthened HST formation consisting of two power cars, two first class coaches, two buffet cars and five standard class vehicles.

Envoi: The Final Years

The introduction of new motive power, in the form of the class '60' Co-Cos, and the continued visits by special passenger trains, served to keep the Wensleydale branch in the public eye - indeed, these developments ensured that the line became known to a younger generation of railway enthusiasts, many of whom had not even been born when the railway lost its passenger services back in 1954.

It seemed, in 1992, that the Wensleydale branch had found a niche in Britain's modernised railway system, and the appearance of class '60's hauling long trains of limestone hoppers underlined the vast changes that had taken place since the demise of steam power. The line was, of course, highly specialised, and little of its former complexity now remained. From Castle Hills Junction the branch extended as a long siding through to Redmire - all intermediate signal boxes having been removed, leaving only Bedale box as a gate cabin. The public delivery sidings at Bedale and Leyburn had been closed with effect from 31st May, 1982, and their demise meant that 'pick-up' goods trains no longer ran. The Wensleydale line was, thereafter, able to concentrate on the carriage of lucrative stone traffic (which, according to the 'Beeching' philosophy, was the kind of bulk traffic that the railways were best fitted to carry).

Unfortunately, the elimination of local passenger and freight traffic was not accompanied by significant investment in terms of loading facilities at Redmire, and prescient observers noted that, on arrival at the stone terminal, the impressive-looking stone trains were shunted in old fashioned sidings so that wagons could be individually loaded. This was not, by any definition, in line with modern thinking, and whereas most of BR's surviving freight traffic was handled on the 'full trainload' system, the arrangements at Redmire were positively Victorian.

In truth, the Wensleydale branch was not as 'modern' as it perhaps looked, and moreover, its reliance on a single source of bulk traffic meant that the railway was left at the mercy of a single customer. The scene was thus set for a major row, and when, in the early months of 1992, British Steel announced that all stone traffic between Redmire and Teeside would be transferred to road transport, it appeared that the railway would have to close. BR's Trainload Freight division stated that the freight service to Redmire would cease at the end of March 1992, though the line would remain *in situ* pending a final decision on its long term future.

The proposed closure was greeted with dismay by local people, who feared that the transfer of large amounts of stone from rail to road transport

Newly built class '60' Co-Co No. 60029 *Ben Nevis* shunts empty stone hopper wagons into the reception sidings at Redmire, soon after the introduction of this class of locomotive. *N. Stead*

Class '60' Co-Co No. 60005 *Skiddaw* nears Preston-under-Scar with a loaded stone train. This was one of the first class '60s' to be completed and was initially allocated to Toton. *N. Stead Collection*

would have detrimental effects throughout lower Wensleydale in terms of increased noise, pollution and road congestion. Few people welcomed the appalling prospect of at least 756 additional lorry movements per week and (with a General Election only weeks away) the controversial plan was deferred for a further six months. The railway nevertheless remained in operation, albeit with the threat of closure hanging over it. The one bright spot, during this period of uncertainty, concerned a proposed re-opening of part of the line as a private railway. The impetus for such a re-opening came from the members of a group known as the Wensleydale Railway Association (WRA), which was formed following a meeting held in Redmire Village Hall on 23rd May, 1990. Encouraged by the successful campaign against closure of the Settle & Carlisle line, the Wensleydale group initially hoped to save the entire Wensleydale line between Northallerton and Garsdale.

An alternative scheme, mooted at this time by a Pickering businessman, envisaged the installation of a narrow gauge line on the trackbed between Garsdale and Hawes - the idea being that former South African Railways Beyer-Garratts (or other colonial locomotives) would be able to show their paces in an appropriately spectacular setting.

The idea of opening the western part of the line was welcomed by a wide range of individuals and organisations, and while British Rail was unable to contribute financially to the project, BR engineers carried out a survey of the abandoned section of line between Redmire and Garsdale. Although the fact that some of the land had been sold to private owners prevented a close examination of every engineering feature, BR concluded that the trackbed and surviving infrastructure was 'in a remarkably good state of preservation'.

One interesting fact emerged from the BR survey in respect of the western extremity of the line between Hawes and Garsdale; this part of the line was said to have been in particularly good order indicating, perhaps, that the engineering and maintenance standards of the Midland Railway had been superior to those of the North Eastern sections of the line (?).

Although the western section of the route was clearly in good condition, the Wensleydale Railway Association subsequently decided that their efforts might more usefully be concentrated on the Leyburn to Aysgarth section; this option would require the reinstatement of just two miles of track between Redmire and Aysgarth, while at the same time the WRA would have a viable operating base at Leyburn.

At this juncture, the proposed closure of the Redmire branch led to suggestions that the Wensleydale group might be able to purchase or rent other parts of the line, though the general consensus of opinion was that BR should be encouraged to use the route for freight traffic. This would keep heavy lorries away from country roads, while the WRA would enter into a working agreement for the use of part of the existing line.

In the event, the line was saved by the Ministry of Defence, which continued to use the Northallerton to Redmire line after the cessation of limestone traffic, and thereby guaranteed the long term future of the route for military traffic. Having made this decision, the MoD invested £750,000

An MoD train with a 'Warrior' armoured vehicle seen during the aborted loading of 'KFA' well wagons on 10th April, 1996. One of the 21 'Warriors' fell off a wagon and the train eventually left empty *(see page 188)*. The train engine, which can just be seen in the distance is a class '47'. *Arthur Hartley*

Class '66' No. 66113 crosses the River Swale at Morton-on-Swale with the Hertfordshire Railtours excursion train from Kings Cross to Redmire on 15th January, 2000. *Arthur Hartley*

in the railway and agreed that the Wensleydale Railway Association and its commercial arm (the Wensleydale Railway Company) would share the line. Army freight on the line was reinstated during 1996.

During this period the membership of the WRA was growing steadily. Membership reached 2,000 during the year 2000, and 3,000 in 2003. Various fundraising schemes were set up, initially in case it became necessary to purchase the line. The association then began the process of acquiring parts of the line to facilitate its future reinstatement. In 1996 the association purchased the Leyburn station site, and land for the planned Castle Bolton Extension. At this time the focus was on the possibility of running a service from Leyburn to Castle Bolton, and then to Aysgarth. Volunteers began clearing the trackbed towards Castle Bolton.

In 1997 the opportunity arose to acquire the station site at Aysgarth, which was achieved with the help of a special bond issue. Work then began on restoring the station buildings at Aysgarth. For a time the WRC ran a bus service in the dale, based on Aysgarth, to emphasise its commitment to restoring public transport and creating integrated services. By 2000 the station buildings and yard at Leeming Bar had been acquired and work began on laying track in the station yard.

In the meantime, the extant section of line between Northallerton and Redmire continued to carry military traffic to and from Catterick; on 9th November, 1998, for example, class '47' Co-Co No. 47051 and class '56' Co-Co No. 56070 worked a trainload of armoured vehicles over the branch, while on 18th January 2000 class '66' Co-Co No. 66011 was noted on the branch at the head of a similar train. Several other class '66' locomotives visited the Wensleydale route during the next few months.

In June 2000 Railtrack, which had taken over the infrastructure assets of the British Railways Board after privatisation in 1996, agreed in principle to transfer the branch to WRC on a 99-year lease. In October 2000 a new public company, Wensleydale Railway plc, was incorporated, and in November a prospectus was published , launching a new share issue with the aim of raising funds for the construction, development and operation of the new railway. (The previous WRC Ltd remained in being as TWRC Ltd). At the same time as the public company was established, the WRA established a charity, the Wensleydale Railway Trust Ltd, which was initially seen as a means to enable the railway to receive charitable gifts. In September 2001 a ceremony was held at Hawes station to mark the donation by Railtrack North West of a mile of track to the Wensleydale Railway.

Unfortunately the proposed transfer of the line was not as prompt or as smooth as had been hoped. A major cause of delay was the decision to put Railtrack into administration. The spread of foot and mouth disease in 2001 would also have made it more difficult to introduce new rail services at that time. However, the delay enabled the company to work on the restoration of Leyburn station, prepare its Railway Safety Case for approval by the Railway Inspectorate, accumulate more rolling stock, further promote the share issue and take over the operation of the kiosk at Northallerton station.

The signing of the lease finally took place on 11th November 2002 but could not be activated until it had been accepted by the Office of the Rail Regulator. Finally the Wensleydale Railway plc took over the Redmire Branch from Network Rail at 10.30 on Monday 12th May 2003. Steve Lupton, Manager of the York IECC (signalling centre) handed over the combined staff and Annets key which locks the ground frame at Castle Hills loop. However, a more exciting day of celebrations took place at Leeming Bar on Friday 6th June, when guests enjoyed food, a jazz band, a fly-past of aircraft from RAF Leeming, a public handing-over of the branch token, and speeches about the project and its future. Amongst the presentations, Jerry Swift of Network Rail was given a copy of an earlier edition of this book.

To realise the scale of the task which confronted the new company, it is worth reproducing part of the final section of the 2002 edition of this book, printed under the sub-heading 'The Railway Today'.

> ...some of the former stations were demolished after the withdrawal of passenger services, while others survived in domestic use. Ainderby, for example, was given a new lease of life as a private dwelling, but Scruton fell into dereliction. At Redmire, the ticket office and waiting room were removed, though the former station master's house survived as a Boy Scout accommodation centre. Wensley was adapted for residential use, while at Askrigg the former station became the offices of a local building firm.

There follows information about the three stations acquired by the Wensleydale Railway Company, i.e. Aysgarth, Leeming Bar and Leyburn. Aysgarth had survived with a tenant in the house and the station buildings converted as a holiday cottage. After its acquisition by WRC, work was done to restore and maintain the buildings, but of course it was, and remains, no longer attached to the running line. Leeming Bar with its listed station buildings and goods shed, had been acquired by the WRC, and Leyburn had been taken over and was being restored. The text continues:

> The erstwhile Bedale & Leyburn stations suffered various fates in the years following closure. Jervaulx station building was an early casualty, but Crakehall remained in being as a house for the Bedale signalman. Finghall Lane enjoyed a brief moment of fame when it was chosen as the setting for scenes in the popular BBC 'Yorkshire Vet' television series *All Creatures Great and Small*. The station was renovated to give it an appropriate 'period' atmosphere - the use of a Wensleydale line station being particularly fitting in this context because James Herriot's best-selling 'vet' books were set in the Wensleydale area. Both of these stations are at present occupied by residential tenants.

The station at Constable Burton was also demolished, and Spennithorne was converted for use as holiday accommodation. The story of Bedale is more complicated. At the time of transfer the platform was still part of the railway, but the station buildings and yard were in use by a private firm.

> At Hawes, the former Midland Railway station and goods yard was acquired by

the Yorkshire Dales National Parks authority for use as a visitor centre and car park. The large goods was extended and converted to form a countryside museum, and in the early 1990s this attraction (actually a branch of the Yorkshire Museum) was being visited by over 20,000 people a year.

Running the Railway

Before any trains could run platforms had to be constructed at Leeming Bar and Leyburn. The revived railway was unique and ambitious. It controlled part of the UK national railway network at local level. At that time it was the only railway which held every type of licence that the Rail Regulator could issue. It planned to extend into Northallerton and to Aysgarth, and in the longer term it hoped to reinstate the line through Hawes to Garsdale, once again linking up with the Settle and Carlisle line.

On 4th July 2003 the first scheduled passenger service ran from Leeming Bar to Leyburn. The opening day was a time for great celebration, and the first train, a DMU set, was flagged away by local MP William Haigh. Then the real work of running a railway began.

On 5th March 2004 the achievement of reopening the railway was marked by an official visit by HRH the Duke of York. Later that year, on 1st August, Bedale and Redmire stations and the five miles of track from Leyburn to Redmire were reopened, though these stations were unstaffed. Later, after restoration by a volunteer group, Finghall was opened as an unstaffed halt.

By the end of March 2004 the share issue which had been launched at the end of 2000 had raised more than £1,370,000. However, it was becoming clear that much more would be needed to deal with the poor state of much of the infrastructure and to maintain the buildings. A further prospectus was therefore issued in April 2004. Although eventually this was successful in raising further large sums, the period which followed was one of great financial difficulty, as it became clear that the company was making significant operating losses. The fight for financial survival came to a head in 2005, when the WRA launched an appeal for 'financial angels', seeking £100,000. At the same time the company had to reduce outgoings in every way possible, and look for ways of increasing its revenue. The wage bill had to be reduced - some staff were made redundant and others worked fewer hours. Plans for an early return to Aysgarth were quietly set to one side, although the company clung on to its hopes of extending its services into Northallerton, with a demonstration of a Parry Light Rail Vehicle running from Leeming Bar to a temporary platform erected at Springwell Lane, near the Castle Hills junction.

Even at this difficult time there were some positive developments. Late in 2004 the company purchased its own DMU set, so that it was not relying entirely on a set leased from a private owner. In May 2005, it ran the first locomotive-hauled trains, using diesel locomotives kept at Leeming Bar by private owners; the charitable trust made proposals to the plc to restore the derelict, but historically important, Scruton station; and early in 2006 the company obtained a licence from Network Rail to enter the South Curve at Northallerton to enable it to clear vegetation and undertake survey work. Bedale station was acquired by Hambleton District Council and after restoration and repair it was leased to the railway in July 2007. The railway's achievements, in no way diminished by its financial problems, were recognised in 2006 when the WRA received the Duke of York's Community Initiative Award. This is not the place for a full and detailed history of the next decade of the reopened railway, but we can mention some of the principal achievements and setbacks.

Looking to the Future

The railway has struggled to establish a clear identity. Is it a public transport service, a community railway, a tourist attraction, or a heritage railway? It is clear now that some of the early aspirations to provide public transport services and commuter trains cannot be fulfilled, and the prospect of dividends for shareholders has also disappeared. For a time, struggling with financial difficulties, the company toyed with a major change to becoming an industrial and provident society, but this proposal could not command general support and instead the company decided in 2014 to make it clear, by changes in its Articles, that it did not distribute profits to its shareholders, and that if it should ever be wound up its shares would not be worth more than their face value when issued. These changes were intended to make it clearer to bodies like local authorities that financial support for projects would not benefit the company's shareholders.

In 2006 the Wensleydale Railway Association (WRA) changed to become a Limited Company. The existence of three companies, i.e. the operating company (plc), the WRA and the charitable trust, made coordination and co-operation difficult, and later, in 2015, following the changes by the plc, the WRA and the trust decided to merge, providing a strong member organisation with charitable status, Wensleydale Railway Association (Trust) Ltd.

In 2009 the company acquired its first, albeit 'acting', general manager. Shortly after he left a new permanent manager was appointed, and since then there has always been a general manager in post to oversee the running and future development of the line. At the time of writing in 2017 Nigel Park has been in post since late in 2011.

The railway is not primarily a steam railway, but it has had to recognise that steam is what attracts passengers. In 2007 it hired a locomotive for a steam experiment in the summer – 'A Whiff of Steam'. This was successful and repeated the following year. However, in 2011 a number of steam locomotives were hired for the season. These succeeded in bringing in more passengers, but were financially crippling. Since then there has been a more judicious use of steam. A good working relationship has been developed with the North Eastern Locomotive Preservation Group and the Group's J72 tank, 69023 Joem, has been seen regularly at the railway for a number of years. Services are therefore provided by a mixture of diesel multiple units, locomotive–hauled trains using diesel locomotives based at Leeming Bar, and steam-hauled trains.

In 2009 the trust completed the restoration of a signal box, brought from Norfolk for erection at Leeming Bar. This was the railway's first project to be supported by the Heritage Lottery Fund. The trust also undertook the restoration of the derelict station at Scruton, with the help of a large grant from the Railway Heritage Trust and a large donation from a private supporter in memory of his son. Scruton Parish Council was a partner in the project and there was a major contribution by the students of Darlington College. The quality of the work done earned a national award from the Heritage Railway Association in 2015. Since completion of the main building new crossing gates have been installed and an extended wooden platform has been constructed to enable the station to become operational. The historic value of the station was recognised by the Heritage Lottery Fund which provided a grant to fund an imaginative heritage education programme in 2016.

It had long been the railway's aim to re-establish a passenger connection with Northallerton. In 2007 staff from Corus, in memory of a colleague who had been a director of the Wensleydale Railway, did detailed work on the options for restoring the South Curve and getting back into Northallerton. Subsequently it became clear that Network Rail would not be willing to allow the line to re-enter the original station site, and the only option available would be to bring a line into land to the west of the low level line and a short walk from the main line platforms, and construct a new station there. This remains the position, but recognising that it would be some time before this could be tackled, the company decided to construct a temporary platform on its existing line, near Castle Hills, which would provide pedestrian access to the centre of Northallerton. Hambleton District Council agreed to provide financial help for this, and a further grant came from the Dales Integrated Transport Alliance. Northallerton West was formally opened in November 2014, and integrated into the scheduled services in 2015.

During this decade the railway has had to overcome some significant problems. An accident at a level crossing in 2011 led to a requirement from the Office of Rail and Road (ORR) that there should be better control of vegetation to ensure that sight lines for crossings were improved. Volunteers put in a great effort to achieve the required standard, and since then the regular volunteer working parties have ensured compliance and greatly improved the trackside. It is a condition of the lease that the line is maintained for the passage of MoD trains when the army wishes to move tanks and other heavy vehicles from Catterick. The poor state of the track, with decayed wooden sleepers, life-expired rail, and poor ballast, has been a constant worry and drain on resources. Again, volunteer working groups have toiled to deal with the problems as they arise. The shortage of capital to invest in the track has made it impossible to plan a systematic programme of replacement and repair.

Early in 2013 there was a major landslip at the embankment at Akebar, just before Finghall going west. This followed a period of very wet weather, and the poor drainage and ballast, much of it made of ash, was unable to cope. An appeal for funds was launched by the trust, and there were no trains at the start of the season. However, the repair was completed in time for the visit of a High Speed Train on a through service from St Pancras on 20th April. Unfortunately, before the end of the year there was a second landslip at the same site, though the earlier repair held firm. Network Rail, the owners of the line, declined to help but money poured in from shareholders and WRA members to support the renewed appeal, and staff and volunteers again tackled the repair. The line was able to reopen in time for Easter 2014.and on 24th May LNER A4 No 4464 'Bittern' pulled nine coaches the length of the line to mark the opening of the Swaledale Festival.

In 2016 the line from Leeming Bar to Northallerton was closed for a time for track repairs. On the day it reopened there was an accident at the Yafforth level crossing and the line was closed again. This has led to a call for the two road crossings on this section of the line to be uprated, and together with the need for other track repairs this section of line to Northallerton has once again had to be temporarily closed, until funds can be found for the work.

Plans have been made for the provision of covered workshop accommodation at Leeming Bar, together with a redesign of the other principal facilities at the station. The plan to progress westwards is dependent on constructing a bridge over the Apedale Beck, and a redundant bridge has been acquired for that purpose. The extension to Northallerton station will be very expensive. These and other plans all require large sums of money to be raised. The Railway must spend heavily on its existing track, buildings and rolling stock in order to keep its present services running, and is therefore unable to press ahead with its plans for the future as quickly as it would like. Nevertheless progress has been made, income has been increased and losses have been reduced, and in the long term this very long railway will become one of the most attractive heritage and tourist railways in the country.

Notes and References

1. G.M. Young, *Portrait of An Age* (1936).
2. It should be noted that the Manchester & Leeds Railway changed its name to the Lancashire & Yorkshire Railway in 1847, and then began to absorb various smaller companies in the Pennine area; it follows that, if successfully completed, the Lancashire & North Yorkshire Railway would have passed into Lancashire & Yorkshire control, and L&YR influence would thereby have been projected deep into NER territory.
3. PRO MT6 12/6.
4. PRO MT6 12/6.
5. PRO MT6 12/7.
6. *The Railway Times*, 21st February, 1857.
7. *The Railway Times*, 24th February, 1866.
8. *The Railway Times*, 24th February, 1866.
9. PRO MT6 169/8.
10. PRO MT6 169/8.
11. See photograph in *The Railway Magazine*, April 1990, p.280.
12. *The Railway Magazine*, January 1966, p.61.
13. PRO MT6 303/4.
14. *The North Eastern Railway Magazine*, November 1915, p.280.
15. Ken Hoole, *Railway in the Yorkshire Dales* (1975) p.43.
16. The LMS also included the London Tilbury & Southend Railway (absorbed by the MR in 1912) and The Lancashire & Yorkshire Railway (taken over by the LNWR in January 1922), together with a number of other companies including the Furness, Glasgow & South Western, North Staffordshire and Maryport & Carlisle railways.
17. Most railways in the LNER group had employed a dark red coach livery prior to 1923, but as pointed out by John Watling in an informative article (GER Carriages in Crimson Lake, *British Railways Journal* No. 11) the LMS group had already adopted Midland-style crimson lake as its standard colour scheme, and as it was vital that the LNER should have a distinctive livery, the company selected varnished teak as its coach livery, at a Board meeting held on 23rd February, 1923.
18. Tom Middlemass, Railway Eclipse, *Railway Magazine*, November 1979, pp.527-29.
19. See letter from H.C. Casserley, *Railway Magazine*, January 1980, p.37.
20. Christine Hallas, *The Wensleydale Railway* (2nd Edition, 1984), pp.64-70.
21. Stanley C. Jenkins, *The Leek & Manifold Light Railway* (1991), p.43 and Basil Jeuda, *The Leek, Caldon & Waterhouses Railway* (1980), pp.24 & 43.
22. Stanley C. Jenkins, *The Fairford Branch* (1985), p.50.
23. H.A. Valance, by Rail Through Wensleydale, *Railway Magazine*, October 1950, p.662.
24. Peter Corbell, The RAF on D-Day, *Air Pictorial*, October 1972, pp.396-401.
25. *The Railway Magazine, passim.*
26. *The North Eastern Railway Magazine*, 1911-1921, *passim.*
27. *Ibid.*
28. *Ibid.*
29. *Ibid.*
30. PRO MT6 1699/4.
31. *The North Eastern Railway Magazine, passim.*
32. Plans of Jervaulx station, now in the Public Record Office at Kew, date from 1857 (PRO RAIL 26/2), suggesting that this station was at least three years younger than its neighbours.
33. PRO MT6 2007/3.
34. *The North Eastern Railway Magazine, passim.*
35. C.S. Carter & A.A. Maclean, LNER Camping Coaches, *British Railway Journal* No. 23, pp.159-66.
36. PRO MT6 190/2.
37. *The North Eastern Railway Magazine, passim.*
38. *Ibid.*
39. *Ibid.*
40. *Ibid.*
41. L.T.C. Rolt, *Red for Danger* (1955) and E.G. Barnes, Disaster at Hawes Junction, *Railway Magazine*, February 1971.
42. *Ibid.*
43. E.G. Barnes, *loc.cit.*
44. L.T.C. Rolt, *op.cit.*
45. *Ibid.*

A Note on Sources

Other sources are, in general, mentioned in the text. These include Acts of Parliament, official documents, Bedale & Leyburn Railway Directors' reports, North Eastern Railway and Midland Railway reports, and contemporary journals such as *The Railway Times*, *The North Eastern Railway Magazine*, *The Darlington & Stockton Times*, *The Sheffield & Rotherham Independent*, *The Railway Magazine* and *The Locomotive Magazine*.

Other useful sources include NER, LNER and BR working timetables and notices, *Bradshaw's Shareholders Guides*, 25-inch, 6-inch and 1-inch Ordnance Survey maps, *Kelly's Directories of Yorkshire*, and local guide books such as *The North Riding of Yorkshire* by Joseph Morris.

This written evidence was supplemented by what (for want of a better term) one might call 'archaeological evidence' - that is to say, detailed examination of surviving bridges and railway buildings in order to obtain clues in respect of construction dates, extensions and additions, and internal layouts. Where buildings have been demolished, careful study of archive photographs from Lens of Sutton (and other suppliers) has, at least to some extent, enabled a similar analysis to take place.

Thanks are due to Lens of Sutton, R.M. Casserley, E.E. Smith, J.F. Addyman, N.E. Stead, K. Taylor, Alan Rimmer, Wensleydale Railway Association and other organisations or individuals who have contributed photographs or information.

Further Reading

The North Eastern Railway was one of the largest and most important pre-Grouping companies, but it has not, hitherto, attracted the attention of writers or historians in the way that the Great Western, Midland or London & North Western have done. There is, in consequence, a dearth of material relating to NER secondary lines such as the Wensleydale route. The following books and articles may nevertheless be of interest to readers seeking further information - though it should be stressed that some of the titles listed are of peripheral interest to the main theme.

Brian Redhead, Dalesrail Excursion, *Railway Magazine*, November 1978.

Malcolm Roughley, Up-country, *Railway Magazine*, November 1978.

Alan Goodyear, Rails to Redmire, *Railway Magazine*, December 1989.

Stan Abbot, A Wensleydale Dream, *Railway Magazine*, April 1991.

'Tynesider', Last Years of the D20s, *Railway Magazine*, January 1990.

J. Walkland, Station on a Bridge, *Meccano Magazine*, September 1959.

Chris Davies, Northallerton, *Back Track*, September-October 1991.

Ken Hoole, *Railways in the Yorkshire Dales* (1975).

C.T. Goode, *The Wensleydale Branch*, Oakwood Press (1980).

Christine Hallas, *The Wensleydale Railway* (1984).

H.A. Valance, By Rail Through Wensleydale, *Railway Magazine*, October 1950.

J.W. Armstrong, The Hawes Branch, *Trains Illustrated*, March 1954.

F. Coulton, Building a North Eastern 'G5', *Railway Modeller*, February 1967.

Nick Campling, NER Class 'X' 2-4-2T, *Railway Modeller*, September 1972.*

W.F. Glasspoole, The North Eastern Railway's 0-6-2Ts, *Railway Modeller*, July 1971.*

M.K. White & D. Permington, A Way Through the Mountains, *Model Railway Constructor*, February-April 1978.*

Joseph Morris, *The North Riding of Yorkshire*.

Peter Baughan, *North of Leeds*, David & Charles.

Peter Baughan, *The Railways of Wharfedale* (1969).

Peter Baughan, Centenary of the Long Drag, *Railway Magazine*, May 1976.

C. Whalley, *A History of Askrigg* (1890).

Christine Hallas, The Social & Economic Impact of a Railway, *The Agricultural History Review*, Vol. 34, 1986.

E.G. Barnes, Disaster at Hawes Junction, *Railway Magazine*, February 1971.

Tom Middlemass, Railway Eclipse, *Railway Magazine*, November 1979.

Cecil J. Allen, *The North Eastern Railway*, Ian Allan, (1964).

O.S. Nock, *Locos of the North Eastern Railway*.

C. Hamilton Ellis, *The Midland Railway* (1953).

J. Routh, *A Guide to Wensleydale* (1878).

W.W. Tomlinson, *The North Eastern Railway* (1914).

Articles marked * contain 4 mm scale plans of interest to railway modellers.

Chronological List of Significant Dates

1841 Great North of England Railway opened from York to Darlington. Northallerton station opened as two-platform stopping place.

1845 The Yorkshire & Glasgow Union, York & Carlisle, Lancashire & North Yorkshire, Lancashire & North Riding Junction, and other companies formed to construct routes through or near Wensleydale.

1846 Northern Counties Union Railway obtains consent for construction of line from Thirsk or Northallerton to Penrith (27th July).
Great North of England Railway leased to Newcastle& Darlington Junction.
Newcastle & Darlington Jn Rly obtains Powers for branch from Northallerton to Bedale (26th June).

1847 Powers granted for line between Northern Counties Union line and Bedale branch (9th July).

1848 First section of Wensleydale branch opened as far as Leeming (6th March).

1853 Bedale & Leyburn Railway incorporated by Act of Parliament (4th August).

1854 Formation of North Eastern Railway (31st July).

1855 Opening of Wensleydale line between Leeming and Bedale (1st February).
Goods services commence between Leeming and Bedale (November).

1856 Opening of Wensleydale line from Bedale to Leyburn (19th May).
Connecting line installed between high and low level lines at Northallerton.

1857 Locomotive shed opened at Northallerton. Bedale & Leyburn capital increased to £60,000.

1859 Bedale & Leyburn Railway amalgamated with NER (8th August).

1865 Incorporation of Hawes & Melmerby Railway (5th July).

1866 Settle & Carlisle scheme authorised, with branch to Hawes (16th July).

1869 Midland seeks Powers to abandon Settle & Carlisle scheme.

1870 NER obtains Powers for new Leyburn to Hawes line (4th July).

1876 Opening of Settle & Carlisle main line (1st May).

1877 Newton-le-Willows station renamed 'Jervaulx'.
Wensleydale line opened from Leyburn to Askrigg (1st February).

1878 Line opened for goods traffic from Askrigg to Hawes (1st October).
Wensleydale line opened between Askrigg and Garsdale (6th August).

1881 NER and Midland companies reach agreement over use of Garsdale engine shed.

1882 New curve opened at Northallerton (March).

1901 Fatal accident at Bedale (December).

1902 Leeming Lane station renamed 'Leeming Bar'.

1908 New agreement between NER and quarry owners at Harmby.
New signal box and loop installed at Leeming Bar (January).

1910 Major accident at Garsdale (Midland).

1911 Harmby East siding installed.
Dairy opened on railway-owned land at Redmire.

1913 Further accident at Garsdale Midland (2nd September).
'Near miss' at Northallerton station (8th November).

1914 Start of World War I: many NER railwaymen enlist in HM Forces (4th August).

1916 Station master killed in fatal accident at Crakehall (24th September).

1917 Garsdale engine shed destroyed by fire (6th October).
Crakehall station closed as a wartime economy measure.

1918 End of World War I (11th November).

1923 NER becomes part of LNER group (1st January).
Crakehall station re-opened (6th February).

1927 Large numbers of people travel to Leyburn to see solar eclipse (29th June).

1933 Camping coaches introduced at Wensley, Aysgarth and Askrigg.

1939 Garsdale shed closed and operations transferred to Leyburn. Northallerton power box brought into use (September).
Start of World War II (3rd September).

1941 New emergency connections installed at Northallerton (November).

1945 End of World War II.

1948 Nationalisation of railways (1st January).

1953 Closure proposals made public.

1954 Wensleydale line closed to passengers (24th-25th April).

1955 The 'Northern Dales Railtour' traverses the branch (4th September).

1956 Scruton station closed to all traffic (May).

1959 Closure of line between Hawes and Garsdale (14th March).

1963 Publication of the Beeching Plan.
Jervaulx closed to all traffic.

1964 Line traversed by the 'North Yorkshireman' tour (25th April).
Line closed completely between Hawes and Garsdale (27th April).

1965	Ainderby and Leeming Bar closed to goods traffic (November).
1967	Line visited by 'Three Dales' railtour (20th May).
	Wensley station closed to all traffic (July 1967).
1970	Royal Train berthed at Bedale (May).
1976	Ramblers' excursion visits Redmire (23rd May).
1977	First Dalesrail excursion (17th September).
1978	Further visit by Royal Train (31st October).
	More Dalesrail excursions (June and September).
1982	Bedale and Leyburn stations closed to all traffic (31st May).
1983	Leyburn de-signalled (26th October).
1990	HST set (power cars 43114/43013) visits Redmire on excursion working (18th February).
	Class '60' Co-Cos introduced on bulk stone trains.
	Formation of Wensleydale Railway Association (March).
	'Wensleydale Explorer' charter train Skipton-Redmire ran using a class '101' dmu. The first WRA publicity was distributed on this train (8th April).
1991	Charter excursion on the branch as part of a 'Railways and the Media' conference (8th June).
1992	British Steel decides to send stone by road; closure of line announced, then postponed for 6 months.
	Wensleydale Railway Co. Ltd formed for the purpose of taking over the line and operating services.
	'Redmire Ranger' charter train by the Branch Line Society (26th April).
	'Wensleydale Ranger' charter train Kings Cross-Redmire using 47501/20092/20169 (20th September).
	The last limestone train 'The Redmire Requiem' hauled by 60086 (18th December).
1993	'The Wensleydale Lament' charter Kings Cross-Redmire using 47820/37884/37714 (2nd January).
	Sidings belonging to British Steel at Redmire lifted by Nottingham Sleeper Co.
	British Steel's loading hopper at Redmire demolished (September).
	WRC bid to purchase the line handed over at BR's York headquarters (13th September).
	First train for 10 months, 'The Phoenix', a ballast laying train, ran as far as Spruce Gill near Finghall but could not continue due to a landslip (10th November).
	First army train from Taunton carrying engineers for Exercise 'Iron Temper' feasibility study, with load of 19 armoured personnel carriers, hauled by 47145 and 47146 (15th November).
	BR takes the line off the market after a deal with the MoD (15th December).
1994	BR staged a controlled 'train crash' between a dmu and car at Yafforth crossing, the climax of 'Operation Zebra' (9th September).
1995	Operation Raleigh volunteers started relaying track, donated by Railtrack, at Hawes station, for the Dales Countryside Museum (20th May).
	British Army release plans to use the Redmire branch as part of a nationwide Army transport network using the East Coast Main Line as the backbone of the system (21st June).
1996	First military train, 'The Boniface' was to have carried Warrior armoured vehicles from Redmire to Salisbury Plain. However one of the 21 vehicles fell off a wagon during loading and the train eventually left empty (10th April).
	Second, successful military train arrived at Redmire with 40 vehicles from Salisbury Plain (11th July).
	WRC leased the section of trackbed at Castle Bolton from the Bolton Estate.
1997	Aysgarth station bought by the Wensleydale Railway Company. It was then fully refurbished and awaits track. Aysgarth signal box restored and fitted with the lever frame from Long Lane on the Northallerton-Middlesbrough line.
1998	Passenger specials resumed with the 'Wensleydale Phoenix' Kings Cross-Redmire with 620 passengers (28th February).
	Two trains loaded with water pipes worked to Redmire by EWS for Yorkshire Water for pipe-laying in Wensleydale (3rd and 6th April).
	RSH 0-6-0 tank 7845/55 arrived at Hawes station as an exhibit for the Dales Countryside Museum. It carries the number and identity of Worsdell 'G5' No. 67345, which worked the final Northallerton-Hawes train in 1954 (29th July).
	The first WRA locomotive delivered to Hawes station, Ruston Hornsby 88DSb No.476141/63, previously owned from new by Markhams of Chesterfield (7th August).
	WRC commence bus services with the 'Wensleydale Tourer' open top bus operating out of Aysgarth station (August).
	WRC commence running Dennis Dart low floor buses along the Northallerton-Garsdale corridor, as a predecessor to a train service.
1999	WRC purchase headshunt section of trackbed at Redmire.
2000	Hertfordshire Railtours excursion Kings Cross-Redmire (15th January).
	Railtrack announces agreement to transfer the 22 mile Redmire branch to the WRC (8th June).
	WRC purchases Leeming Bar station and takes a 99 year lease on Leyburn station. WRC Leyburn shop relocated to the station.
2001	WRC takes over operation of the kiosk in Northallerton station.
	WRC plc completes transfer of the Redmire branch from Railtrack on a 99 year lease, which includes Crakehall and Finghall Lane stations. The branch remains part of the national network.
2002	Wensleydale Railway plc signed lease of the line from Network Rail on 11th November.
2003	On 12th May Wensleydale Railway plc took over the Branch from Network Rail
	On 4th July first scheduled passenger services ran from Leeming Bar to Leyburn

Appendix Two

Facilities at Wensleydale Branch Stations

Northallerton
Up and down main line platforms
Down relief platform and up and down bays
Booking office/waiting rooms/toilets
Refreshment rooms
Coal, watering & locomotive facilities (incl. 2-road shed)
Locomotive turntable (40 ft diameter)
Power signal box and mechanical gate boxes
High and low level goods yards with full facilities
Miscellaneous sheds, huts, stores etc.
Shell-Mex & BP fuel depot
Cow & Gate Dairy (ex-Wensleydale Pure Milk Society)
Staff housing
5-ton fixed yard crane

Ainderby
Single passenger platform on down side
Booking office/waiting room/toilets/
  station master's house
Signal cabin (20-lever frame)
Level crossing
Coal depot
Weigh-house
Cattle pens and loading docks
Permanent way huts, etc.

Scruton
Single platform on down side
Booking office/waiting room/toilets
Level crossing
Lever cabin
Staff housing
Goods siding

Leeming Bar
Up and down platforms
Booking office/waiting room/toilets/
  station master's house
Subsidiary waiting room on up platform
Goods yard
Coal depot
Cattle pens and loading docks
Goods shed
Level crossing
Signal cabin (36-lever frame)
Weigh-house
Private siding to Vale of Mowbray Brewery
  (later bacon factory)
Miscellaneous huts, stores, permanent way sheds, etc.
Water column

Bedale
Single platform on down side
Booking office/waiting room/toilets/
  station master's house
Goods yard
Goods shed
Cattle pens and loading docks
1-ton crane
Coal depot
Weigh-house
Anglo-American Oil Company depot
Miscellaneous huts, stores, etc.

Crakehall
Single platform on down side
Booking office/waiting room/toilets/
  station master's house
Level crossing
Lever cabin

Jervaulx
Up and down platforms and passing loop
Booking office/waiting room/toilets/
  station master's house
Subsidiary waiting room on up platform
Signal cabin (25-lever frame)
Goods sidings
Coal depot
Cattle pens
Weigh-house
Huts, stores, etc.

Finghall Lane
Single platform on down side
Booking office/waiting room/toilets/
  station master's house
Level crossing
Lever cabin (7-lever frame)
Goods siding

Constable Burton
Up and down platforms and passing loop
Booking office/waiting room/toilets/
  station master's house
Signal cabin (28-lever frame)
Goods yard
Weigh-house
Cattle pens and loading docks
10-ton fixed crane
Miscellaneous huts, etc.

Spennithorne
Single platform on down side
Booking office/waiting room/toilets/
  station master's house
Lever cabin

Leyburn
Up and down platforms and passing loop
Booking office/waiting rooms/toilets/offices
Subsidiary waiting room on up platform
Pedestrian footbridge
Goods yard
Goods shed
Coal depot
Cattle pens and loading docks
5-ton yard crane
Goods loading platform
East and West signal boxes (reduced to one in 1936)
Weigh-house
Locomotive shed and coaling facilities
Water cranes (3) and water tower
Locomotive turntable (42 ft diameter)
Various huts, stores & sheds
Rail-connected quarries (West Quarry and
Harmby Quarry)

Wensley
Up and down platforms and passing loop
Booking office/waiting rooms/toilets/
   station master's house
Subsidiary waiting room on up platform
Level crossing
Signal cabin (34-lever frame)
Goods yard
Coal depot
Camping coach
Rail connected-limestone quarry
Huts, stores etc.

Redmire
Single platform on up side
Booking office/waiting rooms/toilets/
   station master's house
Signal cabin (30-level frame)
Goods siding and goods loop
Coal depot
Cattle pens and loading docks
Weigh-house
Quarry sidings
1-ton crane
Huts, stores etc.

Aysgarth
Up and down platforms and passing loop
Booking office/waiting rooms/toilets/
   station master's house
Signal cabin (20-lever frame)
Subsidiary waiting room on down platform
Goods siding
Coal depot
Cattle pens and loading docks
Weigh-house
2-ton fixed yard crane
Camping coach
Staff cottages
Huts, stores etc.

Askrigg
Single platform on up side
Booking office/waiting rooms/toilets/
   station master's house
Signal cabin (15-lever frame)
Goods yard and goods loop
Coal depot
Cattle pens and loading docks
Weigh-house
2-ton fixed yard crane
Camping coach
Huts, etc.
Staff cottages

Hawes
Up and down platforms and passing loop
Booking office/waiting rooms/toilets
Signal cabin (20b-lever frame)
Goods yard
Goods shed
1 ton 10 cwt hand crane
Subsidiary waiting room on up platform
Cattle pens and loading docks
Weigh-house
Station master's house
Miscellaneous huts, sheds, etc.

Garsdale
Up and down platform plus branch platform
Booking office/waiting rooms/toilets
Subsidiary waiting room
Goods sidings
Cattle pens
Locomotive siding (shed destroyed 1917)
Locomotive turntable
Water columns and water tower
Railway staff houses
Miscellaneous huts, stores, permanent way sheds,
etc.

Notes

The term 'coal depot' is used in the NER sense of a battery of raised coal drops for use in conjunction with hopper wagons; where this term is not used it should be assumed that the stations in question were equipped with ordinary coal sidings.

Camping coaches are treated as semi-permanent fixtures, rather than as parked coaches; it thus seems sensible to list them as station accommodation. The term 'goods yard' is taken to mean a single yard containing all or most of the usual goods facilities. Where this term is replaced by 'goods sidings' readers should assume that coal depot or other facilities were dispersed on both sides of the line or at opposite ends of a station (as at Aysgarth). It should be noted, however, that there is no clear-cut distinction between the terms 'yard' and 'sidings'. A similar problem arises in the case of stations such as Askrigg, which had passing loops but only one platform for passenger trains - in such cases the term 'goods loop' has been used because the stations concerned were not used as regular passing places for up and down passenger trains.

All of the stations had small sheds for permanent way men, stores, etc., and no attempt has been made to list these very minor facilities. Weigh-houses have, on the other hand, been listed separately. Signal cabins are included in Appendix Two where stations were also block posts; the term 'lever cabin' is used in all other cases.

Appendix Three

Details of Single Line Operation (1931)

Northallerton High and Northallerton West: Staff with one ring round the middle, and tickets.
Northallerton West and Ainderby: Electric Tablet.
Ainderby and Leeming Bar: Electric Tablet. Passenger or freight trains may approach Leeming Bar from opposite directions at the same time at 'Line Clear'.
Bedale and Jervaulx: Electric Tablet. In clear weather, passenger and freight trains may approach Bedale from opposite directions at the same time at 'Line Clear'. When two passenger trains, or an up passenger and a down freight have to pass, the up passenger must be dealt with at the platform and sent off before the down train (passenger or freight) is allowed to pass the down outer home signal. During fog or snow a down passenger and an up freight, or two freights may approach from opposite directions at the same time at 'Line Clear'.
Jervaulx and Constable Burton: Electric Tablet. Passenger and freight trains may pass each other at Constable Burton and may approach from opposite directions at the same time at 'Line Clear'.
Constable Burton and Leyburn: Passenger or freight trains may approach in accordance with special instructions dated 29th February, 1928.
Leyburn West and Wensley: Electric Tablet. At Wensley, passenger or freight trains may pass each other, and may approach from opposite directions at the same time at 'Line Clear'.
Wensley and Redmire: Electric Tablet. At Redmire, one passenger and one freight, or two freights may pass each other and may approach from opposite directions at the same time at 'Line Clear'. The passenger train must always be turned to the platform line.
Redmire to Aysgarth: Electric Tablet. At Aysgarth, passenger or freight trains may pass each other and may approach from opposite directions at the same time at 'Line Clear'.
Aysgarth to Askrigg: Electric Staff with red handles. At Askrigg, the same instructions as at Aysgarth apply.
Askrigg to Hawes: Electric Staff with green handles. At Hawes, the same instructions as at Aysgarth apply.
Hawes to Hawes Jn: Round black staff.

A 'G5' class 0-4-4T No. 67345 arrives at Redmire with a train for Northallerton on 26th March, 1954. The signalman can be seen on the platform with the electric tablet for the section to Wensley. *R.B. Ledbetter/Alan Rimmer Collection*

Index

Wensleydale Railway Association

Information about the Railway is now available on the Railway's website, www.wensleydalerail.com

You may contact the Railway by email at admin@wensleydalerailway.com or write to the Wensleydale Railway, Leeming Bar Station, Leases Road, Leeming Bar, Northallerton, North Yorkshire, DL7 9AR. The office number is 01677 425805, and the office is normally staffed from 9 a.m. to 4 p.m.